BOUNDARIES

BOUNDARIES

A Casebook in Environmental Ethics

Christine E. Gudorf

and

James E. Huchingson

GEORGETOWN UNIVERSITY PRESS
Washington, D.C.

Georgetown University Press, Washington, D.C.
© 2003 by Georgetown University Press. All rights reserved.
Printed in the United States of America

10 9 8 7 6 5 4 3

This book is sprinted on acid-free, recycled paper meeting the requirements of the American
National Standard for Permanence in Paper for Printed Library Materials.

Library of Congress Cataloging-in-Publication Data

Gudorf, Christine E.
    Boundaries : a casebook in environmental ethics / Christine E. Gudorf and James E.
Huchingson.
        p. cm.
Includes bibliographical references and index.
        ISBN 0-87840-134-2 (pbk. : acid-free paper)
    1. Environmental ethics—Case studies. 2. Environmental sciences—Philosophy—Case
    studies. I. Huchingson, James Edward, 1940– II. Title.
GE42 .G83 2003
179'. 1—dc21

                                                                            2003004438

To our families

Contents

vii

CONTENTS

Introduction

This book began as a conversation on the foundational nature of environmental ethics—by which the authors mean that virtually every area of ethics today involves taking account of the claims of the environment and that, conversely, environmental ethics involves virtually all other existing areas of ethics. At one level the penetration of the environment into the ethics of public policy debate has been clear: We are not surprised to see government offices, the business boardroom, or farmers involved in debates about environmental regulation and ethics. The newspapers and television and radio news are full of such coverage. Nor are we surprised by the expansion of personal ethics among much of the population to include issues such as recycling, not littering, installing appliances (washers, toilets, showers) that conserve water, driving vehicles with high gas mileage, not wearing animal fur or using products utilizing animal testing, and vegetarianism. All of these concerns are well represented among university students, as well as among much of the general public.

Some earlier casebooks in environmental ethics—such as *Watersheds: Classic Cases in Environmental Ethics* by Lisa H. Newton and Catherine K. Dillingham—strongly linked environmental, public policy, and business ethics, focusing on issues in environmental politics that became major media events: Chernobyl, Bhopal, Love Canal, the Exxon Valdez, and others. But technological change has brought other areas of human life into contention with environmental ethics and broken down existing boundaries between ethical subfields. Technologies that allow humans to consider raiding animals for replacement organs, that provide chemically treated fencing to promote coral reef regeneration, that create genetically modified crops and allow scientists to "restore" wilderness all raise anew two issues: To what extent humans are a part of the environment (rather than only the subject that conceptualizes it) and the appropriate limits of human intervention in the environment.

Not all of the cases in this book revolve directly around technology, however. The debate about hunting, for example, is somewhat predicated on the increased power and accuracy of guns and bows—which some critics argue make hunting more a slaughter than a competition between hunter and animal—but depends much more on new and evolving human conceptions of human nature and human civilization. Perhaps what is pushing new perspectives on hunting today is not so much new technologies for hunting but new technologies that have made most citizens into urban dwellers whose closest association with other species is their relationship with household pets.

The decision to name the book *Boundaries* resulted from our recognition of three different kinds of boundaries involved in the cases described here. The first is the boundary between fields of ethics. This type of boundary became most apparent in the xenotransplant case (chapter 13), which is as fully relevant to medical and bioethics as it is to environmental ethics. The case about GMO crops (chapter 11) traditionally would have been a business ethics question; until very recently, the case about rewilding (chapter 10) also would have been cast as a business ethics case—the issue being whether business has any responsibility for restoring damaged or altered environments.

A second type of boundary is the boundary between humans and the rest of the environment. Should humans understand themselves as a part of the environment or as the subject that both conceptualizes and stewards the environment? This issue, of course, is critical in environmental ethics, and it takes many different shapes in these cases. How should the needs of humans count against the needs of other species or individual members of other species? Against the habitats of multiple species? Are humans merely "in" nature or are they truly "of" nature?

A third type of boundary at stake in these cases is the boundary between what is and what could or should be in the environment. What does it mean to "preserve" the environment? If nature is dynamic, how can we know what it should look like in the future? In the case of desertification in China, for example (chapter 9), how can we know how much of the desert was caused by natural forces and how much by human abuse and overuse? Frequently it seems that we lack adequate data on which to pursue any sound projects or policy. We lack the historical data to restore the environment to the shape it had before massive human intervention—assuming, of course, that the appropriate way to understand the environment is entirely without human impact. Not only is nature not static, but we do not know where it is going. If humans really are a part of nature, then our impact on it also is "natural." To say that our impact on nature or the environment is "natural" is not necessarily to say that our impact is good, however; humans could be the part of the environment that is responsible for killing all the rest. We need to use our understanding of ourselves as part of the environment to guide us in restraining our impact on the rest of the environment in ways that allow for sustainability. A major problem is that we do not have enough historical data to allow us to project the direction or pace of natural change—for example, in the size of various animal populations relative to each other—even if we could separate destructive human impact over the past few hundred years.

We could forget the idea of preservation as the center of environmentalism and stick with sustainability instead, but we lack so much data about so many aspects of our world that what is sustainable is extremely difficult to foresee. The principle of sustainability allows us to rule out some technologies—such as fossil fuel dependence—for example, but it doesn't tell us much about population levels to aim for. The (sustainable) carrying capacity of the earth is variously estimated by reputable scientists to be between 2 billion and 30 billion humans. When one considers that the present population is 6 billion, either we need to reduce the present population by 66 percent or we could plan to increase it fivefold—and one could defend both as sustainable. Boundary lines are indeed in question.

Yet we are not of the opinion that the attempt to draw boundary lines should be abandoned. The questions we treat here are vital. The significance of these cases is that they push in the direction of drawing tentative boundary lines where we can, and drawing boundary zones—within which we expect lines to be drawn in the future—in areas in which it is premature to draw even tentative lines today.

We think that this exercise of participating in the social project of conceptualizing the human place in the environment, the understanding of the environment that should guide both public policy and individual lifestyle, and the specific tasks of sustaining the biosphere is an exciting and unprecedented opportunity for students and an exciting responsibility for instructors.

1

Theory in Environmental Ethics

Philosopher Holmes Rolston III makes an important point about environmental ethics when he writes, "Environmental ethics stretches classical ethics to the breaking point. . . . [It] stands on a frontier, as radically theoretical as applied."[1] By *classical ethics* Rolston means systems of morality that apply only to humans; such ethical systems are "anthropocentric." Environmental ethics is not necessarily limited to humans, however. It attempts to expand the circle of moral concern beyond the human species to include at the very least other mammals; perhaps lower animals and plants; and, finally, entire ecosystems.

Classical anthropocentric moral theories are not designed to address or resolve issues that go beyond the narrow circle of human life. These theories can be stretched to include some nonhumans—mostly of the "higher" sort—because such species share important and morally relevant features with ours, but they appear absurd when they are applied to plants or ecosystems. The frontier dimension of classical ethics is limited to areas of human life in which advances in science and technology have created new situations that require attention. This is most obvious in medicine, where novel moral questions are raised frequently in genetics, organ transplantation, and other new fields. Yet even here, moral deliberation often remains within the circle of human life.

1

In contrast, environmental ethics stands on the frontier. It must build whole new arguments to justify and explain why nonhumans should count morally and how conflicts in the environment should be resolved. The theoretical (why) and the applied (how) are not easily separated. Before one can address the dilemma of saving an endangered species or saving jobs that would be lost if that species were protected, for example, the environmental ethicist must answer the question: Why should endangered species count morally at all? Reflection on that question may go far in determining the shape of the resolution to the dilemma. No wonder, then, that Rolston cautions us so strongly. "Environmental ethics requires risk," he warns. "It explores poorly charted terrain, where one can easily get lost."[2] Heeding Rolston's advice, it might be a good idea to orient ourselves in terms of the major moral approaches to environmental problems.

Anthropocentic Ethics

With few notable exceptions, the Western tradition in philosophy and religion is predominately anthropocentric in its claim that moral value is to be found primarily, if not exclusively, in humans. It is possible to argue that although humans are the most valuable beings, some value may be found in nonhumans as well. In practice, this weak form of anthropocentrism differs little from the strong form, which insists that humans alone have moral value. In cases in which the interests of humans conflict with those of nonhumans, the human interests usually trump those of the nonhuman—just as they would in cases in which humans are valuable in the strong sense.

Given the long anthropocentric tradition in Western philosophy and theology, it comes as no surprise that conventional approaches to making moral judgments (also known as moral theories) focus entirely on other humans as the proper objects of our moral attention.

Utilitarianism

Utilitarianism is a moral theory that originally was intended for deciding human moral issues alone. Utilitarianism is a form of consequentialism. Its advocates argue that the proper way to judge the rightness or wrongness of an action is to assess the consequences of the action if it were to occur. Consequences that result in more harm than benefit are judged morally wrong, and those that bring about more benefit than harm are morally right. This approach is easily recognized as a form of cost-benefit analysis. Most actions produce mixed moral results: a combination of harms (costs) and benefits. For an act to be judged as morally right or desirable, the only criterion that must be satisfied is that it should produce a net balance of good consequences over harmful ones. Ethical egoism and altruism are forms of consequentialism. An egoist strives to take only those actions that bring about the greatest benefit and least harm to the egoist alone. The altruist, on the other hand, prefers actions that bring about the greatest benefit and least harm to others, exclusive of the altruist.

Few people embrace either egoism or altruism as a preferred moral philosophy by which to live. We look instead for an ethical approach that includes both our own interests and the interests of others. The Golden Rule ("Do unto others as you would have them do unto you") is a candidate for this inclusive approach, and it does offer powerful intuitive guidance. Many philosophers, however, prefer a more exact and less subjective consequentialist standard. This standard was provided by two nineteenth-century philosophers—Jeremy Bentham and John Stuart Mill—who developed a version of consequentialism that satisfies this criterion of inclusivity. Utilitarianism, as this position came to be known, requires that the good and bad consequences of an action be taken into account for everyone who is affected. Hence the Principle of Utility: Always act to bring about the greatest good for the greatest number of persons who are affected by the action.

It is not enough for utilitarians to speak of benefits and harms. They also must offer some way of determining what is good and what is harmful. One widely accepted approach is simply to define a harm as that which brings about suffering and pain and a good as that which brings about pleasure and happiness. Although pain has no intrinsic value (we never seek it for its own sake), it may have instrumental value. It is instructive; no child willingly touches a hot stove twice. Pleasure, however, has obvious intrinsic value; it is to be sought. It has considerable instrumental value as well. It could be argued that without the pleasure associated with sex the act of procreation, which is necessary for the perpetuation of many species, would be a lot rarer than it is. Although both pain and pleasure may serve as means to human well-being, only pleasure is valuable as an end in itself. Thus, pain is an intrinsic moral evil and pleasure an intrinsic moral good. Now the utilitarian has a standard for judging the moral worth of the consequences of an action. If the consequences, on balance, bring about more pleasure than pain, the action is morally right. If they bring about more pain than pleasure, it is morally wrong. Experience teaches us that one individual's happiness may be another individual's unhappiness because people's desires or preferences vary considerably. This fact presents no difficulty for the utilitarian, who simply alters the Principle of Utility slightly to read, "Always act to maximize satisfaction of personal preferences for the greatest number of individuals affected by the action."

Because utilitarians seek only to maximize the net utility or good of an action, they are willing to accept some harm as well. For example, situating a

3

polluting industry adjacent to a community of color violates principles of social justice. But the cheap land at that location is an attraction to the industry in the first place, and most citizens—including those who live in the affected community—will benefit from taxes paid and jobs provided by the polluting firm. The economic goods will be distributed widely, but the health problems and other harms (the costs of having the industry in town) will be borne disproportionately by the poor and powerless few. Nevertheless, by the standards of cost-benefit calculations, the utilitarian can claim to have maximized the sum of benefits over harms and thus to have done the right thing.

As traditionally applied, utilitarianism clearly is anthropocentric. That is, the Principle of Utility limits the class of beneficiaries of an action to humans alone; the greatest good should come to the greatest number of persons. Because the happiness and pleasure of humans is the only intrinsic value for utilitarians, arguments for the interests of nonhumans rest exclusively on their instrumental contribution to this value. The continued existence of an endangered species—particularly if it is not attractive, charismatic, or valuable to humans for other social or historical reasons—would be difficult to justify on grounds other than hypothetical arguments about its potential contribution to medicine or the gene pool of economically productive domestic species. A small, endangered flower whose vanishing habitat is a gleam in the eye of a land developer will have little chance before the court of utilitarian judgment.

Deontology

Utilitarianism judges the moral appropriateness of an act indirectly by assessing the harms and benefits of its consequences. Another major approach to moral judgment examines the act directly, giving no attention to consequences. This position is called *deontology* (from the Greek for "binding duty") or "Kantianism"—after Immanuel Kant, its most persuasive philosophical advocate. "Binding duty" is an accurate description because this theory requires that to be declared morally good an action must satisfy, fulfill, or conform to some absolute, universal, and unconditional standard usually expressed as a duty—an obligation (that which one must always do) or prohibition (that which one must never do). "Always tell the truth" or "never tell a lie" are good examples of the duty to be honest.

Where are we to find these duties? Their sources are numerous. Such sources can include religion: The Ten Commandments come readily to mind, as do Jesus' Sermon on the Mount and the Hindu Law of Manu. They also may be derived from intuitions associated with our conscience or extracted from the God-given structure of creation (an approach known as natural law theory). Kant, a leading figure of the Enlightenment, preferred the

4

authority of reason to that of revelation. The definitive feature of persons, he reasoned, is that they are autonomous—that is, free and rational. Because they are rational, they are fully capable of determining those universal duties that are binding on all rational persons. Moreover, because I—as a free and rational person—have duties to you, you—as a free and rational person—have equivalent duties to me. We should never lie to one another or to any other person. This reciprocal moral relationship gives rise to the symmetry of duties and rights. I have a duty to treat you in accordance with the same standards (rights) by which you have a duty to treat me. This symmetry leads Kant to the conclusion that persons should never be treated merely as objects—as means only—but always as rational subjects: as ends in themselves.

In its Kantian form, deontology qualifies as a very anthropocentric approach to ethics. Only beings who are capable of reasoning out duties and acting freely upon them—that is, *human* beings—qualify as recipients for the duties of others, as the bearers of rights. Because it is obvious to Kant that no nonhumans possess these qualifying features, they are denied any direct moral standing. By "direct" Kant is referring to ends, not just means. An animal may have indirect moral standing in that by harming an animal (your beloved pet dog, for example) I may indirectly violate some right owed to you—perhaps the right of property. The dog, after all, is your property as well as your companion. Therefore, I am prohibited from harming your dog. I have no duty to the dog apart from my duties to you, however. Kant objects to cruelty to animals for a reason that is consistent with his thinking: Not only is this behavior a bad example, but, Kant reasons, if a man is cruel to animals he may develop cruel attitudes toward other men as well.[3]

Anthropocentric Ethics Extended

For many environmental philosophers, the anthropocentric perspective is sufficiently strong to address any environmental problem, and no further theoretical work is required. In fact, one can reasonably hold to an anthropocentric philosophy and be environmentally concerned. The trick lies in appreciating the importance of a clean, healthy, beautiful environment for human well-being. John Passmore was an early environmental philosopher who took this position.[4] He argued, for example, that industrial pollution is simply a case in which some people were harming the health of their neighbors by degrading the air they breathe. Although we have no responsibilities for the environment in its own right, we do have responsibilities to other persons who can be harmed by the damage we cause to the environment. Hence, the natural world is not valued directly, for its own sake, but indirectly—for the sake of humans who find it valuable for the benefits it brings to them. Passmore's anthropocentrism works well when it is applied to environmental problems, such as industrial pollution, that have clear consequences for persons. It falls short of providing guidance, however, when the benefits to be derived from a particular action toward nature are minimal. For example, the human benefits of preserving the Arctic National Wildlife Refuge from oil exploration seem to be few: primarily the hunting culture of local indigenous peoples, the pristine beauty of a remote place enjoyed by a small number of visitors each year, and perhaps the personal satisfaction we derive simply in knowing that such a unique place exists.

In both utilitarianism and deontology nonhumans clearly have no true moral standing. They are not to be found in "the greatest number of those affected" in the calculation and distribution of benefits and harms, and they are not the autonomous bearers of rights. In either system, nonhumans qualify for our moral consideration only indirectly, as means to human ends. More recently, environmental philosophers have made concerted efforts to broaden the range of moral standing to include species other than ourselves, and even inanimate natural systems. Several thinkers attempt to modify or extend traditional moral systems to include nonhumans. Peter Singer makes this attempt regarding utilitarianism, and Tom Regan does it regarding rights. Because these philosophers are concerned mainly with higher life forms, they may be regarded as biocentrists. Others, including Paul Taylor, see that these two systems are too limited to take us very far and opt instead for other approaches that would justify the inclusion of plants and lower animals. Finally, advocates of ecocentrism, including Aldo Leopold and his disciple J. Baird Callicott, advocate ecosystems as the proper object of our moral attention. One may detect a trend or process in these efforts. To be true to its object, environmental ethics must expand our circle of moral standing to allow for the inclusion of other animals, plants, and systems of plants and animals, not to mention mountains and rivers. Commitment to the project of this *moral extensionism* is the fundamental challenge and a distinguishing feature of environmental ethics.

Peter Singer is a utilitarian philosopher and author of *Animal Liberation*,[5] the well-known "bible" for the movement of the same name. Singer argues for an extension of moral concern to include nonhumans. He argues that we have a fundamental duty to avoid taking actions that bring about harm. He understands harm to mean pain and suffering that comes from unnecessarily violating the interests of beings who are capable of experiencing such violations. Besides humans, many other animal species possess this kind of sentience. Altogether, they and we qualify for moral consideration. Why? Because the only morally relevant consideration is the reduction of suffering or the promotion of happiness. Apart from our sentience, persons have no defining features—not even Kant's freedom and rationality—that confer moral standing. As philosopher Jeremy Bentham put it in 1879, "The question is not, can they reason or can they talk, but can they suffer."[6] Any sentient creature—even if it has wings, four legs, fur, or gills—deserves the same moral standing. Arguments that conclude that humans alone are morally privileged therefore rest on arbitrary distinctions and are guilty of what Singer calls "speciesism."

Furthermore, because sentient animals experience needs and have interests that are similar to our own, they must be given equal consideration. Actions that bring about suffering to nonhumans must be justified to the same degree that they would have to be justified if those actions were directed toward humans. For example, medical experimentation on a chimpanzee must be defended in exactly the same way it would be if a human with equal capacities were substituted for the chimpanzee. Pain is pain, whether it is inflicted on a chimp or a human infant.

Singer's appeal to egalitarianism—the moral worth of all members of the community of sentient beings—is compelling but not without problems. One is that he provides no way to adjudicate conflicts between individuals of different species. It is not clear, for example, whether interspecies organ transplantation (xenografts)—taking the heart of a pig, for example, and implanting it in an infant—is acceptable or not because each of the two parties has a fundamental interest at stake: the interest of not dying. Other philosophers introduce a principle of discrimination that allows for such cases to be resolved. Donald VanDeVeer suggests that level of psychological capacity, roughly equating with the degree of sentience, would be useful.[7] Individual animals with greater psychological capacity would be favored. It is easy to see that this position leads to a kind of *de facto* anthropocentrism because in conflicts in which individual persons (members of a species with unequaled psychological capacity) are competing with a member of any other species, the interests of the person would consistently prevail.

A further problem with Singer's approach is that his reliance on sentience as the basis for equal consideration excludes insentient life forms—lower animals and plants. Because members of these species cannot suffer, they have no moral standing. Singer's efforts at moral extensionism appear to encounter an unbridgeable barrier at this point by including primarily mammals in the exclusive club of morally qualified sentient beings. Perhaps these problems are the inevitable result of applying moral systems designed for intrahuman issues to nonhuman species: An irreducible anthropomorphic bias remains.

Neither of these problems disappears when deontology provides the vehicle for moral extensionism, as it does in the philosophy of Tom Regan.[8] Though inspired by Kant's accounts of universal duties, emphasis on ends

7

rather than means, and human rights, Regan moves beyond Kant's claim that only free and autonomous agents can qualify for deontological benefits. Regan replaces this narrow condition with a broader definition: Any being that has a complex emotional and perceptual life—including pain and pleasure preferences—and the ability to pursue actions and goals with a significant degree of individual independence should be included as the object of our duties. Because many species of mammals fall into this category, they should be included along with humans as candidates for deontological benefits. These "subjects-of-a-life," as Regan refers to them, have inherent value (Regan's term, which corresponds roughly to "intrinsic value"). No being with inherent value should be treated as a means to some end, as a resource or object to be exploited for the benefit of others. Subjects-of-a-life have rights that should be respected by free and rational agents who are morally responsible for our actions. Thus, Regan reaches the same conclusion as Singer, albeit from an entirely different direction. Many mammals have equal worth with humans. Their rights to life, liberty, and the pursuit of happiness must be considered on a par with our own.

Regan faces the same problems as Singer, however. Regan's conclusion that all subjects-of-a-life are of equal worth makes it impossible to resolve some issues. On the other hand, at least his position can speak decisively to the xenograft. A subject-of-a-life—in this case a pig (though it could be a person)—should never be sacrificed for the well-being of another, even as a means to the preservation of the life of a child. With respect to the problem of lower species, Regan finds himself in the same predicament as Singer. Although being sentient and being the subject-of-a-life are not necessarily identical, both require complex psychological capacities. Hence, lower animals and all plants remain excluded from consideration.

Singer and Regan are representatives of a limited form of biocentrism. They wish to extend our moral consideration to nonhumans but can go only as far as their modified anthropocentric ethical systems will allow. Other ethicists—also biocentrists—applaud these efforts but fault them for failing to extend the range of moral standing any further. What about less complex animals and the entire plant kingdom? In the absence of arguments granting intrinsic value, must the justification for their welfare and protection rely exclusively on their instrumental economic or aesthetic value? To make their arguments about moral standing for still disenfranchised creatures, these concerned ethicists must turn to other moral frameworks.

Biocentrism Extended

To extend the circle of our moral concern beyond sentience, a different appraisal of intrinsic worth must be found. Paul Taylor believes he has found such an inclusive sense of worth in his idea of a "teleological center of a life."[9] The Greek word *telos*, meaning "purpose" or "goal," is a centerpiece concept of Aristotle's philosophy of life. All living things (and, for Aristotle, many nonliving things) have a *telos*—an inborn goal that they strive to realize and sustain. That this is true is obvious to any attentive observer. All animals and plants, sentient or not, conduct their lives in a clearly directed way. They grow and maintain themselves specifically in terms of the interests of their well-being. A Monarch butterfly seeks to become a full-fledged representative of its species, as does a live oak tree or a microbe. There is nothing superfluous in the behavior of a living organism in this respect. Its very life is dedicated to—indeed, identical with—its *telos*.

Such a teleological account generates two important observations. The first is that unlike a species' subjective psychological capacity, the *telos* of a species is no secret. It is open to objective description. We can know what harms or benefits an organism simply by witnessing its activities. The second observation is that the organism need not be conscious of its purpose. A plant does not know what it is doing, and it need not know to realize and sustain its full potential as an able representative of its *telos*, the characteristic form of its species—what Aristotle called its "nature." All teleological centers of a life are "good-natured" in the sense that their striving and thriving is good for them. Although they may be unaware, they have interests and needs and act to satisfy them. They have what philosophers call "a good of their own." Such a good is equivalent to being worthy or valuable. Hence, teleological centers of a life are valuable objectively—that is, apart from our assessment or judgment regarding them. Again, they need not be conscious to contain this inherent worth.

It seems to follow that for anyone who adopts what Taylor refers to as "the biocentric outlook," respect for the good of other individual creatures is the proper moral attitude. The biocentric outlook is a sort of creed professing that humans are members of Earth's community of interdependence and equality. That is, the human *telos* is not superior to that of any other living thing, and neither is the *telos* of any sentient nonhuman or subject-of-a-life.

Taylor has taken several strides outward in expanding the circle of moral concern to include ever-greater numbers of nonhumans. He has broken through the confines of subjectivity—the emphasis on consciousness or psychological awareness—as the main qualification for moral standing. Nevertheless, he brings some burdens with him. For example, Taylor's system applies only to individual creatures and requires commitment to the equality of living teleological systems, human and nonhuman, which makes resolving conflicts between them very difficult. Moreover, he has nothing to say about

9

the value of rivers or mountains or of entire ecosystems, except insofar as they provide a suitable environment for the flourishing of teleological systems of life.

Ecocentrism

Biocentrism, or life-centered ethics, is the laudable attempt to extend the circle of our moral concern to include animals and, with some further modification, plants as well. To be true to its name, however, an *environmental* ethic must provide a framework of principles that would justify the further extension of our moral sensibilities to that larger association of animals, plants, and even geologic features (e.g., rivers, lakes, mountains, and valleys) known in environmental science as biomes or ecosystems or generally as "the natural environment."

Establishing such a philosophical foundation—a noble aspiration, to be sure—nonetheless is an imposing task. Ecosystems are loose associations of species, from subsoil microbes to megafauna and great forests, that live together in countless numbers as citizens in a larger community. Arguing for the moral standing for such communities requires a theoretical threshold leap of some distance. Ecosystems are not sentient. It seems absurd to claim that a desert itself can suffer (although, of course, individual members of a desert ecosystem can suffer). An ecosystem does not exhibit a single goal or *telos* toward which it strives as a whole. Instead, its wholeness or systemic complexity is the consequence of the successes and failures of immense multitudes of species over many generations, struggling to adapt to one another and to the inanimate forces of nature. The overall emergent structure of the ecosystem is the consequence of these evolutionary negotiations at the species level. The ecosystem did not grow up according to some preestablished set of commands or inherent tendencies. Unlike a plant (which does have such a normative program—its genetic code), an ecosystem cannot be described easily as a teleological system.

The key to a true ecocentric ethic probably lies in the mind's eye of the ecocentrist beholder. It seems to revolve around one's choice of metaphors with which to characterize the whole. If the preferred metaphor is "community," then the thrust of the moral argument moves toward individual members of that community—that is, toward biocentrism. If the preferred metaphor is "organism," in which the members of the whole are tightly knit in their interdependence, then attention moves toward the entire ecosystem as the object of attention, probably employing some variation of teleological ethics.

Aldo Leopold, a pioneer if not prophet and herald of environmental philosophy, was an early advocate of ecocentrism. His essay "The Land Ethic," found in his classic *A Sand County Almanac* (first appearing in 1949), is the classic expression of the position.[10] Leopold advocates the evolutionary extension of our human ethic toward a land ethic, which "simply enlarges the boundaries of the community to include soils, waters, plants, and animals, or collectively, the land."[11] Although Leopold uses the term "community" to describe the land, it is clear elsewhere that he intends to speak of a highly organized whole, a reality that stands on its own integrity. In other words, the land is "a biotic mechanism." Leopold rightly claims, "We can be ethical only in relation to something we can see, feel, understand, love, or otherwise have faith in."[12] The biotic mechanisms of the Olympic Peninsula, the Florida Everglades, or the Sonoran Desert are more than loosely knit communities. They are entities unto themselves with which humans can relate and toward which we may have direct duties.

Leopold concludes his essay with a succinct expression of his guiding principle of such an ethic: "A thing is right when it tends to preserve the integrity, stability, and beauty of the biotic community. It is wrong when it tends otherwise."[13] At first glance, Leopold's principle appears to be deontological in its appeal to specific ideals rather than to subjective states of happiness or suffering. What misleads us is his casual phrasing. "A thing is right" seems to mean "an action is right." If so, then the outcomes of such actions toward an ecosystem should be judged for their preservation of its integrity, stability, and beauty. Leopold has provided a radical extension of the consequentialist approach as applied to ecosystems. In addition, his inclusion of "preserve" introduces limiting or prohibitory language. The imperative is not to increase these values of the ecosystem but not to decrease them. This emphasis on "do no harm" makes sense within the larger context of the essay, where he relentlessly attacks "the prevailing belief that economics determines *all* land use."[14]

Leopold's commandment defines human duties toward ecosystems, but not in a way that pleases biocentrists. If the ecosystem is the proper and exclusive object of our moral attention, then its contributing components—the vast array of plants and animals constituting the system—must be valued not intrinsically, for their own sake, but instrumentally, in terms of their contribution to its "integrity, stability, and beauty." The ecosystem does not serve individual creatures; they serve the ecosystem and may be treated in ways that violate their individual interests or teleological self-fulfillment when the ecosystem requires.

J. Baird Callicott, a philosopher and disciple of Leopold, endorses a stronger sense of the interdependence of parts in an ecosystem by using the image of organism. "Like organisms proper," Callicott writes, "ecosystems are complexly articulated wholes, with systemic integrity."[15] He does not claim that ecosystems are alive but that they resemble living things closely enough to allow for some real comparisons. For example, organisms can be ill or well. So, "like organisms proper," the health of ecosystems may be assessed by using diagnostic tests that resemble clinical examinations of animals and humans, including monitoring "vital signs" and identifying "risk factors."

What values are attached to ecosystems that make this "clinical ecology" desirable? Instrumentally, healthy ecosystems obviously are vital for the well-being of human cultures, which are embedded in nature. What is less than obvious, however, is why they are to be cherished intrinsically as well. "If our other-oriented feelings of goodwill may extend to nature, then ecosystem health is something we may value intrinsically," claims Callicott. The prior question is, why is this extension of goodwill reasonable? Singer, Regan, and Taylor marshal powerful arguments for the justification of goodwill or moral concern for other species of animals and possibly of plants. Why is it appropriate for ecosystems? An ecosystem is not conscious and would fail to qualify for moral standing under Singer's sentience requirement or Regan's "subject of a life" criterion. It may possess sufficient "systemic integrity," however, to qualify under Taylor's teleological centeredness, especially if Callicott's claims for organic resemblance are persuasive.

Ecocentrism Radicalized: Deep Ecology

The first thing to note about deep ecology is its rhetorical advantage over what would be characterized unattractively as "shallow." The distinction is revealing. Shallow ecology is establishment environmentalism. Its advocates work within the philosophical framework and assumptions of the modern world. These assumptions are primarily anthropocentric, utilitarian, and individualistic. The best that shallow ecology can hope for is to reform this worldview without touching its basic premises. Shallow ecology works within the system; it does not ask whether the system itself is the problem.

Deep ecology is radical to the extent that it intends to correct this blindness by replacing the very foundations of shallow ecology, its prevailing worldview. This approach makes deep ecology more of a "cosmological" (having to do with the whole of the world and not just the human part of it) or "metaphysical" (emphasizing fundamental philosophical beliefs as opposed to the obvious) approach to environmental ethics. The human species does not fare well in this reconstruction project. Deep ecology, like Paul Taylor's biocentrism, proposes that all creatures are equal in intrinsic value—a kind of species egalitarianism. In addition, following the more radical ecocentrists, it argues that the individual is completely subordinated to the well-being of the ecosystem; the whole is of much greater value than any of its parts, including the human parts. The more outspoken deep ecologists sometimes invite the charge that they embrace misanthropy (hatred of humans) in this moral holism by describing the species as a pathogen or plague of the earth.

In addition to egalitarianism and holism, deep ecologists embrace the principle of radical relationality. In their view, one of the most dangerous ideas in the prevailing worldview of modernism is that individuals—whether they are atoms or living beings—are the fundamental units of reality. This position is clearly espoused by Kant and many post-Enlightenment philosophers. Persons are autonomous individuals who control their own destinies through rational decision processes. Thus, the individual takes priority over community, and social relationships are mostly a matter of choice and personal advantage. Physically, we are minds or egos encapsulated by an almost impermeable envelope of skin and separated from all other existing beings as they are from us. Deep ecology reverses this position completely by claiming that any living being is constituted by its relationships: We are our relationships. Evolution teaches us that profound and intricate arrangements between species emerge through processes of natural selection and adaptation. The flower in the meadow is not an isolated individual accidentally growing there. Its very constitution is a consequence of millions of years of active affiliation with other species and with the forces of nature. Even now it transforms sunlight through photosynthesis, attracts insects with its colorful blossom and nectar, and sends its roots deep into the soil for water and nourishment. Its individuality is a minor aspect of its embeddedness in a complex system of relationships. Indeed, reality is a universal river of energy. Individuals are merely local disturbances in that flow. The ethical implications of deep ecology are clear. With few exceptions, individuals and species have little value except within the global context of the absolute priority of the whole. Humans are no different. Thus, implementation of the principles of deep ecology would require a radical transformation of social and economic institutions that are built on the supposition that human beings truly are *different* from the rest of creation.

Social Ecology

Murray Bookchin is a social commentator who agrees with the radical aim of deep ecology to transform society.[16] Bookchin's analysis of these patterns of domination and control draws heavily, however, on the notion of social hierarchy rather than cosmology, or the nature of the universe. Most human societies, he claims, are structured according to levels of power, authority, and control, with those occupying the higher rungs controlling those on rungs below them. According to Bookchin, such hierarchies include "the domination of the young by the old, women by men, of one ethnic group by

13

another, of 'masses' by bureaucrats who profess to speak to higher 'social interests,' of countryside by town, and in a more subtle psychological sense, of body by mind, or spirit by a shallow instrumental mentality." These relational patterns are built into the habitual patterns of belief and action in a culture, so that they become internalized and promoted as normative and beyond question. Given this ubiquitous nature of hierarchical patterns of oppression, the solution lies not in merely changing forms of government—for example, from socialist to liberal-democratic. All forms of social structures are infected. The only cure is a soft form of anarchy. Bookchin envisions a just society that maximizes individual human freedom and establishes the absolute equality of all persons. Only such autonomous individuals are liberated from the psychological inner limits of social conditioning and the institutional outer limits of the authoritative exercise of power and control. They are therefore free to enter into a truly just community of equals with no urge to dominate one another or to dominate nature.

True to its name, social ecology explains the environmental crisis as a consequence of societal patterns and institutions. Social ecologists fault biocentrists and deep ecologists for missing the point. The problem is not to be found in mistaken ethical norms or in faulty worldviews. Instead, the problem is to be found in ourselves, in our social and ideological structures that encourage relations of domination and exploitation—practices we extend to our relations to nature. Environmental destruction is the universal application of the idea that there are superior classes or groups who oppress those whom they determine to be inferior. Ironically, the prevailing attitude of domination is a negative instance of moral extensionism because it takes this ideological framework of belief and action and applies it to the nonhuman world.

Ecofeminism

If men controlling women is a fundamental form of hierarchy, as Bookchin reports, then elimination of such patriarchy would go far toward correcting our exploitation of nature. The primary importance of this project is underscored by a form of feminism known as ecofeminism. Much feminist social analysis focuses of the specific hierarchical notion of patriarchy—the long-standing and traditional domination of women by men. To this extent, feminists agree with Bookchin. They go much further, however, by claiming that patriarchy (the elevated and entitled status of male authorities) is the primary form of social oppression. Eliminating it would go far toward the elimination of other forms of oppression.

Ecofeminists observe that the patriarchal attitude toward women is identical to that toward nature. Nature is addressed as feminine, often maternal—

14

"Mother Nature"; hence, like women, nature becomes the object of "androcentric" (male-centered) subjugation. Although this myth has many variations, the prevailing version—given modern foundations by the philosopher Rene Descartes—is that the mind is fundamentally separate from the body and, because of its rational character, is superior to the material or natural body that falls under its control. According to this myth, men are more rational than women; they transcend the demands of their bodily nature to control its instinctive and emotional drives. Women are closer to nature with respect to their identification with the body. Hence dominance of women (and children and animals) is not to be distinguished from the dominance of nature.

In detecting a kinship between women and nature, some ecofeminists take a part of this modern myth and turn it to their advantage. This kinship, based on the shared powers to give birth and provide nurture and the greater consciousness of women about the importance of the embodied self, allows these ecofeminists to rally their cause in solidarity with nature. Many other ecofeminists strongly deny that any essential attributes of either women or men, rational or biological, are the problem. Instead, hierarchical distinctions of gender are based in social roles. Nurturing is a role assigned primarily to women by cultural expectations and not an expression of any maternal instinct. Oppression will disappear only when these discriminatory roles are abolished. From either of these perspectives, elimination of patriarchy in human affairs also would provide for its elimination in our relations with nature.

Pragmatic Environmental Ethics

According to Bryan Norton, a philosopher who favors a pragmatic or practical approach to moral decision making, environmental ethics is a form of applied philosophy.[17] Very general and abstract theoretical principles—utilitarian, deontological, or teleological—are "applied" to making difficult choices in specific situations. Several problems arise with this "top-down" approach. First, no two situations are alike in all their important details, making it difficult to employ the same "off-the-rack," universal principle unilaterally to every case in exactly the same way. At such times we are forced to fall back on our good judgment alone to make up for the differences. More important for Norton is that not all parties in a dispute are likely to agree on the same fundamental principles. Consensus is almost impossible when the discussion turns from the particulars of the situation to an abstract debate about whose principles shall apply. In fact, the particular case tends to get lost when the discussion turns to abstract argument.

Although Norton does not want to dismiss theories entirely in favor of intuitive responses, he maintains that theory-building takes place when the

15

parties grapple with a common real-world problem. If they share a common goal, even for very diverse motives and theoretical reasons, interested individuals can arrive at a "mid-management" policy for resolving the issue. The broader unity is cemented by a common interest in caring for the environment. Norton uses the example of protecting wetlands habitat for migratory waterfowl. Concerned anthropocentrists favor protection for their own hunting interests. Biocentrists act out of concern for sentient or teleological individuals, and a few ecocentrists intend to preserve Leopold's "integrity, stability, and beauty" of precious wetlands. A strange coalition, to be sure, but it works in terms of real-world politics and habitat management. The key to practical environmental ethics is not insisting on ideological conformity to abstract principles but agreeing as much as possible about values or goals and then devising a set of diverse principles that speak to the issue at hand.

A pragmatic approach that relies on this "moral pluralism" (using a variety of principles that are not deduced from a single master principle) has definite advantages in a world so rich, complex, and varied that no single situation conforms to some abstract ideal. Nevertheless, some moral "monists" are very uncomfortable with the approach. Their concern is that when real conflicts inevitably occur, there are no standards to resolve them. What if I am faced with a dilemma between deciding for humans (requiring an anthropocentric, person-respecting principle) or nonhumans (requiring a biocentric sentience or telos-respecting principle) in an either-or situation with no middle ground? Convivial cooperation is not possible when the value-laden goals of the interested parties are so unalterably opposed. Moral pluralists might rank the two positions and select the one with overriding priority. On what basis do they arrive at such a ranking? For the monist the answer is clear: An appeal to some master standard is the only way to achieve consistency in moral decision making.

Interested Parties

Applied or practical philosophy? Moral pluralism or moral monism? No one ever said that moral reasoning is easy. Moral pluralists are right: Life is too complex to be reduced to a single ethical standard. Moral monists are right, too: Life often requires making hard choices between attractive but exclusive alternatives. At such times, clear thinking requires coherent normative standards. Finally, however, moral judgments are never made automatically, as conclusions to some logical syllogism with principles as its premises. Unless they are disinterested judges sitting in a courtroom pondering the arguments of adversaries, decision makers are almost always personally involved in the dilemmas they face. Their participation means that they must weigh the concerns of all parties—human (possibly including themselves), sentient, or inanimate—and grapple with the decision. Concern and care are appropriate ingredients in the process. The heart and the gut as well as the head enter into the deliberations. More often than not, the decision maker cherishes loyalties to each of the parties affected by the eventual resolution, and working through the competing positions is a labor of anguish as well as love.

Religion and Ecology

What do religious ethicists have to say about environmental ethics? Do religious ethicists—or religion itself—add anything distinctive to the debates? Religious ethicists divide on the foregoing questions: Some support anthropocentrism, some support biocentrism and some ecocentrism, and others support ecofeminism and pragmatic environmentalism. In fact, in the broad sense of *religious*, there may be more religious ecofeminists than nonreligious ecofeminists.[18] This does not mean, however, that religious ethicists bring nothing of their own to the debate. The distinctive element in religious environmentalism is not so much a distinct approach to any of the philosophical questions as an *attitude* toward the environment that not only nuances all of these arguments but also provides motivation for commitment to the welfare of the environment. That is, religious approaches to the environment throughout the world are based in an understanding of the universe either as divine creation or as permeated by divine spirits, or both. In both understandings the environment has standing independent of humanity; in fact, the environment takes on a sacrality that not only gives it standing but demands a kind of reverence from humans. As creation, the natural world reveals the creator; as the realm of spirits, the natural world exudes spiritual power. As we have noted, philosophers have been largely unsuccessful in grounding claims for the nonliving environment as having independent standing. Religious environmentalists have no such difficulty because from a religious perspective the nonliving environment shares the same claim to standing as the living environment, in that both take their standing from their status as created by the Divine.

Religious ethicists offer more to environmentalism, however, than simply a way to offer standing to the nonliving world. They also offer tools for creating and maintaining human support for caring for the environment: the tools of prayer and ritual. Prayer and ritual have reminded believers of their dependence on the gifts of the god(s) that sustain them—on the need to appreciate, care for, be thankful for, and use wisely the bounty of the god(s). Religious systems offer an understanding of humanity not as independent but as both dependent upon the god(s) and as charged with responsibility by the god(s). This state of dependent but responsible humanity is close to the environmentalist understanding of humanity as interdependent. The ecological

crisis has pushed many religious scholars to pay more attention to their doc-
trines of creation. Thomas Berry writes:

> Because our sense of the divine is so extensively derived from ver-
> bal sources, mostly through Biblical scriptures, we seldom notice
> how much we have lost contact with the revelation of the divine
> in nature. Yet our exalted sense of the divine comes from the
> grandeur of the universe, especially from the earth in all the splen-
> did modes of its expression. Without such experience, we would
> be terribly impoverished in our religious and spiritual develop-
> ment, even in our emotional, imaginative, and intellectual devel-
> opment. If we lived on the moon, our imagination would be as
> desolate as the moon, our emotions lacking in the sensitivity de-
> veloped in our experience of the sensuous variety of the luxuriant
> earth. If a beautiful earth gives us an exalted idea of the divine, an
> industrially despoiled planet will give us a corresponding idea of
> God.[19]

Many indigenous religions around the world have become "green" (in the
sense of active environmentally) in the past decades. One reason is that overpopulation and development often have pushed into the marginal spaces to
which indigenous groups had been herded by modernity and now threaten
their very existence by encroaching on the environment on which they are
dependent. The other reason that indigenous communities have become
"green" is that in their religious sensibility, they recognize threats to the
health of their environment—to the rivers and streams; to the animals, birds
and fish; to the air and the soil—as threats not only against their lives and
community but also against a sacred order, against the divine itself. They do
not require the use of logic and philosophical reasoning to recognize that the
obliteration of forests and wetlands, the poisoning of rivers and streams from
mining wastes, and the extinction of millions of species of plants and animals
is wrong.

Within the principal world religions—Christianity, Islam, Buddhism, Hinduism, and Judaism—there are many believers who are environmentalists and
many theologian/scholars who have been presenting arguments for environmentalism based in their religious tradition and attempting to reform aspects
of their tradition regarding treatment of the environment. For a variety of
reasons, including earlier and more thorough industrialization in the West
than in the East, this task of reconciling religious tradition with environmentalism began earlier in the West but now has extended to all areas and religions of the world. Some environmentalists have charged Christianity in

particular as responsible for legitimating environmental devastation through its teaching of the biblical injunction to Adam and Eve, "Be fruitful and multiply and fill the earth and subdue it; and have dominion over every fish of the sea and over the birds of the air and over every living thing that moves on the earth" (Genesis 1:28). Most scholars who have examined this claim have largely dismissed it, noting that the process of industrialization, which fueled overpopulation and maximized human pollution processes, emerged first in the West for a variety of reasons, many having nothing to do with religion at all. Many biblical scholars and ethicists also note that the impact of this quotation need not be destructive at all: It does call for humankind to exercise control, but control can be used for varying interests. They point out that the ethic that early Christianity later developed on the basis of this scriptural assignment of power and responsibility was a stewardship ethic, which it shares with Judaism and with Islam (in which humans are called to be vice-regents of God in conserving the earth).

Today many Christian ecologists understand the scriptural record as reflecting the anthropocentrism of those who interpreted God's interactions with humans within that scripture and regard such anthropocentrism as historically global. Rosemary Ruether presents all inherited wisdom systems as requiring some degree of reform:

> There is no ready-made ecological spirituality and ethic in past traditions. The ecological crisis is new to human experience. This does not mean that humans have not devastated their environment before. But as long as populations remained small and human technology weak, these devastations were remediable by migration, retreat from top-heavy urban centers, or adaptation to new techniques. Nature appeared a huge, inexhaustible source of life, and humans small. Only after the bombs of Hiroshima and Nagasaki did humans begin to recognize the possibility that they could destroy the planet by their own expropriated power.[20]

Ruether goes on to examine both covenantal and sacramental systems for relating to the earth within Christianity, demonstrating the advantages of each and how each requires reform.[21] Other Christian environmentalists, such as Carol Robb and Carl Casebolt, also have presented a reformed version of covenant for dealing with the environmental responsibilities of Christians.[22]

Within a traditional Christian stewardship ethic, several distinctions have arisen under the influence of environmentalism. The most conservative, traditional interpretation of stewardship is that the goods of the earth were given to humans to meet human needs and should be used by all; the only misuse of the earth in this understanding is to squander a resource needed by another human. Other traditional interpretations emphasize the moral requirement that the goods of the earth were given to meet the needs of all, including the poor, and that no human has a right to excess until the basic rights of the poor are cared for. Although both of these interpretations are thoroughly anthropocentric, the latter would effectively preserve more of the environment in that meeting the needs of all people would include protecting the environments on which many indigenous and poor peoples of the world depend.

Many Christian environmentalists have rejected simple anthropocentrism, however—even when, like James Nash, in the end they prefer the claim to life of an individual human being over that of another species. Like many others, however, Nash defends the biotic rights of other species and would place their right to survive as a species ahead of many human interests other than life itself.[23] As the literature in religious environmentalism continues to expand around the world, religionists are replicating the spectrum of ethical stances we have seen among environmental philosophers. The most institutional of the religious responses—especially those issued by officials of the religion—tend to present stewardship models expanded to include both future generations and varying degrees of intrinsic value for other species. On the other hand, in virtually every religion some thinkers have traced through existing tradition a strand from which to challenge the anthropocentrism in the rest of the tradition and have developed an approach that is similar to deep ecology.

Values, Value, and Valuing

Although "value" is a term that appears often in religious and philosophical discussions—including this introduction—its meaning is not always clear. Philosophers have dedicated a subfield called axiology to a discussion of the concept; religions ritualize and confess their values in very public ways. Yet even among these specialists, clarification of the term is sometimes wanting. In philosophy this lack of clarity probably reflects the fact that the notion of value is something of a latecomer in philosophical reflection. In the tradition, self-conscious reflection on value is primarily an aspect of modern inquiry, appearing since the Enlightenment. In religion, a lack of precision is the underside of religion's use of symbolism, which allows religion to make powerful connections between different aspects of reality—connections that involve not only cognition but also affectivity.

Adding to the confusion is the fact that popular expressions of "value" are mostly seen and heard at the local mall or the stock exchange. In its economic or commercial sense, *value* means the worth of a thing in terms of money or the purchasing power of the dollar: fair price or more than fair price. "This new pair of jeans was on sale. What a value." Or, "In this market, devalued stocks are a great bargain."

For philosophers and religionists, the economic understanding of value is uninteresting, for the most part. They prefer, instead, to study its meaning in terms of the worth of an action or object. Our discussion of value is based on this idea of worth. Philosophers are not of one mind about value. Traditionally, value as worth has been understood in two ways. In the first, X is valuable to me if X serves some useful purpose for me—if it performs some function that benefits me or others. A hammer sitting in a toolbox is worthless until I remove it to drive a nail. In this case, the hammer is said to have instrumental value. A second way of understanding value is to assign worth to X in its own right, independent of any usefulness. Specified value becomes a quality carried by X rather than imputed to it, so that even in the absence of anyone to appreciate it, X may be said to be valuable. Instrumental value is easily understood, but this intrinsic or objective value is less clear for two reasons. How are we to understand a value as attached to a being: Is it like a physical property? Second, how is any imputed value truly objective given that a quality is valuable only when it is appreciated by a qualified observer?

These questions are more readily avoided when X is a person. Most of us recognize that others like ourselves possess intrinsic value simply because they are persons. Persons possess inherent dignity and significant worth. Religions have always taught that it is our duty to treat others of our species "with dignity" or in a "dignified way." This means taking no actions that violate others' integrity or otherwise bring unjustified harm to them. Of course, attention to dignity does not prohibit seeing others in terms of their instrumental value. In an economy driven by service industries, such a prohibition would be our ruin. A service worker such as a plumber or electrician voluntarily performs tasks that may benefit me. I should not treat the plumber or electrician as an object of lesser worth than others in my world, however. Furthermore, of course, service representatives should receive fair "value" or wages for their labor.

As we have described in the section on anthropocentrism, problems arise when X is not a person. How are we to understand the value of nonhuman beings or collections of nonhuman beings, species, ecosystems, nature itself? Do nonhuman beings have any value at all? If the discussion is limited to instrumental value, the question is easily answered. Nature provides us with the wherewithal for our secure and comfortable lives. Nature has tremendous instrumental value. In this context, our duty to nature is to conserve it, protect it, and utilize it effectively, lest we do ourselves in. This position is that of John Passmore, who concludes that we have no direct duties to nature, only direct duties to ourselves. That is, we should bring as little harm as possible to natural entities, not for their own sake but for ours. Holmes Rolston III lists several of these instrumental values. He includes life-support value, economic value, recreational value, scientific value, aesthetic value, diversity value, historical value, cultural value, character-building value, and religious value.

Carrying this analysis to the extreme, a philosopher could argue that all values, even objective values, imputed to nature actually are thinly disguised instrumental or subjective human values. Why would I work to preserve the Grand Canyon? Because its grandeur and marvelous vistas trigger a profound response in my psyche. Is all of this beauty merely in the eye of the beholder, and is my duty to preserving the Canyon really only an indirect duty to myself? Although I may be taking actions that protect the sources of my preference for beauty and majesty, I may be doing so because beauty and majesty truly reside in this natural place, to be recognized and appreciated by me. Likewise, because I love and cherish my son I will take every action to assure his fulfillment as a person. Are these duties ultimately based in selfish intentions and egoistic satisfaction? What I value in the Grand Canyon and in my son are not my experience and desires alone but also the very existence of this place and this person. It would seem odd to speak of intrinsic value in any other way.

A religious perspective is very different at this point, however. If one believes that there is a god or gods, then the ultimate perspective is not the human but the divine. Religious scholars such as Thomas Aquinas insisted that God created the world because it pleased him, and the purpose of creation is to glorify God. Creation is diverse, Aquinas wrote, because that diversity testifies to the majesty of God. From this perspective, even within a stewardship framework in which God gave responsibility for creation to humans, humans have no right to decrease either the glory or the diversity of God's creation. From a religious perspective, human responsibility for creation is limited to maintenance and preservation precisely because it would be idolatry—substituting our own judgment for God's—to decide that the only value of the rest of creation is instrumental and indirect, limited to its value to humans.

The implications from this discussion are several. First, values are enumerated as subsequent reflections on the act of valuing. Hence, valuing may be understood as an experiential judgment, a connoisseurship, that involves both the evaluator and some object of evaluation in a relational process. Second, valuing is not limited to the human species. Many sentient creatures clearly appreciate certain experiences for their own sake—such as play and sex—even if these experiences are prepared for and driven by instinct and serve larger purposes (e.g., predatory skills and procreation). Third, the human species shares this natural appreciation of essential goods, but its appreciation of value carries much further into nonessential goods in the creation of culture. Finally, the human appreciation of value in nature entails moral duties with respect to this value. If value is that which is worthy or good and morality is the pursuit, realization, and preservation of the good, then value entails duties. With the recognition of value beyond human culture, our relations with nature become moral.

Notes

1. Holmes Rolston III, "Environmental Ethics: Values and Duties to the Natural World," in *Ecology, Economics, Ethics: The Broken Circle*, ed. Herbert Bormann and Stephen R. Keller (New Haven, Conn.: Yale University Press, 1991), 73.
2. Ibid., 74.
3. *Immanual Kant, Lectures on Ethics*, trans. Louis Infield (New York: Harper and Row, 1963), 239.
4. See John Passmore, *Man's Responsibility for Nature* (New York: Scribner's, 1974).
5. See Peter Singer, *Animal Liberation* (New York: Avon, 1976).
6. Jeremy Bentham, *The Principles of Morals and Legislation* (New York: Columbia University Press, 1945), chap. 17, sec. 1, fn. to paragraph 4.
7. See Donald VanDeVeer, "Interspecific Justice," *Inquiry* 22 (summer 1979): 55–70; reprinted in Donald VanDeVeer and Christine Pierce, eds., *The Environmental Ethics and Policy Book: Philosophy, Ecology, Economics* (Belmont, Calif.: Wadsworth Publishing Co., 1998), 179–92.
8. See Tom Regan, *The Case for Animal Rights* (Berkeley: University of California Press, 1983).
9. See Paul Taylor, *Respect for Nature* (Princeton, N.J.: Princeton University Press, 1986).
10. Aldo Leopold, *Sand County Almanac with Essays on Conservation from Round River* (Oxford: Oxford University Press, 1953).
11. Ibid., 239.
12. Ibid., 251.
13. Ibid., 262.
14. Ibid., 263.
15. J. Baird Callicott, "La nature est Morte, Vive la Nature," *Hastings Center Report* 22 (September 1992): 19.
16. See Murray Bookchin, *The Ecology of Freedom* (Palo Alto, Calif.: Cheshire Books, 1982), and *The Philosophy of Social Ecology* (Montreal: Black Rose Books, 1990).

17. See Bryan G. Norton, *Toward Unity among Environmentalists* (New York: Oxford University Press, 1991).
18. See, for example, Carol J. Adams, ed., *Ecofeminism and the Sacred* (New York: Continuum, 1993), and Rosemary R. Ruether, ed., *Women Healing Earth: Third World Women on Ecology, Feminism, and Religion* (Maryknoll, N.Y.: Orbis, 1996).
19. Thomas Berry, *Thomas Berry and the New Cosmology* (Mystic, Conn.: Twenty-Third Publications, 1987), 17.
20. Rosemary Radford Ruether, *Gaia and God: An Ecofeminist Theology of Earth Healing* (New York: HarperCollins, 1992), 206.
21. Ibid., 205–53.
22. Carol S. Robb and Carl J. Casebolt, *Covenant for a New Creation: Ethics, Religion and Public Policy* (Maryknoll, N.Y.: Orbis/GTU, 1991).
23. James A. Nash, *Loving Nature: Ecological Inquiry and Christian Responsibility* (Nashville, Tenn.: Abingdon, 1991).

I

MAINTAINING AND MANAGING THE ECOSYSTEM

2

Bridge over Troubled Waters: Embattled Community in the Everglades

"Buenos dias, Mr. Harris."

"Hello," responded Kenneth Harris as he stepped from his rental car. "You must be Maria Perez, president of the United Property Owners, and this must be Chakika, Florida."

"Yes, but those of us who live here sometimes refer to this place as 'Pariah,' Florida," said Maria.

Ken Harris smiled. "Pariah" was the characterization he was using in a series of articles for his magazine, *New York Today*, to describe the plight of this small and beleaguered community on the eastern boundaries of the Everglades. As he approached Maria he tried not to step into the muddy potholes at the edge of the unimproved road.

"I see you've experienced the Everglades 'turnpike,'" Maria commented after observing the mud-caked wheels of the car. "I hope the rest of your trip was not that adventurous."

"No, it wasn't," said Ken, "just the last five miles from the bridge on Chapman Drive. I had a few tense moments when I nearly lost control and began sliding toward the canal."

"That's not unusual, even now in the dry season," said Maria. "The community and I do appreciate your willingness to risk your life to hear our side of the story!"

"Well, it's the least I could do in researching the final piece in the series and satisfying that great journalistic principle of fair and balanced reporting," said Ken. "And when you say 'our side of the story,' you mean it quite literally. Chakika is on the west side of this canal, L-31, that marks the development line between suburban Miami-Dade County and the Everglades."

"Yes," said Maria, "and we desperately need the county to fund the rebuilding of a bridge right here where we are standing to replace the ancient rickety one that was condemned and torn down last year. Then the 800 residents of Chakika could drive directly onto Flamingo Road." Maria pointed across the canal to the paved street that dead-ended at its banks. "Unless we get this new bridge, the community will suffer and even disappear."

"The problem is the cost?" Ken asked.

Maria laughed. "Not at all. The county would like nothing more than to see Chakika vanish."

"And I know why," said Ken, recalling the subject of his previous article. "You're called 'a debtor community' because you don't contribute anything to the county in return for public services. In several interviews I was told that the 400 homeowners here should have known better than to buy land from unscrupulous swamp peddlers in a mosquito-infested area that floods seasonally. And now you want the government to bail you out."

"That's wrong," responded Maria. "We pay property taxes—millions of dollars worth in the past thirty years. And we receive little in return. The county does not provide us with any services—garbage collection, street repair. It's a great deal for them."

"Then why do they refuse to rebuild the bridge?" asked Ken.

"That's an excellent question," Maria said, "that can best be answered over a cup of Cuban coffee."

"Here you are," Maria said a few minutes later, handing Ken a small cup. "Sip slowly," she warned. "It's highly concentrated, and the caffeine can give you a real buzz."

"Thanks," Ken said. "So tell me: Why do they refuse to build the bridge?"

"Because there's even more money to be had in seeing us destroyed," Maria exclaimed. "As you landed you may have noticed several large, rectangular lakes west of Miami International Airport. They're open pits filled with water from the underground aquifer. The county offers its land to rock-mining companies that extract huge amounts of limestone for concrete and other purposes in return

28

for millions in leasing permits. The industry is ravenous for additional land, but to get it environmental regulations require that it restore other degraded lands in return. They call it 'land mitigation,' and the land they want is the nine square miles of Chakika."

"And what about the 'swamp peddler' image?" Ken asked.

"That's wrong, too," Maria said. "In the first place, Chakika actually is more than seven feet above sea level. I know that doesn't sound like much, but it means that, historically, this land seldom flooded—perhaps only in a hurricane or other 'one-in-ten-year' storm. Secondly, Chakika is a farming community, not a suburb of Miami."

"But *The Miami Herald* constantly claims in its editorials that Chakika must vanish to prevent urban sprawl from creeping into the Everglades," Ken interjected.

"That opinion is way off base, Mr. Harris," Maria continued with increasing frustration. "The county refuses to allow construction on any plot under forty acres out here. No developer could subdivide enough to make the project worthwhile. The folks who live here are mostly Cuban American. All they want is to be left alone to grow their winter vegetables, harvest their tropical fruit trees—mangoes and avocados—run their plant nurseries, and drive across this canal to the farmer's market in Homestead. Many also make the daily commute to Miami. I'm a registered nurse. We desperately need this bridge. We desperately need to be left alone."

"Now I'm really confused," said Ken. "I've seen pictures of children playing in water up to their waists and canoes floating down the streets of Chakika. Haven't you been seriously flooded at least four times since Hurricane Andrew in 1992? Isn't the image of living in a swamp justified by these floods?"

Ken looked away and began to study a large map of the peninsula of Florida on the wall in the living room of Maria's modest stucco home.

"My living room is the strategy center, or war room, for the property owners' association," Maria said. "This map will help me answer your question. The Everglades—which once spread as far north as Lake Okeechobee, about 100 miles from Miami—actually is a very shallow, very wide river that once ran all the way through the sawgrass down to Everglades National Park and emptied into Florida Bay at the tip of the peninsula."

"But it doesn't anymore, I gather," Ken said.

"That's right. See these red lines?" Maria asked, pointing to the map. "They represent some of the 1,800 miles of canals that were constructed beginning in the 1940s to take this vast sheet of water and divert it to the sea."

"Quite a plumbing project," remarked Ken.

"One of the most ambitious in history," responded Maria. "And it worked. The land was drained, flooding was controlled, and development followed. Now we have six million people living in southern Florida."

"And this red line is the L-31 canal," said Ken, pointing to the map.

"Yes, and we're here just west of it in the historic area of flow," said Maria.

"No wonder you get flooded," said Ken.

"Actually, that's not true," Maria responded. "The reasons are political and ideological, not natural. The South Florida Water Management District—the agency responsible for running this plumbing system—wants us out too. We believe that the SFWMD maintains water levels in the WCAs, or water conservation areas, north of us at unseasonably high levels year-round. So when the rains come—we get 80 percent of our precipitation between June and October around here—the water rises dramatically, mostly through the porous limestone beneath our feet, with devastating consequences."

"And the end result?" prompted Ken.

". . . is to turn us into 'willing sellers'—disheartened homeowners who will sell their land below cost just to get out. Then they and the county would have their so-called degraded land for the rock miners' mitigation," responded Maria.

"The spokesperson for the SFWMD says differently," said Ken, rebutting Maria's claims. "Given the $7 billion effort to save the Everglades—the so-called Modified Water Delivery Project—the agency's new priorities are Everglades restoration and resource management, not flood control. Chakika is seen as blocking the natural sheet flow and seasonal hydroperiods that are so crucial for the health and well-being of the national park. A buyout of the homeowners, they say, is the only way to achieve this flow."

"And I thought New Yorkers were born skeptics," said Maria, "but I guess I should replace 'skeptic' with 'gullible' in my stereotype. The Everglades can never be completely restored. All we can do is use the canal system—the tool that nearly destroyed the Everglades—as an instrument to save it. But what we save will be a remnant and not the magnificent original. And in the original system the elevation of this land lifted it out of the sheet flow. Buying us out won't change that; it would accomplish nothing."

"Then why are you demanding flood protection?" asked Ken, sensing a serious inconsistency in Maria's impassioned account. "I understand that Chakika wants the Army Corps of Engineers to construct a canal and levee on the west side of the community to control flooding. If the SFWMD released all that troublesome water from the WCAs, what flooding would that be?"

"Since I'm a nurse, let me answer you with a medical analogy," Maria responded thoughtfully. "The sad fact about the restoration project is that the Everglades system, a patient now in critical condition, will always require human management or life-support from the SFWMD. This means that all those miles of canals, huge pumps, and massive floodgates will work together to imitate the natural hydropattern. But that includes occasionally storing or releasing water from the WCAs in very unnatural amounts, resulting in the flooding of Chakika. The Corps' canal and levee would prevent most of that."

"Why is the Corps so generous?" inquired Ken.

"It's not generosity; it's law," said Maria, as she pulled a file from her desk next to the map. "Here's a law passed by Congress in 1989. In brief, the relevant section reads as follows: 'If Chakika, Florida, will be adversely affected by the Everglades restoration project, the Secretary of the Army is authorized and directed to construct a flood protection system for that portion of presently developed land within that area.'"

"That's very interesting," Ken exclaimed, examining the document. "What's holding them up?"

"The Department of the Interior refuses to allocate the funds, and I bet you can tell me why," said Maria.

"My guess would be that Interior—like Miami-Dade County, the rock mining industry, the SFWMD, and probably the superintendent of Everglades National Park—prefers a buyout of disheartened homeowners," said Ken.

"Add 'perceptive' to 'gullible' in my stereotype of New Yorkers," Maria said, smiling.

"My experience covering City Hall in New York City taught me that a deceptively simple controversy with two clearly defined opposing sides always conceals more complicated issues and ideologies and a crowd of players," said Ken. "It's no different in South Florida, is it? All these agencies with their missions, ideologies, and vested interests concealed beneath the very simple question of the fate of your small agricultural community—to be or not to be.

"One more question before I have to go," said Ken, glancing at his watch. "I have other interviews before flying out tomorrow. Have we left out anybody in this scene?"

"Just one other player," answered Maria. "Tens of thousands of acres of tribal lands belonging to the Miccosukee Indians lie within or near the WCAs. These lands have suffered considerably from the abnormally high water levels; many tree islands where the Miccosukees located their villages in the nineteenth century are inundated and

31

dead. The tribe has sued in federal court for a permanent drawdown of the water levels and approval of the Corps' plans for Chakika."

"Why are the Indians interested in you?" asked Ken.

"It's obvious. A buyout will take twenty years to complete, but construction of a canal and levee will take only a year or two. Understandably, they want results now," said Maria.

"This has been very revealing," Ken said, preparing to leave. "My next interview is with Gregory Weisman, president of Save the Everglades and chair of the Everglades Restoration Alliance. I gather you know the gentleman."

"Do I!" exclaimed Maria. "We have had numerous encounters— or, more accurately, unfriendly confrontations—in recent years. If you had to name a pure ideologist of the environmental movement, you couldn't do better than Gregory Weisman."

"This is almost as interesting as my beat at City Hall," said Ken, as they shook hands and he walked back to his car.

Maria thought it was unlikely that she would speak to Ken again, so she was surprised when her phone rang later on that afternoon. It was Ken.

"Ms. Perez, I just concluded my interview with Weisman. He informed me that the Department of the Interior has just issued a Jeopardy Biological Alert concerning the Cape Sable seaside sparrow. Apparently, the population of this rare bird is about to crash, resulting in its imminent extinction. An emergency meeting of the Everglades Restoration Alliance is scheduled for tomorrow morning. From what Weisman told me, Chakika is the target in their sights. You should attend."

"Okay, another player enters the scene from stage left, and the drama intensifies," said Maria. "Thanks for informing me, Mr. Harris. I'll be at that meeting."

*   *   *

Maria arrived at the federal building on Biscayne Boulevard an hour before the scheduled meeting, hoping to catch Weisman for a private conference. Luck was with her. He too was an early arrival, and they found a vacant office for their conversation.

"This is an open-and-shut case, Maria," declared Weisman. "You and I both know that Chakika is the problem here. It has always been the problem in our efforts to restore sheet flow to the national park and to Florida Bay in the Modified Water Delivery Project. You are in the way. Now, finally, we have the issue we've been looking for— the imminent extirpation of a rare species. The sparrow belongs in the Everglades; you don't. No longer is the choice between a buyout or the construction of a levee and canal. The only choice is condemnation."

"Dios mio!" Maria exclaimed under her breath. So much for even the minimal congeniality these two adversaries shared in past encounters.

"Gregory," she said, "we both know the history of the sparrow's plight. You may not agree, but its plight is the same as Chakika's. It has to do with too much or too little water."

"We agree about the water," Gregory responded. "The sparrow has three major populations—two north of Chakika near the WCAs, and the other south of the community near Cape Sable and the park. The first two areas are nesting sites where persistent high water has destroyed the marshes and disrupted the nesting cycle. The population to the south is shrinking because the area is too dry and subject to fires that destroy the necessary grassy cover."

"So the plan is to open the floodgates up north and release millions of gallons of water through Chakika on its way to the parched Cape Sable nesting area," said Maria as she completed Gregory's argument for him. Then she added more. "I've followed this case for a long time, Gregory. The population of sparrows is not in a nosedive because of natural forces. You can't blame the weather, drought, or deluge. The sparrow's predicament is the result of political forces and acts of people, not acts of God. It could have been averted years ago, before we arrived at this crisis, if government agencies had simply worked together to draw down the stored water proportionally and over an extended period."

"I can appreciate your point, Maria," said Gregory. "My organization, along with other environmental groups, including the Tropical Audubon Society, repeatedly issued warnings about the sparrow. Nobody was listening."

"And why were you ignored?" persisted Maria.

"Well, I suspect mostly because of ignorance about how the Everglades system really works and because there was no real crisis like this one to which Washington had to respond," said Gregory, in a more cooperative tone.

"Do you know how the Everglades system works, Gregory?" interrogated Maria.

"Of course not. Nobody really does. Local environmental scientists call it a 'turbulent ecosystem' because hydrologically it's exquisitely sensitive to seasonal weather patterns and crisis events like floods and droughts. You try to alter the system so it won't flood by shunting the water out to tide, and you magnify the effects of the next drought. You adjust the system by storing water in anticipation of drought, and you aggravate flooding caused by the next tropical storm. You're either dry or drowning."

"You can add two more reasons to the list," said Maria. "Conflict of interest and lack of communication between the various agencies.

The integrity of a complex ecosystem like the Everglades can't possibly be restored if the responsible agencies go off in different directions to satisfy their own self-defined 'missions.' So now we're in this mess, and Chakika is to be the scapegoat and required sacrifice for all this bungling. Will the SFWMD be represented at this meeting?" she asked.

"Yes, they and the Corps of Engineers will attend, along with the city manager of Miami-Dade County, who wants a soapbox for the L-31 bridge issue. The Miccosukees are sending their attorney," answered Gregory.

"And what position will he take?" asked Maria, feigning ignorance just to provoke Gregory.

"This may surprise you, but I'm not sure of their position. The Indians are caught in the middle. On one hand they're pleased that their waterlogged tribal lands may finally be drained. On the other hand, they realize that it may happen so quickly that the Corps of Engineers won't be able to construct that protective canal and levee that you and the tribe want so badly. So they're afraid that they'll be caught in an extended and messy legal dispute between Chakika, the government, and themselves."

"And that's okay with you?" asked Maria?

"Yes. At this moment, our interests lie exclusively with the sparrow. You know how strongly I feel about endangered species, even the marginal and minor ones—those whose disappearance nobody would notice because they aren't symbolic and charismatic, like the bald eagle, or winsome, like the manatee. The death of a form of life is much more serious than the death of an individual of the species because, in that case, other individuals can carry on its kind. Loss of the sparrow is the death of life itself, irreversible and unforgivable." Gregory hesitated, "I'm sorry, Maria. I should save my sermons for the meeting. But you can tell where my sympathies and passions lie."

"That's never been my problem with you, Gregory. But the ease with which you're willing to sacrifice an entire community of families, depriving them of their homes and livelihood, is very bothersome. I'm sympathetic to the predicament of the species, but it's difficult for me to grasp how the rights of the sparrow trump the rights of the citizens of Chakika, no questions asked. That kind of justice is so cruel as to be inhuman."

"Oh, you retain your rights, Maria," corrected Gregory. "In fact, I believe that some time ago everyone living in Chakika was sent a copy of the federal pamphlet, *The Rights of Displaced Persons,* at the request of the SFWMD. "

"Dios mio!" exclaimed Maria, realizing that the phrase was becoming a habit. "Where is your soul, Gregory?"

"Don't act like such a victim, Maria. You don't *belong* in the Everglades." With this remark, Gregory turned and entered the conference room.

Maria turned to see Colonel Terry Price of the Army Corps of Engineers approaching the conference room. Just behind him was the lead attorney for the Miccosukees. Maria's spirits brightened. She and the people of Chakika were not alone, after all. She would testify with the same enthusiasm as Gregory. Then, she thought, we would see who the victims are.

Commentary

This case reflects real-life situations in its complexity. It involves individuals, communities, governmental agencies at several levels, and an endangered species. Each of these "players," as Maria refers to them, has interests and intentions—or, in the case of the Cape Sable seaside sparrow, advocates with interest and intentions. If the situation were a simple conflict between two opposing positions on an issue—for example, whether to release water to save the sparrow's nesting territory—a straightforward weighing of the claims of each side theoretically would lead to some resolution, even if a true dilemma were present. But moral situations, particularly those involving public policy, often are more complicated. Not only do the numerous parties frequently engage one another in contradictory ways, they also interact in ways that sometimes cancel and sometimes aggravate consequences. The Indians have an interest in saving inundated tribal lands by forcing the release of massive amounts of stored water. The Army Corps of Engineers seeks to construct a protective levee and canal for Chakika as part of its instructions, based on a law of Congress. The SFWMD has the opposite intention—which, according to Maria, is to force the homeowners to become "willing sellers" by maintaining unnaturally high waters levels in the community. Others, including aggressive environmental groups, rush to save the sparrow through the immediate strategy of releasing water.

One can only imagine what the superintendent of Everglades National Park must think of all this. After all, the overarching goal of the Modified Water Delivery Project is to implement the $7 billion Everglades Restoration Project, which some observers have called the largest public works project in history. It is unclear whether the park would welcome or regret the sudden release of water into the several "sloughs" or shallow rivers that would carry it through the park into Florida Bay at the tip of the peninsula. Too much water would be as disruptive to wildlife, especially wading birds, as too little. The conflicted engagement of these players could lead to actions that would benefit the park only marginally, if at all.

35

The little community of Chakika is caught in the middle of these brawling factions. As represented by Maria, it is characterized both unsympathetically as a villain and sympathetically as a victim. Public opinion (yet another player) is represented by the editorial opinions of the local newspaper (although news media shape public opinions as well as reflect them). If its readership consists of a representative cross-section of Americans, this opinion is unlikely to favor Chakika. Research and polls consistently show that the public has embraced environmental values wholeheartedly. If this were not so, Congress would not have underwritten the massive and very expensive Everglades Restoration Project, and the government of Miami-Dade County would not apply pressure to the community by withholding services and refusing to rebuild the community bridge. To the newspaper and the public, Chakika is indeed the villain—by insisting on building in the Everglades floodplain, its homeowners interrupt sheetflow of water to the park and contribute to the extinction of an endangered species. Their continuing resistance to moving reflects a selfish and obstructive attitude that can only bring harm to the public good. Ken Harris, the out-of-town reporter, is at least willing to listen to Maria's claim that none of this is true. Maria's defense is that the *Miami Herald*, the county, and other agencies arrayed against Chakika misrepresent and distort the facts in accordance with their own goals. How is it possible to receive a fair hearing in any public forum when your community has been demonized by the press?

Recall the discussion of Murray Bookchin's social ecology in chapter 1. Bookchin places the blame for the environmental crisis on social and ideological structures that encourage domination and exploitation. He concludes that the way we treat nature is an extension of the way we treat one another, especially through our institutions. The institutions in this case are no exception.

Social institutions—governmental or the media—often seek to achieve desired results through the application of power, bureaucratic or public, that comes with such organizations. The county has the power to build bridges across canals, or not to build them, as a means to gets its way. The SFWMD may withhold or release water into the canal system in accordance with its goals. In this case, the goal of both institutions is to force the vacancy of the land on which the 400 homes of the community now sit. The justification of this selective application of power lies in the desired consequences. Ostensibly, each of these governmental entities serves the public—in this case, the citizens of South Florida. Clearly, however, they do not serve all of the citizens all of the time. The county, for example, aims at filling its coffers with monies gained from land leases to the rock-mining companies (commercial institutions with power and goals of their own). Ideally (and we realize that politics seldom approaches the ideal), this money will then be allocated by responsible public officials—the mayor and county commission—to public projects that will bring benefits to the millions of people who live in Miami-Dade County. Achieving this goal requires the denial of funding for the new bridge because its construction would contradict the strategy of using the land as environmental mitigation for the mining companies. Although this situation does not seem quite fair, its moral justification clearly lies in the utilitarian perspective of most government agencies—which, as we recall, is to maximize the good in the form of desirable consequences that benefit the largest number of persons. To put it in blunt terms, sometimes it can be reasonably argued that the ends do justify the means, even if those means result in some harm. But to make that argument is to minimize or even set aside concerns for justice.

The intentions of a public institution do not always correspond to public needs. Social groups, including highly organized groups—particularly government agencies—frequently take on identities and lives of their own. An agency is given a "mission" or a specific set of assignments it is mandated to carry out and upon which its very existence depends. Sometimes such missions are elevated to the level of ideologies and implemented with a dedication and passion that resembles religion. Sociologists Peter Berger and Thomas Luckmann write that an ideology arises "when a particular definition of reality comes to be attached to a concrete power interest. . . ."[1] In this case, more than one power interest seems to be in play. Indeed, each institutional entity wishes to reinforce its power by successfully achieving its particular mission or assignment.

This situation corresponds nicely with Bookchin's analysis, but with an important twist that he apparently did not anticipate. Except for Chakika, the feuding institutions and agencies involved in this case appear to share a common view of a value-laden "reality"—namely, that the Everglades and its endangered species should be preserved and restored. This position is best represented by Gregory Weisman. Thus, an environmental ideology is embraced as the source of the rules of the game by which all players should abide. Other interests, though not subordinated to the environment, must be pursued within the context of the common ideology. For example, the county and the rock miners serve particular major interests—generating funds or profits—but each must pursue these interests by conforming their actions to environmental assumptions. In their actions to fight eviction and save their community at the edge of the Everglades, the homeowners of Chakika appear to oppose this ideological stand. This stance probably is the primary source of their demonization.

This pervasive political and environmental philosophy has not always been the case in Florida. In fact, some of the confusion in this case arises because the missions of several agencies have changed radically as a result of this shift in public values. Before the 1960s the emphasis had been on treating natural systems as resources to be extracted and managed. "Conservation" was the term most frequently used to convey this approach. In the spirit of Gifford Pinchot, who established the U.S. Forest Service during the administration of Theodore Roosevelt in the first decade of the twentieth century, conservation of timber and other resources was prudent and carried out not for the sake of preserving nature but instrumentally for the sake of providing resources for future generations. Economic development fit nicely into this theme. The original intention of the massive canal system in the Everglades was to construct an "engine for economic growth" that would effectively control the seasonal flow of water and maintain it as an abundant resource. The missions of the SFWMD and the Army Corps of Engineers reflected this national ideology. Indeed, they were designed to carry it out.

As the priorities of Americans moved from the exploitation of nature to the enjoyment of nature and, hence, its preservation, the missions of these agencies were altered in kind. Originally intended for flood control and water supply, the task of the SFWMD came to be restoration and resource management, with special emphasis on the Everglades ecosystem. The Corps of Engineers reoriented its functions from channeling rivers to reintroducing original meandering riverbeds and regenerating long-lost marshes. Such projects—for example, the Kissimmee River basin in central Florida—have been grand successes.

The great irony—or tragedy, as seen through the eyes of the homeowners in Chakika—is that the community is a success story in the context of the drain-and-build philosophy of development. In the new scheme of Everglades restoration, however, it stands as a pariah, blocking water flow to a parched park.

Grave difficulties remain to be overcome before restoration is a success, regardless of what happens to Chakika. More than half of the historic Everglades system has been lost to agriculture and urban and residential development. Much of the remainder has been "balkanized," in the words of one environmental scientist.[2] That is, a seamless region has been fragmented into compartments for which various governmental agencies are responsible. These agencies, in turn, fail to communicate effectively, much less collaborate on a common goal. This lack of coordination is reflected in the disarticulation of the once highly integrated natural system they were designed to manage.

Furthermore, these agencies—reflecting the character of most formal social institutions—are highly centralized. Management is by a technocratic elite (i.e., "experts") that revels in tight regulations and an engineering mentality. It also tends to establish momentum in a single direction that is difficult to alter unless confronted by a crisis. Restoration of the ecological integrity of the Everglades system is not well served by this approach; neither is the future well-being of Chakika. Success in this grand project requires a sensitive awareness of the dynamics of natural systems and particularly the willingness to adapt or co-evolve within the system in addition to plumbing or managing it.

The ancient Chinese philosophy of Taoism[3] questions the highly centralized divide-and-conquer approach that is oriented toward unilateral application of power and scientific knowledge for the sake of mechanical control. This style corresponds to the assertive yang energy of Taoism. The yang must be balanced by patience, flexibility, and sensitivity—the yin of Taoism. A Taoist master might say that each of these fundamental attitudes must be present in proper proportion to the particular requirements of the situation for success to be realized. In the case of Chakika and Everglades restoration, the balance should tilt decidedly in favor of yin to redress the destructive tendencies of the modern scientific and technological age that, to attempt a pun, suffers from its "yang-ups."

Application of a yin approach is especially important for the Everglades—an ecosystem whose central feature is the presence or absence of massive volumes of water. Crisis events—floods, droughts, or storms—define human responses. Historically, however, these responses have done little more than reinforce the unpredictable effects of the next crisis event. Now that the human species has inserted itself into a radically disrupted ecosystem, both natural and human-induced changes must be factored in. Thus, to a significant extent, nature has been politicized.

The Everglades is neither a pristine wilderness nor a mechanical plumbing system. It is a highly complex system involving human and natural components in a dynamic and evolving relationship. Chakika's plight represents the struggle of very finite and fallible human beings to reverse destruction that they have caused without leaving further destruction in their wake.

Questions for Discussion

1. Who are the "players" in this case? Rank them according to the importance of their interests or purposes (e.g., economic, political, environmental). Justify the order of your ranking.
2. The important role of governmental agencies and their policies often is neglected in environmental ethics. Describe the policy or "mission" of

the agencies in the case. Are these missions only political, or do they also promote hidden environmental philosophies?

3. Many metaphors have been used to describe the Everglades, including "swamp," "river," "patient," and "garden." How does each of these promote a particular attitude toward the ecosystem and encourage particular actions toward it? Explain.

4. The billions of dollars allocated by Congress for Everglades restoration make the project the largest and most expensive ever undertaken. Compare the environmental and ethical issues raised here with those faced in chapter 7, as well as in the much smaller project in chapter 10. Note important similarities and differences.

Notes

1. Peter L. Berger and Thomas Luckmann, *The Social Construction of Reality: A Treatise in the Sociology of Knowledge* (New York: Anchor Books, Doubleday, 1966), 106.

2. Stephen S. Light, Lance H. Gunderson, and C. S. Hollings, "The Everglades: Evolution of Management in a Turbulent Ecosystem," in *Barriers and Bridges to the Renewal of Ecosystems and Institutions,* ed. Lance H. Gunderson (New York: Columbia University Press, 1995), 130.

3. See Lao Tsu, *Tao Te Ching,* trans. Gia-Fu Feng, and Jane English (New York: Random House, 1972).

For Further Reading

Berger, Peter L., and Thomas Luckmann. *The Social Construction of Reality: A Treatise in the Sociology of Knowledge.* New York: Anchor Books, Doubleday, 1966.

Florida International University. Everglades Information Network, www.fiu.edu.

Fortin, Madeline. "Pariah, Florida: Hopelessness in the Face of Bureaucracy." Master's thesis, Florida International University, 2002.

Light, Stephen S., Lance H. Gunderson, and C. S. Hollings. "The Everglades: Evolution of Management in a Turbulent Ecosystem." In *Barriers and Bridges to the Renewal of Ecosystems and Institutions,* edited by Lance H. Gunderson. New York: Columbia University Press, 1995, 103–68.

Lodge, Thomas E. *The Everglades Handbook: Understanding the Ecosystem.* Delray Beach, Fla.: St. Lucie Press, 1994.

Nelson, Robert H. "How Much Is Enough? An Overview of the Benefits and Costs of Environmental Protection." In *Taking the Environment*

Seriously, edited by Roger E. Meiners and Bruce Yandle. New York: Rowman and Littlefield Publishers, 1993, 276–301.

Switzer, Jacqueline Vaughn, and Gary Bryner. *Environmental Politics: Domestic and Global Dimensions*, 2d ed. New York: St. Martin's Press, 1997.

3

For Ecological Health or Profit?
The POPs Elimination Treaty

"This is a heavy responsibility, and I need help from all of you to fulfill it," announced Diego Sandoval solemnly as he looked around the room at the senior staff of *Medios Nuevos*, the nongovernmental organization (NGO) by whom he was employed. Diego had just been appointed to the Peruvian delegation to the fifth session of the Intergovernmental Negotiating Committee (INC-5) for an International Legally Binding Treaty to Eliminate Certain Persistent Organic Pollutants (POPs), which was to take place in November 2000 in South Africa. Diego was the head of the environmental department of *Medios Nuevos*—a department that had expanded fourfold over the past five years under the international funding he had obtained for regional environmental research and implementation. It was the staff opinion that Diego's two latest projects in Lima's northern cone— one a pesticide education project for local farmers and their families and the other a plant that recycled sanitary sewer water from local neighborhoods for irrigation of park and (inedible) garden land—had caught the eye of someone in the government and resulted in this appointment. Diego had assembled the senior staff from all of the departments to ask for help in developing a comprehensive position.

"Much of the information available on these POPs emerges from the situation and perspective of the developed nations and does not represent our situation here in Peru," Diego went on. "There are many delegates from developing nations who, like me, come from NGOs. I want to network with them and share information, but I need you to help me gather as comprehensive a set of data as possible as our contribution. The questions involved in eliminating these POPs involve many of your areas of work, as they affect public health, the welfare of infants and children, human rights, agriculture, and labor rights, to name just a few. I know that all of the departments are busy with their own projects and face their own deadlines. I thank you for coming today to share some initial information and an overview and ask that we reassemble in five weeks to share the fruits of our research in our various departments relative to these negotiations. Is that agreeable?" All present nodded acquiescence.

"Maria Amparo has done some initial information gathering on the status of the negotiations. Maria?"

Maria Amparo read from her notes: "Previous meetings agreed on a list of POPs called the 'dirty dozen,' which are the immediate target of the treaty. These dirty dozen include eight pesticides (aldrin, chlordane, DDT, dieldrin, endrin, heptachlor, mirex, and toxaphene), two industrial chemicals (hexachlorobenzene [HCB] and polychlorinated biphenyls [PCBs]), and two unintended by-products (dioxins and furans), all of which are used—or, in the case of dioxins and furans, produced—in Peru. The issues still being debated when the group last met in March 2000 in Bonn included whether all of these chemicals should cease being manufactured, all their stockpiles destroyed, and contaminated sites cleaned up; to what extent the Precautionary Principle should be used in adding new pollutants to the list of the dirty dozen; individual and general exceptions to the bans; how to fund the transition in the developing nations; and how this treaty would relate to the World Trade Organization (WTO)."

"How did Peru stand at the previous meetings?" Diego asked.

"Solidly with the other seventy-six developing nations on the funding issue, demanding that the developed nations contribute to a specific fund to cover the costs of the transition in developing nations," Maria replied. "Canada offered to donate $10 million, but the United States and the European Union (EU) only offered pocket change—less than a million apiece. Probably because of the mining companies, Peru was unwilling to give blanket authority for banning new chemicals. The mining industry doubtless will be even more concerned after the big mercury spill June 2 at the Yanococha gold mine in Chorapampa. I understand that the financial arm of the World

43

Bank, the International Finance Corp., owns a piece of that mine and is very worried—a 330-pound spill with sixty people already affected could become a major problem. On the other issues—the severity of the ban, the question of exceptions, and the interface with the WTO—I found nothing."

"Well, we can understand the mining companies' interests," Diego said. "And the miners' unions certainly would support them, too. Can you imagine if the mines were shut down because new regulations on chemicals made them not profitable enough to operate? We have less than half of the national workforce in full-time employment now, and mining is a big piece of that!"

Jose, head of the Department of Public Health and Nutrition, spoke up. "Does the debate over the exceptions involve the use of DDT for malaria control?"

"Yes," Maria answered. "South Africa, where the next session will be held, banned DDT in 1974, but has just begun spraying it to combat a 100 percent increase in malaria deaths over the previous year. They reintroduced DDT largely because the mosquitoes had become resistant to the other pesticides they had been using. This use of DDT is only for public health reasons; agricultural use is still banned. South Africa is not the only developing country with an escalating malaria problem; several million people die every year from malaria, 300–500 children under age five die every hour, and the death toll is rising, largely because of strapped public health budgets and growing mosquito resistance. Several other developing nations also use DDT for malaria control, including China, India, and Mexico."

"Yes," Jose responded, "but you need to look carefully at Mexico because they have become a major producer of DDT—they have a vested economic interest in its continued use. And there is evidence that at least in parts of Mexico DDT is no longer effective; their mosquitoes, too, have become resistant."

"You all read the initial report from our pesticide education project," Diego said. "That project was begun following the deaths in Tauccamarca last October[1] and aimed at assessing the level of safety common in pesticide usage in Peruvian agriculture and then introducing safer practices around pesticides. The problems we found were immense: We have illiterate and semiliterate peasants buying and using increasing amounts of dangerous chemicals without any instruction or any ability to read directions and warnings. Moreover, even if they could read the directions and warnings, they would be unable to carry them out. Many peasants—for example, here in the northern cone—have limited access to water, which they must buy by the liter from trucks, so they cannot wash after applying pesticides. Worse, many store the drinking and cooking water they buy in empty pesticide containers! Most sleep in the same clothes they wear to apply pesticides because they have at most one other set of clothes. Because pesticide application does not require great strength, children and pregnant women often are given this chore, and they seem to be most vulnerable to health damage, at least based on the medical research that has been done. Women often go straight from pesticide application to food preparation.

"The education project has had limited success. We have succeeded in convincing farmers to store the pesticide as far as possible from food, drinking water, and livestock; to avoid whenever possible direct contact with skin or food; and to keep pregnant women and very young children away from pesticides. But protective gear—gloves, masks, special clothes—these are simply out of the question for virtually all."

Juan Francisco, the head of the agriculture department, which had cooperated with Diego's environmental department in the pesticide education project, now joined the conversation.

"You know, in the last few years several MIP projects in the mountains have been pretty successful. I have been looking at a program at the University of Cusco that teaches peasants to use the old Indian methods to control pests. The experimental fields have actually decreased pest damages to crops by 12 percent after two years of substituting MIP for pesticide use. As one peasant tries it successfully his neighbors take it up voluntarily, so the method is steadily spreading."

"But what is MIP?" Jose asked. "I don't know much about agriculture."

"It's a combination of methods called Integral Plague Management," Juan replied. "The basic method is crop diversification and rotation, supplemented by one or more of a variety of methods. Sometimes one borders a field with plants that repel particular pests; at other times and situations one uses pest traps, sexual pheromones, and even farm-produced baculo-virus—which is made from larvae from damaged potatoes, ground and mixed with talcum powder, and then spread at the edges of the fields. In the past three years these methods have been more successful than pesticides in combating the resistant 'gorjogo' giant potato moth infestation that appeared in 1998. Crop damage was reduced from a 44 percent level with pesticide use to 8.5 percent with MIP. But it is still experimental; some critics charge that farmers using MIP are obtaining benefits from their neighbors' use of pesticides and that if the majority switch to MIP the results will be much worse—though it's interesting that MIP farmers have *higher* yields."

"I'd like to know more about the extent of the danger in these pesticides and how important they are for maintaining crop yields," said Xavier, who headed the human rights department, which engaged in popular leadership training and human rights education work. "*El Senor*, the Lord, knows that the *campesinos* can't afford to lower either their caloric intake or their marketable crops."

"Do we have an agreement to research these areas, circulate our findings, and meet again in five weeks with suggestions about what the Peruvian position at the INC-5 should look like?" asked Diego. All the heads in the room nodded. "In the meantime I will initiate contact with the minister and see how open he is to preparatory discussions within the delegation. I also will find out from our NGO Internet network who the NGO members of other Latin American delegations are so that I can contact them and work out information sharing. Thank you all for your help."

*   *   *

Five weeks later, half an hour into the meeting the debate was loud and divisive. Diego finally stood and quieted the room.

"Let me see if I can fairly summarize the two positions I have heard. Maria Amparo, Juan Francisco, and Xavier propose that Peru should refuse to agree to a total and immediate ban on the dirty dozen and refuse to support the creation of any body that could add other chemicals to the list. Instead, they argue that we should support a more gradual shift away from use of these chemicals, demand economic aid from the developing nations to fund this gradual transition, regulate national pesticide sales to ensure that safety directions in Spanish are included with each purchase, inspect to ensure that the pesticide application processes on large farms protect worker health, and immediately begin large-scale pesticide safety instruction for *campesinos* throughout Peru. They think we should move more gradually to a phaseout and reserve the right to use one or more of these chemicals when needed either to promote public health or to combat agricultural threats. Maria Amparo points out that these pesticides have never been so harmful in the developed world as they are here and that we can lower harm here by attacking overuse of chemicals and poor handling techniques.

"These advocates offer several compelling reasons for this position. First, they point out that the developed nations that are pushing this ban eliminated virtually all of these chemicals from use in their own nations many years ago. They do not use these older, broad-spectrum organo-phosphate agents; they use more herbicides, which tend to have lower acute toxicity. Virtually all of the older, broad-spectrum agents that the rich nations want globally banned have moved out of patent protection and are cheaply made locally. The newer pesticides we would be forced to substitute for the dirty dozen are still under patents owned by the developing nations and are much more expensive than the 'dirty' ones. As with other technologies, the developed nations invented these pesticides, got rich selling them to the rest of the world, and now want not only for us to pay all the costs of cleaning up the toxic mess their products created but also to dictate when we abandon them and which of their new toxic technologies we buy to replace them.

"The supporters of the gradual phaseout also point out that Peru does not have the capacity to effectively enforce either an import ban or a manufacturing ban; an immediate ban would only worsen the present black market in these chemicals. Moreover, we do not have the capacity to test the toxicity or environmental harm of the new substitutes, either. Perhaps with a slower phaseout we could move directly from these pesticides to more natural methods like MIP."

Maria Amparo, Xavier, and Juan Francisco all nodded their approval of this account.

"On the other hand, Rosaria, Jose, and Jaime propose that Peru support an immediate ban on the dirty dozen. They argue that mobilization of the nation is difficult and expensive and that it should only have to be done once, not first to ensure safer handling of dangerous pesticides and then later to shift to alternative methods of pest control. Instead, they think we should use the discontinuation of these pesticides as the opportunity to move immediately to MIP methods."

"We think that MIP is not only safer, avoiding all the health hazards of the POPs, but that it has great potential for increasing the status of and appreciation of Indians and Indian culture in Peru," Rosaria said. "The Indian population has been discriminated against for centuries, their religion and culture persecuted and denigrated. The mountain terraces that we inherited from our Indian ancestors are still the basis of Peruvian agriculture, however, and the crop diversification and rotation that are the foundation of MIP defined traditional Indian agriculture on those terraces. Think what effect it will have on Indian communities to have national agricultural agents teaching that the pesticides and large-field monoculture that have represented modern scientific agriculture are more toxic and less productive than the traditional Indian practices! There will be boomerang effects on the status of village leaders; on *curanderos/as*, or native healers; and maybe even on the preservation of other cultural practices such as regional costumes and dances. We think that all of these factors are important if the Indian population is to be included in the national project."

Jose nodded and said, "One of the articles sent to me by a Brazilian researcher in our network concerned the potential effect of discontinuing organo-phosphate pesticides on the fishing industry. Fish are even more sensitive to pesticide residues than birds, and there is a great deal of evidence that points to the tremendous increase in pesticide levels in freshwater and oceans as a primary cause of decline in the fish stocks of the world. Certainly mountain trout have been disappearing in Peru as the use of pesticides rose in the past twenty years, and the coastal fishing industry is in even worse shape. The evidence suggests that pesticide accumulation in fish weakens their immune systems and makes them vulnerable to a host of other threats. Our Humbolt current brings us frigid waters from the Arctic, to which pesticides tend to migrate, so the fish in the current have higher levels of pesticides than those in warmer currents. The bulk of our population lives in the coastal cities, and fish—now contaminated with pesticides—were a staple in the coastal diet until the fishing industry went into decline from lack of fish. Stopping pesticide use here would bring back our native trout, but with global action the ocean fish stocks also could be restored."

"Juan Francisco," Rosaria said, "I understand and share your resentment at the developed nations, which always seem to be on the profitable end of things. They invent these POPs, make tons of money on them, and when they decide they are too dangerous to use at home they continue to sell them to poor nations for twenty years until they think they can make more money selling us new replacements for them—all in the name of our own welfare! But the health costs of these pesticides are real here in Peru. We can debate how we should weigh the welfare of other species against the welfare of human communities, but we must all take seriously health risks to people. I know we can greatly decrease incidents of pesticide intoxication that result in death, blindness, and neurological damage by teaching safer handling techniques. We have to be concerned not only about workers who may get directly overdosed but also with chronic, low-level exposure of our whole population. You saw the Chilean study of newborn children of workers in fruit orchards: almost double the national rate of serious birth defects, and the national rate also included other high-risk agricultural populations. In Ecuador a 1994 study found exceptionally high rates of organo-phosphates in children working in orchards. And our own 1996 Peruvian study found that the pesticide levels in men, women, and children living in three valleys with high pesticide use was so high as to seriously impair quality of life. Eighty percent showed signs of chronic agrochemical absorption, and 72 percent had toxicity resulting in memory loss, depression, anxiety, language deficits, and other signs of neurological dysfunction. Seventy-five percent of breast milk samples—and 95 percent of cow milk samples in this Peruvian study—contained toxic chemicals in concentrations that exceed tolerance levels. The literature from the North is full of accounts of animal and some human studies of endocrine disruption and weakening of the immune system by

pesticides. We have not done many of these carefully controlled studies here, but our Peruvian study showed a 2.7 percent rate of defective newborns born to agricultural families in these valleys with high
pesticide use. The majority of our population is already at high risk of
malnutrition, tuberculosis, parasites, dysentery, and malaria; they cannot survive with weakened immune systems. Is your proposal aimed
more at resisting further manipulation by the developed nations than
at protecting the welfare of the people of Peru?"

Juan Francisco paused, then responded.

"We think that resistance is a survival factor. We think that it is important not to tie ourselves to decisions we might regret. With global
warming, our malaria problem may be moving out of the jungles of
Iquitos and up the lower slopes of the Andes. Are you sure that you
want to renounce all use of chemicals such as DDT, even if we may
want to discontinue agricultural use, or even regular spraying? We
don't know what kinds of problems will come along, and DDT, for
example, is cheap, it can be manufactured locally, and its acute [im-
mediate] toxicity is relatively low for humans. We want to keep these
options open while we move in safer directions. Some of our public
health officials in the jungle want to continue spraying residence walls
because they find high resistance to the bednets that have been introduced as protection against malaria. The nets are too expensive for
many families to afford one for every member, but it is usually too
hot to sleep many persons under one net. Which is better: malaria
deaths or the long-term risks of sprayed walls?

"Furthermore, you do not know how safe replacement pesticides
will be. I e-mailed you the October 1999 speech by Lynn Goldman,
the assistant administrator of the U.S. Environmental Protection
Agency (EPA) Office of Prevention, Pesticides, and Toxic Substances,
which I found on the Internet. Did you notice where she said that of
the 3,000 chemicals that the United States imported or produced in
amounts in excess of 1 million pounds per year, the EPA has found
that 43 percent have *no* testing data on basic health and environmental effects, and only 7 percent have a full set of basic data? Although
the United States requires any pesticide that touches food to have basic health and environmental testing, that does not cover all pesticides. We have no way of knowing that these dozen are any dirtier
than any of the others."

Maria Amparo jumped into the discussion.

"You know perfectly well that you can explain to miners and their
families, or to *campesino* families, that these chemicals may cause mis-
carriages, a higher risk of defective children, and health risks to workers—tell them everything researchers suspect. But if their choice is
between using the chemicals with all their risks and not having jobs

or not producing so much potatoes and maize, they'll choose the chemicals regardless of the risks. Because hunger is the bigger risk, the more immediate risk, the one they know."

At that Diego stood up. "We are almost out of the time we agreed to. This has been most helpful in getting all the issues out in the open. What we need now is some way of choosing between the positions or finding a compromise between them. Can we use the remaining half-hour to reach a decision? Do we want to discuss the possibility of compromise first? All in favor, raise your hands."

Commentary

The discussion of the POPs treaty and process at *Medios Nuevos* probably would surprise and disturb many observers in the developed world who thought they understood the issues involved in the POPs treaty. The issues can look very different, however, from the perspective of developing nations. For many observers in developed nations, the POPs treaty looks like a "no-brainer." Who could possibly object to banning chemicals that we know are dangerous not only to humans but also to virtually every animal species ever tested, from fish and birds to all the animals that eat them, all the way up the food chain? Many Americans thought most of these chemicals had been banned throughout the world when DDT was banned decades ago in the United States and only learned of their continuing sale and use in the developing world when media coverage of the POPs treaty began.

Perceptions of the POPs treaty as completely noncontroversial were heightened in the United States by the stance of chemical companies. Chemical companies in the developed world generally have supported the banning of the dirty dozen, though they have demanded assurances that their interests would be protected in any process that was developed for banning other chemicals in the future. This feature, however—the support of chemical companies for the banning of the dirty dozen—was very much a local phenomenon, limited to large multinational chemical companies headquartered in developed nations, few of which produced many of the dirty dozen, and all of which stood to gain sales of their patented next-generation chemical pesticides and herbicides that would replace the banned substances. In the developing world, many of the medium-sized and "mom-and-pop" chemical companies that have been producing the POPs chemicals since the patents of the multinational companies lapsed would be forced out of business or to black market operation by a worldwide ban.

Just as the stance of chemical companies differed between developed and developing nations, so did the stance of farmers. There was no great opposition to the POPs treaty from farmers in the United States, where most of the chemicals to be banned had been made illegal and unobtainable decades before. In developing nations, however, farmers stood to lose the cheapest pesticides available to them—and in many cases the only affordable ones. At the level of public health officials as well, the United States had no attachment to any of the chemicals in the dirty dozen, whereas several developing nations were facing an upsurge in malaria deaths from strains of the disease that were resistant to newer, more costly pesticides that were preferred for human and environmental health and safety reasons. In those nations, health officials wanted to be able either to use DDT in limited malaria-control operations now or to reserve the possibility of restricted malaria-control operations in the future.

The desire to use DDT is not based primarily on its low cost, though that is a factor. The primary reason for reserving rights to use DDT for malaria control is precisely because in many nations it has not been used in decades, so the mosquito population no longer has any resistance to it. That is, in any initial use of pesticide, the vast majority of affected mosquitoes will die, but a small amount—often those on the edges of the sprayed area—will survive, recover, and reproduce, passing on some resistance to the pesticide. With each application the number of survivors increases slightly, requiring heavier and heavier applications to achieve the same level of effect, until most of the mosquito population is resistant to this particular pesticide. Thus, although public health officials, like farmers, want to use a pesticide that is effective, their long-range goal must be to have lined up and waiting in the wings a pesticide or two or three to which their pest targets have no resistance.

Cheapness of POPs Pesticides

In developing nations, the fact that the pesticides that the POPs treaty would ban are cheaper than the available replacements is a critical fact that tremendously alters the general perception of the issue at stake in the POPs process. The increased cost of replacements has the potential to lower or even prevent pesticide use altogether, thereby lowering crop yields—which, in turn, lowers the amount of food that farmers have to eat and to sell to markets. In developing nations, the environmental advantages of the treaty are more easily outweighed by the specter of mass hunger than in the developed nations, where any disadvantages are of much less import. This calculation is true even when some of the environmental disadvantages from the POPs chemicals—such as health effects on humans, especially farmers—loom much larger than they did in the developed nations even when these chemicals were common there.

Farmers in the developed world who used these chemicals usually did not have to contend with acute water shortages that prevented them from washing the chemicals off of their bodies and clothes after application, as is often the case in developing nations such as Peru. Farmers in developed nations were less often illiterate than those in developing nations. Furthermore, U.S. and European farmers were seldom faced with having the directions for preparing and using pesticides and other chemicals printed in foreign languages they could not decipher, as is the norm in many developing nations. In Peru, for example, one of the reasons many farmers preferred DDT made in Mexico to other imported pesticides that scientists consider to be much safer and are not too much more expensive is that Mexican DDT came with very simple directions printed in Spanish about how to prepare, apply, and store the mixture. This was a contrast to directions for pesticides imported from the United States, which not only printed directions in English but also gave directions in such obscure scientific language that even most English speakers could not decipher them.

For the staff of *Medios Nuevos,* and probably for many of their fellow Peruvians, the highest and most compelling good is the immediate welfare, the survival, of the human population—especially poor people, whom they understand to include many different groups of the most vulnerable. In this case the staff clearly understands the most vulnerable individuals to be small farmers, especially Indians, who invariably are living below the economic median. Thus, the approach of the staff is not only anthropocentric but also typical of the Latin American religious movement called liberation theology. For the liberation theology movement, the God of Christians and Jews has historically professed and demonstrated a preference for poor people on the basis of their suffering and has called humans to respond with their own preferential option for the poor. Because so many poor people in many nations of Latin America are Indians whose spirituality is largely based on nature and whose welfare is closely connected to the welfare of the ecosystem, environmentalism is not alien to liberation theology. Concern for the environment in liberation theology clearly takes a backseat, however, to concern for human beings. For most theologians of liberation, so much of the local human population lives on the edge of physical and psychic survival that it would be inconceivable that the needs of any other species could take priority over those of humans.

Nevertheless, it would be simplistic to characterize the basic difference between U.S. and Peruvian views as biocentrism versus anthropocentrism. The more one has, the less costly generosity is. As the scene shifts from the United States to Peru, the level of prospective damage to humans and other species increases dramatically in all possible POPs outcomes. If developing nations support the POPs treaty and it is enacted, most small farmers will not be able to afford POPs substitutes, and it is unlikely that there will be sufficient MIP instruction for them to switch systems. These farmers, then, will either suffer decreased yields and increased hunger or continue to make, or to buy on the black market, banned chemicals—with deleterious health effects on their families; other species of animals; and the health of the land, rivers, streams, and oceans. On the other hand, if POPs chemicals are not banned, even if the Peruvian government and NGOs do begin an MIP program, that program will take years—probably decades—to include the entire farming population. In the meantime, massive damage to the health of agricultural families will decrease only very gradually, even if the caloric levels of agricultural families do not decline. Moreover, DDT and other chemicals will continue to accumulate in fish and birds, multiplying at every step up the food chain, decreasing the sizes of animal populations and very possibly making some species extinct—not to mention increasing the rates of sterility, spontaneous abortion, and birth defects in the human population.

Both stances developed by the staff at *Medios Nuevos* focus on the need to protect human farmers and their families. They consider the dangers to trout, ocean fish, and other animals in the context of their importance as human resources. Within the Peruvian perspective this attitude is not regarded as a conflict, as it often is in the United States—where the livelihood of one segment of a local human population is pitted against destruction of the environment of the last representatives of an endangered animal species. In a developing nation such as Peru, farming is not just one occupation among many others (as logging, for example, is in the United States). Farmers make up half or more of the population, and any failure of small farmers would cause a rise in food prices that would disastrously impact another quarter or more of the population—poor urban dwellers—as well.

On the environmental side, Peru—even more than most developing nations—has lacked the resources to map and catalogue its ecosystem. Peru has three distinctly different types of ecosystems: the coastal deserts, the Amazonian jungle, and the Andean Altiplano, all of which are internally diverse as well. None of these ecosystems has been well mapped for plant and animal species. Like several other Latin American nations, Peru has even been unable to police the botanical piracy that has developed over the past decade and a half by pharmaceutical companies and freelance botanists. These botanists not only fail to contribute their findings to any national database; they have been known to appropriate large stocks of plants and to deliberately destroy any remaining examples of the species growing in the wild to prevent competition.

Lack of Baseline Data

Knowledge of the status of local species and their ecosystems is rudimentary to any effective environmental policy. Scientists know that many Peruvian animal populations—including mountain trout and coastal fish, as well as the national icon, the condor—have declined drastically, but for most species little is known about the size of remaining populations or the extent of the decline in population size; much less are environmentalists able to point with any certainty to most of the causes of decline. One question in this case is how this lack of information should be interpreted: Should we treat all species in decline as if they are endangered, or should we reserve endangered status for species that have been proven to be endangered? Without the resources to investigate the level of threat, a nation that chooses to assume that no species is threatened without clear and convincing proof of the threat risks many extinct species. Yet there are definite human and economic costs to assuming that all species in decline are threatened. The paucity of environmental data in many developing nations is an additional factor—in addition to the extreme vulnerability of the majority poor—helping to perpetuate anthropocentric approaches to environmental questions. The less we know about the environment, the less weight the environment can have in our decision making. The information we need involves not only mapping various species' populations and health but increased data about the interrelationships between species within ecosystems—including relationships of humans within ecosystems.

Paths to MIP

One of the more interesting aspects of this case is that the immediate question—whether Diego Sandoval and his fellow Peruvian delegates to the POPs conference should support the POPs treaty—is largely instrumental. The ultimate "answer" is agreed upon by both sides at *Medios Nuevos*. Both sides agree that the nation needs to move toward MIP as the basic approach to pest control in farming. They disagree about whether signing the POPs treaty will move them toward MIP more quickly and with least suffering. MIP certainly is the cheapest method of pest control for individual farmers and for the Peruvian economy—assuming that it is as effective as the existing studies suggest—and it certainly is the safest for the farmers themselves, as well as for other species. In terms of the environment the philosophy of MIP largely parallels what we have learned about ecosystems in general. MIP utilizes principles of diversity (crop rotation and diversification) and particularity (treating specific pests with their natural controls). By working with nature instead of against it, MIP avoids triggering nature's response of escalation (pesticide resistance), which demands heavier and heavier pesticide application at greater and greater cost to achieve the same or diminishing results.

MIP is one example of an agricultural system that meets the ecological paradigm proposed by Joe Thornton.[2] Thornton advocates replacing the risk paradigm that until now has been used to regulate and manage chemical pollution, one chemical at a time, by allowing chemical discharges as long as they don't exceed a numerical standard of "acceptable" contamination. Thornton's new paradigm is based on the precautionary principle but specifies three additional principles that direct us in choosing action: zero discharge, clean production, and reverse onus. *Zero discharge* means that we eliminate rather than allow the release of substances that persist or bioaccumulate; their persistence tells us that nature does not have any means for handling them. *Clean production* means not using or producing toxic chemicals, but using alternative products and processes. *Reverse onus* means that the burden of proof that a new product is safe is shifted to those who want to produce it; it is not up to society to prove that it isn't safe.

Interestingly, the reason for favoring MIP that receives the most emphasis within the case itself is cultural, not environmental or public health-oriented. This fact probably seems strange to North Americans accustomed to scientific approaches to questions such as POPs. The argument is that MIP is merely an update on traditional Indian methods of pest control that originated before the Spanish conquest of the Americas. Adoption of MIP would be interpreted as a vindication of Indian culture in a Peruvian—and, indeed, Latin American—historical tradition that has seriously and continuously devalued and even degraded Indian culture.

The masses of the Peruvian Indian population have lived in the Andes, while the descendants of the Spanish have settled disproportionately in the major cities on the coastal plain. The descendants of the Spanish on the coastal plain have controlled national government, which has consistently distributed government services—including electricity, sewers, running water, health clinics, schools, universities, and hospitals—disproportionately, favoring the Spanish on the coast at the expense of the Indian populations in the mountains, where the worst national poverty has been located. For the most part, in Peru "farmer" has been synonymous with "Indian," and both have been terms of derision. Although it is true that national assertion of the superiority of traditional Indian MIP over imported, scientifically produced chemical pesticides could support Indian pride, it cannot be assumed that all Indians therefore would embrace MIP. Given the centuries of domination and degradation of the Indians that have driven many Indians to dissociate from their traditions, one could expect tremendous resistance to MIP from farmers, including many Indians, who would refuse to believe that anything traditional or distinctly Indian could be superior. One also could be sure that advertising by the chemical companies would support that prejudice. This is not an argument against the value of MIP; it is merely a suggestion that a transition to MIP undoubtedly will encounter obstacles that the case itself does not mention.

Once past this initial self-deprecatory suspicion of MIP, however, Indian farmers may well be easy converts to MIP. The geographical divide in Peru between the dominant *criollos* of the coastal cities and the subordinated Indians of the Andean valleys preserved not only a dominant anti-Indian prejudice but also many subtle and not so subtle aspects of Indian culture in the mountains. Those cultural aspects include close and reverential—even religious—attitudes toward all aspects of the natural environment, beginning with the mountain winds and the mountains themselves. This environmental awareness not only offers a platform on which to found an MIP program; such environmental awareness also would almost certainly be expanded and deepened by extended exposure to and use of MIP. MIP could support a shift in the very agricultural ideal from the massive fields of chemically treated monoculture promoted by "scientific" farming in the developed world to a historically grounded local ideal of mountainsides of small terraces planted in different crops and varieties of crops, with pests controlled by alternative borders and crop rotation. Such a shift in the ideal could promote restoration of more ancient terraces and creation of new ones, instead of disastrous attempts by poor farmers to plow up the hillsides of the Andean valleys, which promotes erosion of topsoil, flooding, and silting of rivers and streams.

It is difficult to avoid the conclusion that the one issue on which the developing nations had agreed at the previous POPs meeting is indeed crucial: funding for the transition from POPs in the developing nations. If the POPs process supported by the developed world really is about environmental protection rather than about forcing the poor nations to give up cheap, locally manufactured—in some cases even homemade—pesticides in favor of expensive pesticides imported from the rich nations, then rich nations should be willing to fund an open-ended transition from the dirty dozen. Their aid should not take the form that so much aid to poor countries does: funding for commodities that must be bought from the nation giving the aid. Instead, the developed nations should be willing to fund a transition from POPs to nonchemical alternatives such as MIP.

Questions for Discussion

1. What do the *Medios Nuevos* staff suspect are the motivations of the developed nations in the proposed POPs treaty? Why?
2. In what ways is the approach of the staff anthropocentric? Is this appropriate or not? Why?
3. Spokespersons for developed world chemical companies have called the approach of the staff in this case "antitechnology" and "antiscience." Do you agree? Why or why not?
4. What is MIP? To what in U.S. agriculture is it analogous?

Notes

1. On October 22, 1999, thirty schoolchildren died after sixty ate milk and cereal laced with rat poison at a school in Tauccamarca in the province of Cusco, Peru. One of the children had mistakenly picked up the poison-laced milk her mother intended to use to kill wild dogs ravaging her livestock and took it to school, where she added it to the milk used in the communal breakfast. The poison initially was reported as insecticide.
2. Joe Thornton, *Pandora's Poison: Chlorine, Health and a New Environmental Strategy* (Cambridge, Mass.: MIT Press, 2000).

For Further Reading

Ashford, Nicolas, and Miller Claudia. *Chemical Exposures: Low Levels and High Stakes.* 2d ed. Van Nostrand Reinhold, 1998.

Hallman, David G. *Ecotheology: Voices from South and North.* Maryknoll, N.Y.: Orbis/WCC, 1994.

Krimsky, Sheldon. *Hormonal Chaos.* Baltimore: Johns Hopkins University Press, 1999.

O'Brien, Mary. *Making Better Environmental Decisions.* Cambridge, Mass.: MIT Press, 2000.

Peterson, Anna L. *Being Human: Ethics, Environment and Our Place in the World.* Berkeley: University of California Press, 2001.

Thornton, Joe. *Pandora's Poison: Chlorine, Health and a New Environmental Strategy.* Cambridge, Mass.: MIT Press, 2000.

U.S. Environmental Protection Agency. "Priority: PTBs: Dioxins and Furans." Persistent Bioaccumulative and Toxic Chemical Initiative report, 15 November 2000. Available at www.epa.gov/opptintr/pbt/dioxins. htm (accessed February 9, 2003).

4

Heart Thieves: Preserving Endangered Ecosystems or Endangered Cultures in Madagascar

Herbert stepped out of the van, happy to put his feet on the ground after a long and bumpy ride. Madagascar, he thought, is a much larger island than it seemed on the map. Perhaps its location some 500 miles off the eastern coast of Africa gave a false sense of minor proportion when compared to that great continent. And the ride from the airport in the capital, Anatananarivo, to this remote village of Ranovao in a celebrated *taxi-brousse*, a wreck of a passenger van, reminded him just how far he was from his work as a tropical botanist with the Missouri Botanical Gardens.

"Are you exhausted, Dr. Jenkins?" asked Lucianne as she stepped from the van. "The flight from the United States is long and demanding. I know. I've made the trip on several occasions. And having to come straight from the airport to Ranovao is hardly a proper Malagasy welcome."

"Are my aches and pains that obvious? It would have been worse if I had not enjoyed the fine company that you and Jean-Amie provided."

"*Merci*," said Jean-Amie as he emerged from the open rear of the van carrying several small suitcases. "You Americans are as generous with your praise as you are with your money."

Herbert laughed. "Well, it's not exactly my money, you know, nor is its source exclusively American. After all, the checks I write draw on the accounts of the World Fund for Nature, which taps into purses from many countries."

Several young boys ran across the dusty plaza to take the bags from Jean-Amie and carried them to a modest but comfortable-looking mud-brick bungalow near a stand of large trees at the edge of the village.

"So that's our abode for the night," said Herbert, "and our offices as well."

Herbert knew that the three had their work cut out for them, and the workday was about to begin.

"Dr. Jenkins, please come and meet our host," said Lucianne.

Herbert turned and was confronted by a distinguished gentleman dressed in traditional Malagasy attire and carrying a wooden staff, which he recognized as a symbol of village authority.

"Dr. Jenkins, please meet Hanairivo Rahandraha, senior elder of Ranovao and former government magistrate, among other distinctions," said Lucianne.

Then, turning to Rahandraha, she shifted from English to Malagasy. "Dr. Jenkins is the American scientist and representative of the World Fund for Nature. He is the real reason we are here."

Herbert was pleased to have someone as competent as Lucianne at his side. She was a Malagasy who had trained with him in tropical botany on an international fellowship at the Missouri Tropical Gardens. Her fluency in several languages and her experience as a government official in the Departement des Eaux et Forets made her perfectly suited for the difficult task that lay just ahead.

"And this is Jean-Amie Decary from the Institute for the Conservation of Tropical Environments in Antananarivo." Although Jean-Amie was of French extraction, he was a fourth-generation Malagasy whose family had long abandoned any loyalty to the land of their origins.

Rahandraha nodded to the three of them and then, with a sweeping gesture, ushered them into his home and to a large table—obviously the conference room for important discussions among the elders of Ranovao.

"Herbert, please, you must sit here, between Jean-Amie and me," said Lucianne, directing Herbert away from the nearest chair to another on the opposite side of the table.

"Oops, was I about to violate a taboo?" asked Herbert.

"In a way," responded Lucianne. "The cardinal directions are very important to the Malagasy and especially to this tribal group, the Tanala. They consider north and east to be superior to south and west. We are sitting on the northeast side of the table—a place reserved for dignitaries and other distinguished guests in the village."

"I gather that tradition is important here," said Herbert.

"Yes," Lucianne answered, with a touch of apprehension in her voice, "in ways you may find difficult to appreciate. And that fact won't make our job any easier."

"I realize that as one whose own upbringing was in a village like this," Herbert said to her, "you are sensitive to the villagers. But we have a larger perspective and a very important goal: preservation of the forests for all humankind. Achieving that goal may bring discomfort, and that is to be lamented. But such, as they say, is the price of doing business."

"I hope you realize that your tone is a little callous, Dr. Jenkins," Lucianne responded, with her characteristic honesty.

"I know, and I regret the evident lack of compassion in my remark. But we have to prepare ourselves mentally for the announcement we've come to make."

"Obviously you believe deeply in what we're doing," Lucianne said.

"Yes," Herbert replied. "So let's get started."

After an initial period of social conversation, Lucianne addressed Elder Rahandraha, again in Malagasy. "I am sorry to have to tell you, sir, that the central government has decided, for reasons Dr. Jenkins will explain, to relocate the people of your village from Ranovao, here in the east central highlands, to land and new homes in the western sections within the coming year."

Rahandraha's eyes grew wide with shock.

"Once the move is completed," Lucianne continued, "you will be provided with all that you need until the crops and harvests are sufficient to support the village. We believe that the living conditions in your new home, including health care and education, will be greatly improved. And the opportunities for your children will be greater, too."

Rahandraha's immediate response was one of sadness. His remarks were sharpened by anger and frustration as well, and he looked straight at Lucianne. "I have been expecting the government to take some action, but certainly not this radical. You are intimately familiar with Malagasy traditions, Dr. Randrianasolo. They are your own—or, perhaps I should say, they were your own before you were trained to embrace other values."

"Yes," countered Lucianne, "but I recall that you yourself spent many years in a distinguished career that took you at least as far from this village and into a different world."

"True, but I finally left my position with the government to return here because I was forced to think and act in the clever and crafty ways of the Europeans and the Americans, who are full of tricks, full of *vazaha*. In our new place, far from the forest, the government will provide for us to become *vahiny*, strangers to our traditions, to this land of our ancestors—just as you have become a stranger to yours."

Lucianne winced. The elder's remarks cut deeply. In her home village she was received coolly when she returned to visit her family, as if she no longer qualified as *havana*, or kin—the only ones who can truly be trusted. She thought briefly of her own young children and what they might have lost permanently in her neglect of those who were their ancestors as well as hers.

Rahandraha continued, turning his attention to Herbert, who needed no translation to understand the elder's intense emotions. "I have two sisters whose rice plots are entrusted to me on that hillside outside this village. What will happen to them if they become widowed and have nothing for support? I have obligations to work that land and keep it productive for my kin. If I fail, I am guilty of a sin as great as any claimed by you from Christian countries. I have ancestors resting in the big tomb house you will see over there." He gestured to the northeast. "I am head of the tomb group. What will happen to the *razana*, the ancestors, if I am no longer here? This village is *tanindrazana*, the place of the ancestors and my true home. If we are forced to live far away, and the village is destroyed, all of us will be *vahiny*, with no tomb to live in when we die."

The elder fell silent, and Lucianne continued to translate his statements to Herbert, who took a deep breath before beginning his response. "It is not possible for me to appreciate fully what will be lost in this relocation," he said. "But I hope to help you understand why this action must be taken."

"I will listen," Rahandhraha said through Lucianne's interpretation, "but my appreciation of your justification may be lacking as well."

"The World Fund for Nature is one of many international organizations that have given priority and major funding to rescuing the remaining rainforests of Madagascar," Herbert said. "I have been authorized to work with the central government in this task. Ranovao is located in a section of rainforest that is currently intact but gravely threatened by growing human population pressures and farming practices that threaten to cut it off from the strand of forest that connects it to the special preserve of Manombo, some fifteen kilometers to the west. If this happens, the isolated section will be fragmented and destabilized, and the animals now inhabiting the fragment will be unable to move back and forth to the preserve. These animals include a recently discovered and very rare subspecies of the Aye-Aye lemur, which will undoubtedly become extinct unless urgent actions are taken to preserve its habitat." Herbert hesitated, wondering if he had omitted anything important in his statement. He sat silently as Lucianne completed her translation to Rahandraha.

Turning to Herbert, she whispered, "I'm not sure if that was an explanation or an ultimatum." There was no hint of humor in her voice.

The elder responded. "What you say is true, I'm sure, but the situation is not the fault of the people of this village. Certainly, for generations we have burned sections of the forests to clear land on the hillsides and produce fertile soil. But we allowed the forests to recover for five or ten years before taking any other action. Nothing was permanently destroyed by this process. And our irrigation of rice paddies on the slopes of the hills and mountains is as permanent and natural as lemurs eating nuts from the trees. The forest provides us with so much. Why would we destroy it now?"

Rahandraha thought for a moment and then answered his own question. "The problems were not caused by the people of Ranovao. They were caused by too many people moving here from the lowlands in search of land for their zebu cattle and rice. They were caused by the needs and demands of the growing cities of this great island. But mainly they were caused by Europeans and others like them." He turned and spoke directly to Jean-Amie. "First the French and then others brought great *vazaha* to the Malagasy, with your knowledge of things but your ignorance of tradition and custom. You are witches and *mpakafo*, heart thieves, and you have stolen the heart of the Malagasy. And so Ranovao must be sacrificed. Is that justice? I thought justice was precious to you. Obviously, it is not as precious as cleverness."

Now it was Jean-Amie's turn to wince. He wanted to respond; his sympathies lay with the plight of the village and not with Jenkins. But he kept silent for the time being and allowed Rahandraha to speak for him by speaking against him.

There was little more to say. The bad news was delivered, and Herbert's responsibilities were completed. Rahandraha ushered other villagers into the house. The table was transformed from a place of debate to one of social exchanges, and dinner was served. Even strangers bearing bad news must be treated with traditional hospitality.

As night fell, several young boys with lanterns led the way for the three guests to their bungalow for the night. The evening was not yet completed, however. Lucianne and Jean-Amie, still feeling the emotional wounds inflicted by the village elder, needed to talk. Lucianne initiated the conversation.

"I think I've answered my own question to you, Dr. Jenkins," she said. "Your statement was an ultimatum, wasn't it?"

"I'm not surprised at your comment, Lucianne. I have felt for some time that your frustrations might result in some criticism of my approach. And that's understandable."

"Sometimes my work is very difficult," Lucianne responded.

Herbert continued. "You're caught in the middle—a Malagasy who is Western-trained and yet respectful of her traditions. That's why I made this trip from the United States just to announce the decision to move the village for the sake of saving the forest tract. I carry a delegated authority as an advocate for preservation, and I'm not shy in wielding it."

"But that's the problem, now, isn't it?" said Lucianne. "Conservationists are not democratic, nor do they seek a balance between the traditions or life ways of a people and the need to rescue threatened biodiversity. Biodiversity always trumps. Your political, economic, and social agenda for the people of Madagascar revolves around the value of biodiversity."

"I recognize myself in your description, Lucianne," Herbert responded. "I don't relish the task of bringing bad news to the village, but removing these people is a necessary step in protecting some of the richest rainforest in the world from the ignorance of those who have lived with it for thousands of years."

"Is it really worth it, Doctor?" Lucianne pleaded.

"Certainly," Herbert replied. "The Manombo preserve contains ancient botanical and zoological riches—dozens of species of orchids, for example, that are found nowhere else on earth. Relocating the people of Ranovao is the lesser of two evils, with the greater being the unthinkable and eternal loss of those orchids and all the other incredible life that thrives in the forest."

"There is something to be said for the preservation of our rich traditions as well, but they will vanish—'eternally,' as you say—with the forced removal of the villagers from the land of their ancestors," said Lucianne.

"Perhaps, and you've introduced another good point. Those very ancestors, so rightly venerated, were responsible for the original destruction of the vast wilderness of Madagascar with the introduction of zebu cattle and the practice of *tavy*, periodic burning, around 900 years ago. The old biblical adage about the sins of the fathers being visited upon the children is true here. Perhaps, with the loss of attention to their tomb dwelling once the village has been relocated, the ancestors will finally receive the consequences of their actions."

"But we're talking about the living, Dr. Jenkins," said Lucianne. "We may successfully save this patch of rainforest, but at the cost of destroying the rich cultural heritage of these people."

"I understand that," Herbert said. "But even that culture is a present danger to numerous species in the forests. That newly discovered subspecies of the Aye-Aye lemur is a case in point. The villagers fear the animal and declare it to be taboo. They kill individual lemurs that stray too close to the village, and many are hunted down as a way of dispelling bad luck."

Herbert hesitated thoughtfully for a moment before delivering his harsh conclusion. "Undoubtedly, it is best that some traditions, the destructive ones, be put to rest in the tombs with the ancestors."

Jean-Amie, who had been listening quietly, could no longer restrain himself. "The question goes far beyond custom and tradition and whatever 'ignorance' you find in it, Dr. Jenkins. It has to do with the right of our people to decide their own destiny, apart from some other destiny not of our own choosing imposed upon us by foreign ideologies."

"But without intervention," Herbert responded forcefully, "the Malagasy will persist in and even amplify actions that eventually will destroy priceless natural treasures. Look," he continued, "forest loss is not the only environmental problem on this island. Eighty-five percent of the land is burned annually—85 percent! The great and growing herds of cattle graze along the margins of the forest and encourage the herders to slash and burn new pastures. Exotic species are flourishing everywhere, and endemic species are being harvested at alarming rates."

"That's true," Lucianne interjected. "I was in the capital this week at *zoma*, market day, and saw several shops that were displaying great numbers of mounted butterflies for sale. Many were from gravely endangered species."

"These are urgent causes for alarm," Herbert continued. "The world has taken notice and, through organizations like the World Fund for Nature, has taken action as well. Our position is that nature should not always be sacrificed to human folly and that a portion of the costs of its preservation should be borne by those responsible."

Jean-Amie smiled at the idealist purity of Herbert's comments. "What you say about responsibility is the truth, but not the whole truth. One must use a mirror to see the whole truth. Many of these problems are not of Malagasy making."

"How do you mean?" said Herbert.

"The responsible parties live across the seas. Our overpopulation, crowded cities, increasing demands for material goods, economic displacement, and abject poverty—the average annual income of the Malagasy is under $300—are consequences of imported ideologies and influences. For example, Madagascar cannot afford to buy much oil for the generation of energy for our rapidly growing cities; so we burn charcoal, which is made from an introduced species of rapidly growing tree, the eucalyptus. It is tragic that our rich native forests are being replaced by a single alien species that is good only for burning. The village elder was right when he characterized Western influence as *vazaha:* admirably skilled but full of clever tricks. My French heritage is implicated, and now so are your American attitudes. Modernization and development are the really dangerous exotics that destroy this land. Should the village be sacrificed at the command of those whose culture introduced the evil forces that created the problem originally?"

"I can't deny that, Jean-Amie," said Herbert. "My presence as a representative of the values of preservation is partially in recognition of our complicity and yours in creating this situation. And we are moving to correct it."

"But it is a goal to be achieved at considerable cost to those who have had little to do with its creation," Lucianne persisted. "Let's look clearly into Jean-Amie's 'mirror.' I traveled to America several times for study. I saw your impressive affluence. But it is accompanied by arrogance and ignorance. Americans generate more global environmental damage in a single day with their SUVs than the Malagasy contribute in a year of burning of forests and grasslands. I recall seeing one SUV with an environmentally friendly license plate that read 'Save the Rainforests.' And speaking of ignorance, that's worse than ignorance; it's schizophrenia. Perhaps our passion and attention should be as devoted to threats that Miami poses for the Everglades as they are to the threat that Ranovao and other villages pose for the Manombo Preserve."

"Some of the sources of your frustration are now clearer to me, Lucianne," said Herbert, who couldn't resist a smile as Lucianne concluded. "I can't deny the irony of your example, but American hypocrisy does not cancel the truth."

"No, but it contributes to the truth," replied Lucianne.

"Listen to me, Lucianne," Herbert continued. "The rainforests do not belong to the Malagasy alone. Their importance goes far beyond national sovereignty and the customs of a single culture. They belong to all humankind. You and I are merely the custodians of these treasures. And it's time that they are permitted advocates to defend them against the claim that nature must always be sacrificed to cover human incompetence."

"Your single focus is admirable," Jean-Amie responded. "But my work in the conservation section has shown me the wisdom of attacking the problem not narrowly with strategies based on ideology but along a broad front. We are working to increase the productivity of domesticated lands so the farmers and herders won't have push further into the forests. We are working to improve the lot of women through education and better medicine so that they and their families will not find it necessary to have a large number of children simply to get by. In time, the birth rate will fall, and with it the pressure on the forest preserve will diminish."

Lucianne added her thoughts to Jean-Amie's point. "And we can teach the people—or remind them—of what their ancestors once knew but they have forgotten: that the forest is a friend and self-renewing resource. Forests can attract tourists and provide medicines, food, and other nondestructive products for local communities, like Ranovao. Destruction of villages and traditions or the degradation of forests is not our only choice, Dr. Jenkins."

"In the long run, probably not," Herbert replied, "but the situation is critical. We simply can't wait for these long-range programs to bear fruit. Mounting population pressures on the remaining 10 percent of the island's original rainforests are unavoidable. Perhaps we can slow, but nothing can stop, the island's population from doubling in the next twenty years, given the staggering 2.8 percent growth rate—one of the highest in Africa."

"We must work with the people, or we will compound the wrong and invite disaster," said Jean-Amie.

"Averting disaster, that's why I'm here. Not to negotiate, but to announce," Herbert said. "Yes, some people, such as those in Ranovao, will be victims in that they must bear the costs of actions intended to bring about our immediate goal—to save this fragment of rainforest and the endangered species, the lemur and the orchids, for which it provides a shrinking habitat. These battles must be waged now, or else it will be too late, and all humanity will be tragically and irreversibly diminished."

In the face of Herbert's impassioned dedication to the cause as he saw it, Lucianne and Jean-Amie were silent for a moment. The day had been exhausting, and a long ride back to Anatanarivo awaited them in the morning. Finally, Lucianne concluded the discussion. "Perhaps the best we can hope for is that these people will be treated with some sense of compassion because all they seem to have left is the traditional Malagasy exhortation: *malemy, malemy,* 'Be gentle, be kind.'"

Commentary

Madagascar, the earth's sixth-largest island, has some of the richest treasures of biodiversity in the world. It also has one of the poorest economies.

Originally Madagascar was part of a huge landmass connecting Africa and South America. As the continents drifted into their current locations, the island separated and stood apart, marooning many species. Although many of its plants and animals are African in origin, some species are found only in South America and Madagascar. Evolution on the isolated island also led to a great number of insects, plants, fish, and reptiles that are found nowhere else. Amazingly, all sixty-six endemic land mammal species are unique to the island. The rainforests alone contain 900 species of orchids. Many of these plants and animals are not only unique but also endangered.[1]

One island species that is not endangered is *Homo sapiens*—humankind. Madagascar is peopled with immigrants from Asia and Africa, making it unique in another way. Although there are distinct tribal cultures, especially in rural areas, the Malagasy share a strong panislandic identity and a common language. Another thing they share is poverty. The average per capita annual income is less than $300. Eighty percent are subsistence farmers. As in many other developing nations, the population of Madagascar is burgeoning. It increased a staggering 550 percent from 1900 to 2000. By 2025, its current number of 14 million is expected to double, thanks to an increasingly healthy and youthful population. Many of these people will choose to live in cities, placing additional stress on the already burdened social and economic infrastructure.[2] The country is even too poor to import the oil it requires. Consequently, 80 percent of its domestic fuel needs are met by charcoal made from felled trees.

Given the rich but vulnerable biodiversity of Madagascar and its increasing population and economic pressures, no prophetic powers are needed to predict impending environmental disaster. Even now an astounding 85 percent of the island is intentionally burned each year in a traditional agricultural practice known as *tavy*. Herdsmen burn the grazing lands in the belief that a new and more nutritious carpet of grass will replace that consumed by fire and provide nourishment for increasing numbers of zebu cattle. Rural villagers living at the edge of the rainforests burn trees to make way for rice paddies or other crops. In the past *tavy* could be sustained because the burned areas were allowed to replenish themselves through rotational burning over a period of years. Population pressures have destroyed this rhythm, however, and many Malagasy have abandoned traditional environmental wisdom in the face of urgent needs for immediate survival.

Alarmed by this situation, powerful international environmental organizations have responded. With the cooperation of the government of the island nation, they have set up several natural parks and preserves and initiated studies to determine which species are in greatest danger. In our case, Herbert Jenkins represents the environmental NGOs, and Lucianne and Jean-Amie represent the government's interests in the preservation of the rainforest. Their meeting with the village elder, Rahandraha, reveals additional moral quandaries in this already difficult situation. The continuing presence of this village—and presumably others abutting the endangered section of rain-forest—threaten its survival and the survival of specific plants and animals that live in it.

Removal of the villages—to a better place, presumably—would seem to be beneficial to the endangered environment and to the villagers. The elder's angry response is based primarily on beliefs arising from his tribal traditions, which are representative of a large portion of Malagasy culture. The principal issue is the status of the ancestors—who, as we learn, are interred in a local tomb dwelling that is far more than a mausoleum. In Malagasy culture, the departed have not yet parted. They "live" in the tomb dwelling in the middle of the village and influence their neighbors and surviving kin through the substantial power they wield, ironically, as suppliers of life. To touch the tomb or to pay homage through small offerings left in its entryway assures fertility. The dead, not the living, are the source of vital energy. By residing close to this center of power, the living derive blessings that are necessary for a good life. They also bear considerable civic and ceremonial responsibility, however, for the upkeep and maintenance of the tomb dwelling. Failure to fulfill these obligations results in considerable *tsiny*, or guilt.[3]

Of equal importance is the intimate relationship between place and iden-tity, both personal and communal. If the inhabitants of Ronavao are forced to abandon the village and the tomb, they face psychological and spiritual de-privation. Their center of the world, or *axis mundi*—the place where the an-cestors lived and still abide—suddenly will be far away, and they will be like Lucianne: *vahiny*, or strangers in their new place.

With these observations, it becomes clear why Rahandraha responds so strongly to the government's removal order. He is far from finished, how-ever. After chastising Lucianne as *komo*—one who has not fulfilled her tradi-tional obligations to her village kin—he turns his attention to Jean-Amie. Jean-Amie's ancestors, the French, were the early colonizers of the island. They introduced European ways and religion and opened the way for the re-ception of Western ideas of materialism and individualism. By describing these modern values and practices as *vazaha*, or crafty, the elder is expressing his mistrust of and disdain for European and American cleverness. He also is expressing his belief that such alien ideology (emphasizing material posses-sions over traditions) and urban life (emphasizing individual liberty over village and tribal customs) are major contributors to the current plight of Madagascar. Later, Jean-Amie and Lucianne echo these points. It seems paradoxical to them that Herbert, an American, is so concerned for the rainforest that American values have put in danger. Lucianne's poignant example of the sport utility vehicle with an environmentally promotional license plate sharpens this contradiction.

Along with paradox and contradiction comes ambiguity. Jean-Amie recognizes that Western ideology carries tremendous practical power; *vazahna*, cleverness, has its beneficial side. Agricultural, social, and marketing strategies can make a huge difference in the preservation of the island's environment. Providing the Malagasy with better education and access to basic medical care will go far in reducing birthrates and mortality rates for children. By encouraging consumer-oriented Americans to live out their contradictions by using their affluence to travel to Madagascar to enjoy the lemurs and the orchids in the rainforests, ecotourism promises to improve the ailing economy of the island dramatically. The ambiguity cuts both ways. Herbert notes that local beliefs about the Aye-Aye lemur as a demon-like creature, based on the bizarre appearance of the animal's huge eyes and large paws, constitute a real danger for its survival. Not all customary practices or long-standing beliefs of indigenous peoples are necessarily harmonious with or favorable to the natural environment.

Herbert's ideology is an additional important factor in the discussion. By acting locally in the village, he is thinking globally in terms of working assumptions and moral principles to which he is dedicated. One assumption is that the natural heritage of the earth is the common possession of all peoples throughout all generations. It follows that the obligation of those who are entrusted with these treasures, including the government and citizens of the nation within whose boundaries they lie, is to maintain them in a state of health and well-being. The responsibility of trained professionals like Herbert, Lucianne, and Jean-Amie is to be vigilant in their assignment to monitor ecosystems at risk.

This position calls into question a fundamental supposition of the modern nation-state system: that a nation-state is sovereign over all activities that take place within its recognized borders. This notion of sovereignty is being honored less and less as the world changes politically, economically, and technologically. It is weakened especially by the international "war on terror," the emphasis on human rights, communications technologies, and transnational corporations. Preservation of environmentally valuable places may be added to this list as well.

Herbert's philosophical position also holds that a specific value is paramount and decisive in determining action. This value, discussed in the introductory chapter as biodiversity—the variety of living things in a single

69

region—guides his moral judgment and determines his strategies. Although biodiversity, like beauty, often is regarded as an intrinsic value (it is inherently good, for aesthetic or other reasons), Herbert does not argue exclusively from this claim. Instead, he begins and ends with a tacit appeal to universal human rights. All humankind has the right to enjoy its common heritage and to have it protected from the destructive actions of a few. This right is bestowed not by virtue of membership in a society or political group (perhaps in common agreement as a social contract) but by virtue simply of being a human citizen of planet Earth. Thus, it is nonnegotiable ("unalienable," according to Thomas Jefferson's words in the Declaration of Independence) or "natural" in the sense intended by natural law ethics.

But what about the rights of the few—the Tanala of Ranovao for whom maintenance of the Manombo rainforest's biodiversity is particularly costly? There seems to be something inherently unfair about destroying a village and displacing its inhabitants for the sake of the sensibilities of patrons of a botanical garden in St. Louis who fill its parking lot with gas-guzzling SUVs. Herbert concedes that this blatant hypocrisy exists and includes the oddly illogical situation of the people of the earth contributing to the destruction of the common heritage they wish to rescue, but he does not allow it to derail his argument. Neither the questionable intentions of some people nor the outright confusion of others negates the moral end of his project: saving the rainforest from human folly regardless of its numerous sources, including the *vazaha* of Western influence and the environmentally dysfunctional tribal customs of indigenous Malagasy.

Despite its complicity, the village cannot be blamed entirely nor even primarily for the diminishing rainforest. Indeed, we learn that it has tried to live peacefully within its natural surroundings. Yet it finds itself in this difficult predicament. Why must the villagers bear the cost for the consequences of actions taken principally by others? Herbert would counter with a question of his own: Why must "nature . . . always be sacrificed to cover human incompetence"? The village is caught in the middle. For Herbert, however, its relocation is the lesser evil that will bring about the greater good—the rescue of the rainforest.

Perhaps other, less disruptive alternatives are possible. Jean-Amie argues for social and economic programs that would rescue the people and the environment. These programs will take years to implement, however, and by then this section of the rainforest will no longer exist. "These battles must be waged now," Herbert concludes, "or else it will be too late, and all humanity will be tragically and irreversibly diminished." Lucianne probably is accurate in her final observation: For the people of Ranovao it seems that all that is left is to make the appeal, *malemy, malemy.*

Questions for Discussion

1. Describe Dr. Jenkins's position. Do you agree with Lucianne that he is rigid and ideological, or is he merely steadfast in protecting rare and endangered ecosystems for the sake of all humanity? Give reasons for your choice.
2. What reasons does the tribal elder give as he resists being moved to a new location despite promised improvements for his community? Do you agree with his position?
3. In Madagascar the ancestors are understood to possess tremendous power. Maintenance of their tombs therefore is an important responsibility for the living. What is the modern secular understanding of the dead and their burial grounds? Would you favor, for example, the removal of buried remains from Arlington National Cemetery for any reason? What weight should be given to such ancient cultural beliefs in modern attitudes toward the protection of the environment?
4. Jean-Amie argues for a strategy that involves economic development and social advance in Madagascar as a way of curbing environmental destruction. Is his proposal realistic? Explain.

Notes

1. Harry T. Wright and Jean-Amie Rakotoariso, "Cultural Transformation and the Impact on the Environments of Madagascar," in *Natural Change and Human Impact in Madagascar,* ed. Steven M. Goodman and Bruce D. Patterson (Washington, D.C.: Smithsonian Institution Press, 1977), 309.
2. Claire Kremen, "Traditions that Threaten," available at www.pbs.org/edens/madagascar/paradise.html (accessed February 9, 2003).
3. Maurice Bloch, *Placing the Dead: Tombs, Ancestral Villages, and Kinship Organization in Madagascar* (London: Seminar Press, 1971), 163.

For Further Reading

Bloch, Maurice. *Placing the Dead: Tombs, Ancestral Villages, and Kinship Organization in Madagascar.* London: Seminar Press, 1971.

Goodman, Steven M., and Bruce D. Patterson, eds. *Natural Change and Human Impact in Madagascar.* Washington, D.C.: Smithsonian Institution Press, 1997.

Gradwohl, Judith, and Russell Greenberg. *Saving the Tropical Forests.* Washington, D.C.: Island Press, 1988.

Gupta, Avijit. *Ecology and Development in the Third World.* New York: Routledge, 1988.

Jeffery, Leonard H., et al. *Environment and the Poor: Development Strategies for a Common Agenda*. New Brunswick, N.J.: Transaction Publishers, 1989.

Jolly, Alison. *A World Like Our Own: Man and Nature in Madagascar*. New Haven, Conn.: Yale University Press, 1980.

Meyers, Norman. *The Primary Source: Tropical Forests and Our Future*. New York: Norton, 1984.

Nations, James D. *Tropical Rainforests, Endangered Environment*. New York: Franklin Watts, 1988.

Rolston, Holmes III. "Feeding People Versus Saving Nature," in *World Hunger and Morality*, ed. James Aiken and Robert Lafollete. Englewood Cliffs, N.J.: Prentice Hall, 1996, 143–65.

5

Must Java Have No Forests?
Nature Preserves and
Human Population Pressures

The Indonesian heads of twenty different environmental groups, including national and international nongovernmental organizations
(NGOs), began to filter into the conference room at the offices of
the Indonesia Environment Forum in Jakarta to begin a planning
meeting on responding to the recent Jakarta floods. Beginning in the
last days of January 2002, the rivers and streams around the capital
city of Indonesia, swollen with monsoon rains, overflowed their banks
and inundated streets and homes in low-lying districts throughout
large portions of greater Jakarta—home to 11 million people. The
floodwaters in many places rose more than a meter and a half (almost
five feet). The first wave of flooding crested on the third day and by
the eighth day had receded from most parts of the city. As the rains
continued into February, however, the flooding returned in three
new waves; some parts of the city suffered a fourth wave. Each wave
lasted for days.

Jakarta has a history of flooding on a five-year average, but the
2002 floods were by far the worst ever to hit the city, and they were
the result of only slightly higher than average monsoon rainfall. The

73

floodwaters were full of mud, snakes, and dead animals, from rats to chickens. They also contained petroleum products, chemicals, and other pollutants from factories, businesses, and homes, not to mention thousands of tons of rotting garbage. At least twenty-two people drowned in the floods. Hospitals were crowded with thousands of patients complaining of respiratory ailments from exposure to the water, mold, and rot; of dysentery from contaminated drinking water and spoiled food; and of skin irritations and infections from contact with the floodwaters. A hundred or more young children died of dysentery directly related to the flooding.

The losses from the flooding were enormous. Many millions of households had all their possessions ruined. Clothing and furniture rotted because there was no way to dry them even after flooding receded, as a result of continuing monsoon rains and then new waves of flooding. As the floodwaters drained into the Java Sea, they carried the garbage, chemicals, and debris with them. Fishermen were forced to move far from the shore to catch anything at all.

Nor did the flooding affect only poor Jakartans. Many hard-hit areas were rich neighborhoods of upscale villas. By the end of February, outbreaks of malaria and dengue fever, both spread by mosquitoes, and leptospirosis—a disease spread by contact with rat urine—were under way throughout the city. The rat population, displaced from some locations by floodwaters, multiplied rapidly as garbage collection ceased. Mounds of garbage still filled the streets six weeks after the floods began.

This March 2002 meeting of officers of twenty environmental organizations was brought to order by the director of the Indonesia Environment Forum, Iqbal Soetarto, who began by reminding the group that by the second week of flooding, many of the same environmentalists gathered here had been saying that the prime reason for the flooding was the failure of the government to enforce its environmental plans and laws.

"We all know that this is true," Iqbal said. "I think most of us can agree on at least three main enforcement failures within Jakarta itself, as well as several other failures of implementation upstream from Jakarta. Within Jakarta, we could name illegal development in areas designated as catchment areas, the failure of developers in other areas to build the canals and catchment ponds that were part of the permits approved for their buildings, and the excessive number of golf courses in Jakarta (thirty-one!)—most of which had not followed the environmental specifications in their permits. Harwanto Amin, Elys Muhammad, and Acik Mentuto have pointed in particular to Puncak, as well as Bogor and Cianjur, as examples of areas upstream of Jakarta where the villas of the rich had been built onto hillsides and in forests that were designated as catchment areas for streams headed for downstream Jakarta. As those areas were cleared and built on, local streams became filled with silt from erosion and the rainfall that could no longer be absorbed."

Iqbal then recapped the widespread discontent in Jakarta with the ineffectiveness of local government in predicting, preventing, or responding to the flooding. In the aftermath of the flooding, as property values dropped precipitously in all the flooded areas—affecting rich and poor alike in a nation still reeling from the financial crisis that had hit in mid-1997—demands were heard on all sides that the government do something to prevent such flooding from ever occurring again.

"This is our chance," Iqbal said, "while the population is paying attention to the suffering from the floods, to achieve a coordinated environmental plan that will prevent this kind of disaster, allow for planned growth in Jakarta, and protect the environment surrounding Jakarta. How should we proceed?" The group was silent. Finally, someone spoke.

"Many of our groups have different foci," Elys said, "especially divided between the urban planning issues in Jakarta and the preservation of forests in the upstream areas. The floods involved both our interests. At a more fundamental level, we are all aware that our efforts face the same basic problems: the corruption of government officials at all levels and the widespread public feeling that now that the repressive centralized government of Suharto is replaced by democracy, all national resources belong to the people—which often means whoever seizes them first."

"And some people began seizing public resources immediately," said Acik, who recounted his findings in Puncak: "About 4,000 new villas have been built in the past four years, since the New Order government fell. Many not only are large homes with patios, some have tennis courts, garages, even swimming pools. Some of them have additional small guest houses around the main house. There are, of course, long roads, some portions even paved, leading to the villas, and the buildings, tennis courts, and roads all prevent water absorption, increasing the flow in the Ciliwung River. Many of these developments have replaced natural lakes. Bogor had 122 lakes in 1949; today it has 102. The situation is much worse in other upstream areas: Tangerang had 45 lakes and Bekasi had 17 in 1949; today Tangerang has 19 and Bekasi has 8. Furthermore, the most popular places to build the villas are along the banks of the Ciliwung, so the increased surface flow goes directly into the Ciliwung, with no chance to be absorbed by surrounding land.

"According to the locals and the records I checked, most of the villas are owned by generals, politicians, and rich people connected to the military and government," Acik continued. "Only about 40 percent have building permits, and those permits are illegal because the land belongs to the government and is clearly designated as either protected forest or community forest. A protected forest, as we know, is one in which all human activities are prohibited; a community, or traditional, forest is one that may not be cleared and in which people may not live or farm, but from which they may take deadfall wood and in which they may allow small animals such as chickens to feed and gather. The local forestry officials will not do anything to enforce the law, however, against either villa owners without building permits or those with permits obtained through bribery. They say the villa owners are too powerful, that those people never lose. If the cases go to court, the charges are dropped, or the judges are bribed. And most forestry officials in Puncak are locals—many of their relatives are employed at the villas as cooks or drivers or guards, so they don't want to see the villas destroyed. And they are afraid of the local officials who sold the building permits in the forest. Citing the villas for the illegal permits would be an attack on the local officials who sold them."

As the group pondered Acik's words, Iqbal responded.

"Yes, we have the same basic problem in Jakarta," he began. "Though many new housing and commercial developments in the areas designated for water catchment have illegally purchased permits, many do not but were developed by rich persons, often army generals or politicians. Police and other government officials won't issue either demolition notices or warrants or arrests that might offend powerful persons. In addition, the increased density caused by building in the catchment areas has caused another problem with water. Jakarta has virtually no septic sewers; it relies on septic tanks. Because the city gets 70 percent of its water from groundwater—much of it from shallow private wells that are far less than the recommended 10 meters from septic tanks—the quality of much of the city's water is deteriorating. Furthermore, we have pumped so much groundwater that seawater subsidence has reached the Monas [a well-known public monument in the center of Jakarta], and moves inland 40–80 meters annually, contaminating our water."

"But surely there are some places to start in putting together a plan," said Herman Suparjo, an officer of an international NGO. "The city has announced that it will destroy two golf courses and make them back into catchment, and the central government has announced that it will suspend new building permits for six months until a study can be done of the catchment needs in Jakarta and build five new dams to control flooding. Surely those are a foundation."

There was an angry buzz of voices as Herman concluded. Elys leaned across the conference table toward Herman and said, "But

Herman, the Jakarta governor refused to agree to the suspension in building permits as soon as the developers and construction unions protested that suspending building permits for six months would throw 900,000 people out of work. With the unsettled state of the autonomy law, the legality of the national government's suspension is not even clear. Besides, do we want to side with the central government here?"

"That's an important issue," insisted Anchu Pamin, "because most of our groups are clear that the central government is good at issuing environmental plans and orders but has neither the resources to enforce them nor the will to prevent bribery from undermining them. Our only chance to protect remaining forests, reefs, and fisheries is to work with local populations and officials who have an interest in their preservation and helping them see short-term as well as long-term benefits from preservation."

In the previous four years, since the New Order government had fallen, environmental policy had disintegrated in Indonesia. National forests all over Indonesia's thousands of islands had been stripped by logging companies that had encouraged villagers to log the forests at cheap wages, assuring them they could build and farm on the cleared land. The few projects that had been successful in stopping incursions—and only after massive local forests had been cleared—were those in which environmental groups and forestry officials had worked out compromises that allowed villagers to expand onto the outermost parts of the cleared forest, worked out with all concerned groups the boundaries between protected and community forests, and found external funds to pay villagers to replant core forest areas that had been cleared and to assist forestry officials in detecting and preventing incursions by logging crews. A general consensus had emerged that there was simply no other way to prevent the total destruction of Indonesia's forests and wildlife habitats in the absence of effective legal enforcement. Yet there was still great discontent, especially on the part of many international conservation groups, over the environmental concessions those compromises entailed and the precedents they set for the future.

Iqbal called for attention. "In talking with several organizations prior to this meeting, it seemed to me that the most contentious issue is the five dams. Perhaps we should turn to that now."

Willis Brecht, from the Urban Planning League of Jakarta, spoke first. "I will not pretend that these five dams are the best environmental answer to the situation we face in Jakarta. Ideally, we all know that it would be preferable to restore the catchment areas in the 1999–2000 Environmental Master Plan by bulldozing illegal residential and commercial developments and forcing the developers to

77

install the drainage and canals that their permits called for. Politically, however, that will not happen. At most a few token developers will be forced to add drainage canals. There simply is no way any Indonesian government will destroy subdivisions or shopping centers of 200–500 acres because they were built illegally on state land designated for catchment. So the five dams, the four new water-pumping stations, and the continued acquisition of land for the East Flood Canal offer the best plan for dealing with flooding in Jakarta."

Elys faced the group around the conference table. "I don't believe I just heard this," she sputtered. "This is not an environmentally sound proposal at any level. And it's not even the issue of dams in themselves. Like most of us, I'm skeptical about using dams. But these proposed dams, with one exception, are not even to dam up rivers but only excess runoff. They will barely make a dent in any real flooding. Perhaps if the population of Jakarta stayed constant and there were no new development, these dams and new pumps could prevent flooding in a third to a half of the areas affected this year. But we continue to lose catchment areas to development every year in Jakarta. In another year, two at most, the increased loss of catchment will exceed the capacity of these dams, and we will be worse off than this year. The proposal for the dams is simply public relations—an attempt to fool the public into believing they will be safe."

"I'm not so sure, Elys," replied Agus Winik, who worked with the Wildlife Conservation Fund. "It seems to me that any plan with a chance of success will be cobbled together out of many pieces, and these dams may have a role. Virtually none of the common objections to dams apply here—they will not inundate large areas, they will have minimal displacement effects on animals and humans, and they do not affect the normal flow of rivers. Although I agree with you that the catchment areas are vital and we cannot simply concede their loss, it seems to me that building the dams could give us a little extra margin in trying to preserve and reclaim catchment. Most important, I think, is to not be coopted into what, as you say, clearly is an attempt by the city government to persuade the people that the dams are enough to protect them. We must press for preservation and restoration of catchment."

Bodies settled back in their chairs and heads nodded as Agus concluded. There was a moment of silence, then Herman spoke. "We may all agree that the catchment areas should be restored and, of course, remaining catchment preserved. But how do we see that being done?"

Iqbal intervened. "Lunch has arrived. Let me suggest that we divide into groups that are appropriate to our particular organizational strengths and interests and talk over lunch. How about one group on the upstream clearings, one group on Jakarta catchment, and a third group on dams, canals, and land procurement for the East Flood Canal?"

Everyone agreed, and he continued. "Jakarta catchment meets here, upstream clearings in the reception area, and dams/canals in my office. We meet back here in an hour. Okay?"

When the groups came back from lunch, both the dams/canals group and the Jakarta catchment group had agreed on a plan, and both plans were acceptable to the conference as a whole. The conference would support the city's building of the floodwater dams, and organizations in the dams/canals group would use the media to target ten to twelve of the largest, best-financed developments that had not built the canals required in their building permits and lobby the city administration to either require the developments to install the canals or fine them to finance city installation of the canals.

The Jakarta group also was in general agreement that the basic issue was catchment within the city. The agencies concerned had divided up the various tasks. One agency agreed to push for and oversee the promised destruction of the two 36-hole golf courses the city had promised to destroy, installation of drainage basins, and restoration of the original topography. Two other agencies agreed to research developments in the north and west of the city that were built in violation of the 1999–2000 Master Plan and to assess in each case the viability of demolition, the possibility and cost of ameliorating the lost catchment, and the political feasibility of pushing for either in each specific development. Three agencies jointly took up the formidable task of monitoring development plans and building permits that might be planned for remaining catchment areas in Jakarta and, using Indonesia's watchdog press, lobbying against such projects. Though there clearly were not enough hands to do the tasks that had been delegated, much less the ones that remained unclaimed, there was a general sense of satisfaction in the two groups.

The upstream clearing group, however, had come to an impasse, which quickly involved the entire conference. The division originally arose over whether the agencies should insist on adherence to the 1999–2000 Environmental Master Plan for West Java. Some members argued that all of the "green" areas marked in that plan should be retained. Others argued that this approach was no longer feasible and that environmental concerns had to be integrated with population, poverty, and development concerns. Anchu rose and began to speak.

"Of the 13,600 islands of Indonesia, Java has less than 7 percent of the land mass but has 60 percent of the population of Indonesia," he said. "Only 39 percent of Java's 128 million people are urban; the rest live in villages and towns and are agricultural. The Indonesian population program has been very successful, for a developing nation: The fertility rate is 2.9 children per woman—down from almost 7 per woman forty years ago. But it will be another twenty years, if that, before Java hits the replacement level of 2.1 children per woman, which means that population growth will be strong in Java. Without quick industrialization, those excess people will have to support themselves in agriculture, and already these past three years we have been importing rice, the basic staple. People need space in which to build homes and plant crops, and that space must come from clearing forests. We must manage such clearing well, but we cannot simply put all the forests off limits as if we had a stable population size. Furthermore, if industrialization is to occur and Indonesia is to benefit from it, the capital for industrialization must come from the sale of natural resources such as lumber, oil, and mining. Even the Master Plan has some areas designated as 'production forest.' Just because that designation has been interpreted in these last years since the fall of the New Order government as meaning that such forests belong to anybody with a chainsaw does not mean that production forests should be written out of the plan."

Anchu sat down, and Elys began.

"We cannot allow the possibility that Java will be left with no forests, that all of its rivers will be polluted with pesticides and fertilizers from agriculture, simply because of population growth. Javanese—whole villages of Javanese even—have been migrating to other islands for centuries in search of new land to cultivate; there is no reason to destroy the ecosystem here to prevent migration within Indonesia. Each of our islands needs to preserve its own forests and animal habitats. By what right do we put these interests of humans ahead of those of all the other species of animals and plants on Java? Would Java still be Java without its flora and fauna that figure so heavily in its cultural symbols, its foods, and its legends? Why should we preserve forests, animal habitats, and rivers only on large and sparsely populated islands such as Papua, Sumatra, and Kalimantan? Should we just surrender to extinction all the endangered species here on Java? What kind of environmental policy is that? Whatever plan we have for Java should be based not on what 'green spaces' can be spared from industrialization, housing, and agriculture for humans or on what will protect Jakarta from flooding but on what protected spaces are necessary to allow other species to be self-perpetuating."

The two sides were deadlocked. As Iqbal adjourned the meeting, he asked that both sides from the upstream clearings group bring back the following month their proposals for a master plan, in hopes that agreement was possible on some aspects. As he walked out of the meeting with Acik, however, both were depressed.

"If we can't even agree on whose environment it is," Acik mourned, "how shall we ever agree on how to care for it?"

Commentary

The deadlock issue in this case is not new or unique in environmental ethics. It is the basic question underlying the entire field (as laid out in chapter 1): What priority, if any, is to be given to humans over other species? Underneath a great deal of consensus among environmentalists about the interdependency of the entire biosphere lies a spectrum of positions concerning the role of humans. Although virtually all environmentalists reject blatant anthropocentrism, in which the earth exists to serve the needs of human beings, most argue that the human species must take precedence over other individual species—but that humans must use that precedence responsibly. James Nash, for example, argues that all creatures are entitled to "moral consideration" but that not all have the same "moral significance," arguing against biotic egalitarianism.[1] John Hart argues that all living beings have intrinsic value, not merely instrumental value:

> The fact that a part of creation comes to have instrumental value does not negate the fact that it has intrinsic value. Individual members of a species might retain their initial intrinsic value until their life ends, not experiencing a change in value status until they become food for vultures and microorganisms. Ecosystem integrity and Earth's greater well-being would result if humans were to learn to acknowledge and respect the intrinsic value of all creation, and convert a creature's value from intrinsic to instrumental value frugally and responsibly, and only when necessary to sustain life or to enhance human cultural development.[2]

An example of rare, responsible conversion of an entire species from intrinsic to instrumental value might be eradication of the smallpox virus or the anticipated elimination of the human immunodeficiency virus (HIV), in which the negative consequences of the virus for humans outweighs their intrinsic value. Environmentalists such as Peter Singer argue that all sentient species have a right to exist that equals that of humans but that an individual's right to exist—for humans and other species—ultimately is functionally, or instrumentally, based. Thus, they reject arguments of intrinsic value for individuals of any species.

Although Nash argues for the greater moral significance of humans, he nevertheless argues for biotic "rights"—in opposition to Holmes Rolston III, who understands rights as applying only within the human political community.[3] Nash replies that the debate about the value of species and individual members of species takes place only within the human political community, and it is necessary to use the language of that community:

> The stress on nonhuman rights is a way of saying that all life is sacred or intrinsically valuable and worthy of being treated as the subject of human moral consideration. Indeed, the acknowledgment of intrinsic value in nonhuman creatures seems to be implicitly an acknowledgment of their legitimate claims for appropriate treatment from the human community, and, therefore, of some level of rights and responsibilities. The underlying concern seems to be human responsibility for nature, and the stress on rights provides an objective moral basis for this responsibility. . . . Advocacy for the rights of nature is the contention that environmental concern is not only an expression of benevolence, but also an obligation of justice—not simply justice to human interests, but also justice to the interests of other creatures. In Western cultures, rights are important; no rights suggests no moral consideration.[4]

In Indonesia, little environmental consciousness survives from tribal religious culture after the relentless missionizing of Hindus, Buddhists, Muslims, and Christians that began almost 3,000 years ago. What little tribal environmental consciousness did survive often is visible only when villagers regard local resources as under their ultimate control and as important for sustaining their own lives and those of their children. After Indonesia achieved independence following World War II, its resources too often were controlled by the central government, and today many observers fear that the present democracy—and the promise of local autonomy—is too fragile to endure. Thus, many villagers regard massive resource "harvesting" (as in logging of forests) as their only chance to benefit from what originally were permanent sustainable resources for their communities.

Indonesia is a very religious nation, with a large Muslim majority but with significant populations of Christians, Hindus (especially on Bali), Buddhists, and Confucians. The environment has not been a primary focus of Indonesia's religions, although that is beginning to change. Yet even as religions in Indonesia begin to include the environment alongside concerns such as religious tolerance and peace, education, and development, they are hampered because the religious resources for dealing with the environment are some-what ambiguous.

Both Islam and Christianity teach an ethic of "stewardship" or "regency": Humans are caliphs, or regents, over the earth in Islam and stewards in Christianity, charged with managing the earth well for Allah or God. The historical development of the role of steward/caliph in both religions, however, has emphasized management in the interests of humans, to use and preserve the earth for the use of all humans now and in the future. In addition, both traditions have emphasized the superiority of humans over all other species.

The situation in Indonesia's other religious traditions is not much different. Hinduism, which provides the predominant underlying cultural values for most of the Indonesian people despite their Islamic faith, retains in ritual many elements of early nature worship. Forests, in particular, have been important in supporting meditation, and there is a basic understanding in Hindu philosophy of the oneness of existence that could form the basis for an environmental ethics. For the most part, however, creation has been valued for its use value. Confucianism focused on social relationships, from the family to the empire; other than understanding nature as modeling peace and as conducive to contemplation, it does not offer much with which to construct an environmental ethics—especially because the Chinese Confucians in Indonesia tend to be urban, middle- and upper-class business and commercial investors. Many are Christian as well, with little Confucian cultural tradition remaining in the young.

Buddhism—the smallest of the five official religions of Indonesia (Protestantism and Catholicism are legally recognized as separate religions, and Confusianism does not have full recognition)—offers the best grounding for an environmental ethics in its principle of codependent origination. This principle is tempered, however, by its understanding of the material world as ultimately illusion and by its history, in which nature has been primarily appreciated for being conducive to meditation—the path to nirvana. Internationally, all of these religions are struggling toward an environmental ethics that draw on their traditions and meets the needs of the environmental crisis. This work is beginning in Indonesia, but it is not yet well developed and has not much influenced public opinion. However, the high degree of religiosity of Indonesia, especially the increasing levels of Islamicization, indicates that environmentalists in Indonesia should support the development of religious environmentalism as an avenue to creating environmental consciousness.

The crux of the debate in this case, however, may not be this foundational question about whether or to what extent humans take precedence over other species. The crux of the debate may be the different context of environmentalism in Indonesia. There may be a significant difference between environmentalism in a developed nation such as the United States and a developing nation such as Indonesia. Do the claims of human beings on the environment carry any more weight when the bulk of that population lives at great risk than when the bulk of that human population lives comfortably, at little risk?

In Indonesia and other developing nations, individual survival is more at risk than in the developed nations. Whereas in the United States only 8 of every 100,000 women who give birth die in childbirth, in Indonesia more than 650 women in every 100,000 die in childbirth—only one-third of whom are assisted by trained personnel.[5] In the United States—which has one of the highest infant mortality rates among developed nations as a result of inadequate prenatal care for poor women[6]—7.1 of every 1,000 infants die within their first year. In Indonesia, on the other hand, 46 of every 1,000 infants die in the first year. In 1999, the last year for which World Health Organization (WHO) figures are known, more than 175,000 Indonesians died of tuberculosis—a disease of poverty that has been virtually eliminated in the United States. These deaths are in addition to tropical epidemics plaguing Indonesia, such as malaria and dengue fever, not to mention more exotic diseases such as the leptospirosis generated by the floods.

The per capita gross national income of the United States is more than $31,000; that of Indonesia is $2,660. Of course, per capita gross national income in itself affects access to health care as well as education. In Indonesia, 11 percent of the population is completely illiterate, and only half of the youth go on to attend secondary school.

As noted in the case, the population figures for Indonesia show a total fertility rate of 2.9 children per woman. The 2001 population was 230 million people, with a population density of 280 persons per square mile—1,000 persons per square mile in Java, more than the highest rate in the most populated European nations. By comparison the U.S. population in 2001 was 284 million, with a density of 77 persons per square mile. Because Indonesia's fertility rate is still well above replacement levels (2.1 children per woman), the country's population is expected to be 272 million in 2025 and 304.8 million in 2050; a disproportionate part of that growth will occur in Java.[7]

Indonesia's hope of providing jobs, health care, and education for its underserved present population, as well as for its increasing population, depends on its ability to meet its own basic needs (especially food) and earn capital. Among its principal methods of earning capital is sale of wood, sand, and tropical fish and birds. There is a great deal of difference between arguing that comfortable populations with the highest degree of luxury in the world should make some sacrifices to accommodate what is necessary for other species to survive and arguing that to help other species of animals and plants survive, significant numbers of human beings may die or lack minimum levels of development we associate with basic human needs.

Even in the face of dramatic human need, some environmentalists may argue for other sentient species having equal claim to that of humans on the environment. Certainly, however, many who might cede priority in a developed context to the survival of other species in the case of the developing world will reluctantly side with a compromise that gives priority to meeting basic human needs such as food, shelter, health, and education. In the United States we might decide that increases in regional levels of unemployment resulting from inability to log remaining forests in the Northwest should be addressed through retraining and/or relocation of affected workers, whose suffering was not sufficient to justify turning the remaining forests and the animals and plants whose habitats they are from intrinsic to instrumental value. We might decide that the level of suffering from malnutrition, high infant and maternal mortality, disease, and illiteracy was too high, however, to justify a ban on logging in some regions of Indonesia. When the threat level to human groups increases, the level of threat that is acceptable for other species seems to rise as well. But to what level of threat?

Elys's group raises the issue of migration as the answer to Java's particular problem. Should that proposal be interpreted as sheer callousness to the plight of the landless farmers, or is it an acceptable answer to an unevenly settled nation of more than 13,000 islands? Perhaps both. It is true that Javanese have been settling on other islands for more than two centuries in search of land and businesses. The Dutch moved 605,000 people from Java to Sumatra to become plantation workers beginning in 1905, and after independence in 1950 the central government resettled 7 million people, mostly from Java and Bali. The resettled population consisted mostly of poor, landless (inexperienced) farmers who often used unsuitable farming methods and ended up as poor as before. About 10 percent of the resettled were urban poor people from Jakarta, most of whom could not adjust to the new location and eventually made their way back home.

Since 1990 government *transmigrasi* programs have slowed dramatically, both because family planning programs have been much more effective in reducing population growth in Java and because transmigration itself created many problems. The Javanese often have been resented on other islands. Indonesia is a multicultural nation *par excellence*. Its people speak more than 300 different local languages, in addition to the national language of Indonesian, and identify themselves in dozens of ethnicities; they are divided religiously among Islam, Christianity, Hinduism, Buddhism, and Confucianism—as well as tribal religions (where they survive). Movement of groups with different ethnicity, language, and religion from one island to the other—especially from Java, which always is resented on the other islands for its concentration of wealth and power and its control of the central government—can be like putting a fuse to dynamite. In March 2002 Indonesia was simultaneously conducting human rights trials against military and civilian officials for militia massacres of Catholics in East Timor, in truce negotiations with warring Muslim groups in Aceh, reconciling warring Christian and Muslim groups in the Maluku Islands, and dealing with attacks on Christians in Bali, along with slow reconciliation between Chinese and other groups that destroyed the Chinese areas of Jakarta, killing, beating, and raping Chinese in the riots of 1998. Certainly no Indonesian government today will easily accept a policy of urging Javanese to migrate en masse to other islands. Especially since the end of the New Order government and the signing of the Autonomy Law (though it has never been fully implemented, and confusion reigns about how it should be interpreted in various areas), Indonesians understand local resources—the most prominent being forests—as belonging primarily to the local people. If the central government were to intervene and give parts of forest in Riau to Javanese, the people of Riau would protest—and probably would disregard government policies restricting their use of local forest. Although individual Javanese will continue to migrate to other islands in search of economic opportunity, large-scale government transmigration policies are not a real possibility.

What does this mean for the forests of Java? Will the last few remaining Javanese tigers and orangutans disappear? Possibly. In the eastern United States many species of plants and animals became extinct in the process of settlement. While environmentalists attempt to prevent such extinction from occurring all over the world, local peoples living in poverty object that it is unfair of the developed world to impose on the poor, undeveloped nations of the world the burden of preserving global biodiversity when carrying that burden results in the perpetuation of poverty and its attendant evils: high infant and maternal mortality, illiteracy, epidemics, malnutrition, and unemployment and underemployment.

Yet at a very practical level there obviously are some areas of agreement possible between the two divisions in the upstream clearings group. First priority should go to preserving forests that serve the interests of both humans and other species by preventing flooding and preserving animal habitats. If the remaining habitats of endangered species on Java are sufficient to preserve those species, then protecting those habitats from further incursions also should be a top priority. In the 1999–2000 Master Plan, a common strategy was to indicate a core area of protected forest, surrounded by a ring of mixed community forest and production forest. As long as the core area is large enough to sustain the species of plants and animals found there and the core area can be protected from community and commercial incursions, such demarcations should continue to be acceptable to both sides, as they were in 1999–2000. As the case presented in this chapter indicates, protection of all three types of forest from illegal invasions of loggers and settlers will depend on enlisting local populations in monitoring the forests—which means that the local population must understand themselves as having a stake in the forests and their preservation. The core will be protected only if the production and the community forests that surround them are protected, if the logging companies in the production forest carry out replanting policies, and if the communities abide by the restrictions on clearing of community forest for houses or farming. If local populations believe that the benefits of deadfall wood, gathering, hunting, and grazing small animals in the community forest will be recognized and protected for them and for their children and grandchildren and if they are hired to do the logging and replanting in the production forests, then the core forests can remain intact.

The issue of how many protected core areas there should be, and how they should be distributed in Java, is more difficult. At the very least, efforts should be made to protect every different type of forest habitat, with some concern for geographical distribution throughout Java. Community forests should be available for as many village communities as possible. Production forests for logging should be in areas where agricultural land is scarce and needed and where cleared forest would be appropriate for farming or in areas that can be replanted relatively easily, where erosion from extraction will be minimal, and where extraction (via roads or rivers) will not cause incursions into nonproduction areas. (Such incursions have been a significant problem in that logging crews have claimed that they could not find, or got lost finding, areas marked for production, and instead logged areas that were more easily accessed, especially by rivers.)

Notice that what a developed nation would consider an immediate crisis issue—fouling of the drinking water for a city of 11 million people with sewage and seawater[8]—is ignored completely. There are several reasons. One is that information about seawater incursion is very new. Another is that there is general agreement that the only way to address sewage contamination is to build a sanitary sewer system, which is entirely beyond the resources of the city or the nation. Jakarta has trouble securing enough water and already is drawing on the resources of other West Java areas; it will not be able to avoid using groundwater and is far from being able to supply water to replace city wells if it were to forbid well use. The agencies represented at this meeting simply do not have the resources to take on other issues. They must be selective.

Another reason that the issue of drinking water may not have been addressed is that the people at this meeting undoubtedly are among those who can afford to buy bottled drinking water. Indonesia now ranks among the top ten nations of the world in bottled water consumption (5,000 million liters in 2000). Growth in the bottled water market in Indonesia between 1999 and 2000 (63 percent) was second only to that in Pakistan (140 percent).[9] The majority poor, however, cannot afford to buy their drinking water.

Ultimately, the question of how much of Java's forests will remain at the end of the twenty-first century—when the Indonesian population is expected to have completely stabilized and, it is hoped, the bulk of the population will have been lifted out of poverty—is not one that any group can answer now. It will be answered again and again, in many series of decisions by the central government, by local governments, by logging companies, and by innumerable villages across Indonesia, one stand of trees at a time. Environmental consciousness must become one part of the policymaking process in twenty-first-century Indonesia—a consciousness of the intrinsic value of every living thing. The decision to regard a forest as having instrumental value rather than intrinsic value—which in Indonesia today means to log it—is irreversible. The forest can be replanted, but if the species of plants and animals that populated it died when their habitat was cut down, the uniqueness of the original forest is lost for all time. This is a tragedy. It is not the only tragedy, of course. Dying and hungry children also are tragic, and like irreplaceable forests, hungry children pass tragic legacies to the future. The human task is to make decisions in the present that grant as much equity across the spectrum of species as possible and help create a future with less tragedy for all species.

Questions for Discussion

1. What were considered the main causes of the 2002 floods in Jakarta?
2. How is the context for public policy decisions regarding the environment different in the United States and in Indonesia? How is the task of environmental groups more difficult in Indonesia?
3. Which of the final arguments, Anchu's or Elys's, more closely resembles environmental stances within the United States? Why might they both represent environmental thinking in Indonesia?
4. Why do the authors urge Indonesian environmentalists to involve religions and religious leaders in environmental issues? What might these bring to the situation?

Notes

1. James Nash, *Loving Nature: Ecological Integrity and Christian Responsibility* (Nashville, Tenn.: Abingdon Press, 1992), 181.

2. John Hart, "Salmon and Social Ethics: Relational Consciousness in the Web of Life," *Journal of the Society of Christian Ethics* 22 (2002): 67–93.
3. Holmes Rolston III, *Conserving Natural Value* (New York: Columbia University Press, 1994), 106.
4. Nash, *Loving Nature*, 175.
5. Population Reference Bureau, 1998 statistics; available at www.prb.org.
6. Other industrialized nations often have infant mortality rates that are almost half that of the United States.
7. Population Reference Bureau, 1998 statistics; available at www.prb.org.
8. Soeryo Winoto, "Conserving Groundwater Easier Said Than Done," *Jakarta Post*, 22 March 2002, B13; "Seawater Intrusion Worsens Drinking Water Quality," *Jakarta Post*, 21 March 2002, A6.
9. Sudibyo Wiradhi, "Growing Sales of Fake Bottled Water Raise Health Concerns," *Jakarta Post*, 22 March 2002, B13.

For Further Reading

Forests for the World Campaign, Environmental Investigation Agency. "The Final Cut: Illegal Logging in Indonesia's Orangutan Parks." Environmental Investigation; available at www.eia-international.org.

Menotti, Victor. *Free Trade, Free Logging: How the World Trade Organization Undermines Global Forest Conservation*. San Francisco: International Forum on Globalization, 1999.

Nurbianto, Bambang, and Theresia Sufa. "Environmental Damage Unabated." *Jakarta Post*, 7 March 2002, A14.

Potter, Lesley, and Simon Bradcock. "Reformasi and Riau's Forests: A Weak Government Struggles with 'People Power,' Poverty and Pulp Companies." *Inside Indonesia* (January–March 2001); available at www.serve.com/inside/edit65/potter.htm (accessed February 10, 2003).

Potter, David. *NGOs and Environmental Policies: Asia and Africa*. London and Portland, Oreg.: F. Cass, 1996.

"Pulp Mills Put Heavy Pressure on Forests: Study." *Jakarta Post*, 9 February 2002, B11.

Sharp, Ilsa. *Green Indonesia: Tropical Forest Encounters*. Kuala Lumpur and New York: Oxford University Press, 1994.

6

Buried Alive: Future Generations and Permanent Underground Disposal of Nuclear Waste

"I can think of better things to do in Las Vegas than waiting in this small conference room," said David, glancing at his watch impatiently.

"Are you saying that our royal tour of Yucca Mountain this morning wasn't worth the trip?" replied Stephannie.

"That's no big deal," continued David. "During my twenty years with the Nuclear Energy Institute I've seen the storage facility many times. Still, with each visit I've become more confident of its function as the deep geological site for permanent disposal of high-level nuclear wastes. That's why I feel this meeting is unnecessary, even absurd. The problem of where to store spent fuel rods from nuclear plants has been solved. Now it's time to get on with the project, not to revisit old debates."

"You're right, the debate is old. People have been arguing the merits of permanent geologic disposal for forty years, but you must agree that this meeting adds a new twist," said Stephannie.

"I'll say," agreed David. "Not only new but completely bizarre. As representatives of the NEI and the Department of Energy, our assignment is to make the case of industry and government to somebody who officially represents future generations. What was the president thinking when he established an office of advocacy for future generations in the Environmental Protection Agency, and what was Congress thinking when it confirmed his nonsense?"

"He's up for reelection next year, of course," said Stephannie, reciting the obvious. "The 2012 elections are a vote of confidence by the public on Yucca Mountain. If he's reelected, we'll continue to inter tens of thousands of tons of spent nuclear fuel at the desert site. If he loses, the next president may well halt the project and throw the whole industry into jeopardy."

"Sure, but why all the attention to the future? I've never understood that," said David.

"It's a riveting attention-getter," continued Stephannie, "and the stakes are sky high. With the effects of global warming accelerating around the world, nuclear energy is a perfect way to generate all the power we need without releasing a whiff of greenhouse gas."

"Yes, added David, "and the industry has responded heroically by putting ten new reactors on line in the past nine years."

"Visibly parading all the highly radiotoxic waste they generate from all points in the country for burial at Yucca Mountain has given people pause, though" said Stephannie. "The media picked up on it big time, particularly when they were told that the waste would be dangerous for at least 10,000 years, and some of it for far longer. In their view, Yucca Mountain is a huge radioactive landfill that we are passing on to our children and grandchildren and their children and grandchildren pretty much forever, as history goes."

"So the advocate for the future somehow speaks for all those potential people?" asked David, whose background in engineering had ill-prepared him for these kinds of intangibles.

"That's exactly right," answered Stephannie. "She's a proxy or public defender for the future."

"That description applies to us," David added. "You and I are as intent on defending future generations as they are. We believe there are many good reasons to pursue the nuclear option and permanent storage here—good for us and good for unborn generations. We're not sweeping radioactive waste under the rug to be dealt with by future occupants."

Two individuals entering the room interrupted their conversation.

"I'm so sorry we're late. I'm Carry Delling, Principal Advocate Secretary from the EPA, and this is Dr. Nawaraj Sharma, who teaches in the departments of philosophy and anthropology at the University of California at Berkeley."

"Hi. I'm Stephannie Hightower from the DOE."

91

"David Earl, Nuclear Energy Institute," said David, extending his hand. "Dr. Sharma, don't I know of you as a distinguished futurist?"

"Well, you may have come across my name in that regard. It's my field of research," said Nawaraj.

"I've never quite understood the concept of future studies. How can you study something that hasn't happened and doesn't exist?" asked David.

"I get that question all the time," responded Nawaraj. "Let's just say I study a history yet to be."

"Okay," nodded David. "It seems like so much science fiction."

"I'll accept that," agreed Nawaraj, "but with the emphasis on science rather than fiction."

"I'd emphasize the fiction," mumbled David to himself.

"Why don't we start our fact-finding session?" said Carry. "I understand we're scheduled to tour the Yucca Mountain site later today, so our time together is somewhat limited. Let's begin with what some people would call the science fiction of secure permanent geologic storage of radwaste."

"Yes," agreed Nawaraj, "futurists are as interested in what we can't know about the future as what we can know. That's why, as a philosopher, I'm very interested in understanding the logic behind your overwhelming confidence in the very long-term safety of Yucca Mountain."

The question was tailor-made for David. "The potential performance assessment included in the site-suitability report issued by the evaluation committee back in 1992 gives very positive long-term geologic estimations for hydrology, volcanism, seismic activities, and other possible vulnerabilities with respect to radionuclide release and leachate transport. . . ."

"Please, Mr. Earl," interrupted Carry. "I'm very much a layperson with respect to these technical terms. My training is in theology, not geology—African American Womanist theology, to be exact. I deal in social oppression, not seismic compression. And though I make every effort to comprehend your technical jargon, my role here is to assure intergenerational equity."

"But intergenerational equity has a great deal to do with site integrity, doesn't it?" asked Stephannie.

"It certainly does," said Nawaraj, reentering the discussion, "and the integrity of Yucca Mountain as a geologic repository is exactly the question. We are working in a time frame not of decades or centuries, in which we have some confidence in our predictive powers, but in millennia and tens of millennia—many thousands of years. We have no experience with this extraordinary time horizon, which is longer than all of recorded history. Even the pyramids of Egypt were constructed only about 4,000 years ago. You are burdened with assuring the integrity of Yucca Mountain for at least 6,000 years longer than that!"

"You're being overly dramatic, Dr. Sharma," said David, a bit offended. "There has been no volcanic activity in the vicinity of Yucca Mountain for the past 10,000 years. No indication of earthquakes has been discovered either. We're in the middle of an ancient arid desert with sparse rainfall. And even in the unlikely case of increased precipitation, hydrological studies show no indication that water corrosion of the storage canisters and migration of that water into the very deep aquifer are reasonable concerns. Besides, opponents frequently overstate the size of the waste to be stored. Certainly its weight is considerable, in terms of thousands of tons, but the volume is quite small because nuclear waste is twenty times as dense as water. We estimate that the entire volume will fit into a cube about fifty feet on each side. This volume is much easier to protect than one would expect. I have ample documentation of my claims in these research reports." David reached into his large briefcase and removed two imposing bound volumes.

"Thanks, Mr. Earl, but I'm quite familiar with the massive technical research done on the suitability of Yucca Mountain over the past twenty-five years. Our office has a technical staff that assists us in its familiarity," said Nawaraj. "Again, my interest is in the underlying logic of these data and your stated conclusions."

"Umm, can you give us an example, Dr. Sharma?" asked Stephannie.

"Yes; your risk estimations for geological activity are based on a predictive model. But geology as a science is explanatory, not predictive. It is very accurate in describing how a particular geologic feature—a canyon or a range of mountains—came to be, but it cannot predict precisely where the next canyon or range of mountains will occur. Efforts to develop a predictive geology for volcanic eruptions or earthquakes are notorious for their range of error. If we can't predict when an existing volcano will erupt, how can we predict the appearance of volcanoes yet to be? And your estimates of the likelihood of surface water infiltrating the rock, invading the canisters of radwaste, and leaching into groundwater are based on no experience of the Yucca Mountain site, and certainly on no experience of the behavior of the geology and hydrology of such sites over extremely long historical periods. You are merely extrapolating from the present into the far distant future, and that introduces subjectivity into your conclusions and a range of uncertainty that is highly questionable. Any futurist will tell you that such assumptions of uniformitarianism are folly."

"Futurists such as yourself have their field of expertise, Dr. Sharma, and I would never presume to share that experience and knowledge," David responded politely but with mounting indignation. "In like manner, perhaps you should be reluctant to issue hasty and ill-spoken judgments of the considered conclusions of hundreds of experts in all relevant fields over several decades of scientific inquiry into the suitability of Yucca Mountain."

"In other words, all of this science gives us the range of actual risks, Dr. Sharma," Stephannie interjected, "while the layperson can have only perceived risks. I think you know which of these is more accurate and hence preferable.

"Look," continued Stephannie, "we all can agree on one fact. Over time, the radioactivity of the stored material will diminish. In just 1,000 years most of it will carry no more risk for humans than that of uranium ore, which occurs naturally. If that normal exposure is acceptable now, why would it not be acceptable in 1,000 years?"

"Let's see," said Nawaraj, taking a pose of feigned reflection, "how many cancers in the United States each year are caused by naturally occurring background radiation, Ms. Hightower?"

"I'm not sure," answered Stephannie; "several hundred?"

"I believe the numbers are in the thousands. Are they acceptable?" Nawaraj continued.

"Of course not," said Stephannie, "but there's nothing we can do about it, so we must accept them."

"I think your logic is questionable, Ms. Hightower," Nawaraj responded. "To accept a risk or harm does not mean to sanction or approve of it. What is normal, like background radiation, is not necessarily neutral in terms of value. I run a 'normal' risk of contracting lung cancer from secondary cigarette smoke. Should I accept that risk simply because it is normal? You also seem to assume that background radiation from geologic sources is normal because it occurs naturally. Since when do we appeal to nature for our value judgments?"

David took the opportunity of Stephannie's silence that followed this question to seize the offensive. "Whatever you may think about our interpretation of the science, one thing is certain: We have identified no credible mechanisms that would lead to unacceptable radionuclide releases over the time frame in question. Thus—and here I quote from memory reports from the DOE—'the evidence does not support a finding that the site is not likely to meet the qualifying condition. . . .' This is all anyone can ask for, given the incredible complexity of the task, and for most of us it is good enough."

"It might be good enough if the stakes weren't so high," said Nawaraj, "but when I hear a statement like that, which derives a positive conclusion from two negatives, I can think of only one thing: an appeal to ignorance. I'd feel much more secure if your quote had read, 'the evidence supports a finding that the site is likely to meet the qualifying condition.' Instead, you turn lack of good data and great uncertainty in predictability into a virtue."

"Do you intend your condemnation to apply to the scientific enterprise in general, Dr. Sharma?" David asked. "Because that's exactly what you're proposing. For all of its considerable power, science is powerless to prove anything. All it can do is incrementally increase the confidence we have in a theory by testing it over and over and seeking evidence supporting its contrary—that is, to disprove it. Our confidence in a theory grows with our failure to dethrone it, but there's always the chance that tomorrow something will be discovered that will disqualify it. Yucca Mountain is the most thoroughly researched geological plot of ground in history. I stand by our scientific appraisal. We have found nothing to question our confidence in the theoretical proposition that Yucca Mountain is a safe site for the disposal of radwaste for the indefinite future. The theory is robust. Science has given us great confidence in the integrity of permanent geologic disposal. That's why we unconditionally endorse the word 'permanent.'"

"Speaking of unpredictability, have you considered the predictability of human intrusion into the entombed waste?" asked Carry.

"Certainly, Ms. Delling," said Stephannie. "The fundamental premise of permanent geological disposal is to maximize the isolation of the radwaste to assure that intrusion, by accident or intention, will never occur. This is our responsibility to future generations."

"We'll talk further about our duties to future generations in a moment, but now I'm concerned with the potential for human compromise of the storage site," said Carry. "Once Yucca Mountain is sealed, do we have the technology for mining and drilling so that we could reenter if we wished?"

"Yes," answered Stephannie.

"Why wouldn't they possess at least the same capabilities?" continued Carry.

"If they do, then one assumes their entry would be for good reason," said Stephannie.

"I can think of several scenarios in which a future society might possess sufficient technology to breach site containment, yet endanger themselves by doing so," objected Carry. "They could be seeking mineral resources, ignorant of the presence of dangerous radiological materials. There are such resources documented within striking distance of Yucca Mountain. Or they could be directed by a totalitarian despot, the future equal of a Stalin or Hitler, intent on using the radioactive materials for weapons."

"Please excuse me, Ms. Delling, but aren't your scenarios highly imaginative and unlikely?" asked Stephannie, in clear disagreement. "The last 300 years have been a record of social, scientific, technological, and even moral progress. It is more plausible, is it not, to construct our scenarios of future societies as more advanced than we are and thus better able to handle the radwaste if they choose to."

"Of course my visions are speculative and unlikely," Carry responded, "but no less likely are your more optimistic images of future societies inhabiting Nevada. Who could have predicted a half-century ago that the fastest growing metropolitan area in the United States would be Las Vegas, here in the middle of the desert? In truth, human institutions are not very predictable even for historical periods of moderate length. I think we must agree: Our ignorance of the form of future societies that might be affected by the risks posed by deep geologic disposal of thousands of tons of the most durable and toxic materials ever produced is close to complete."

"Yet the president has given you the power of a cabinet officer to represent these unknowable, faceless persons," said David, shaking his head incredulously.

"Yes," said Carry, "but they are by no means all faceless. Future persons are being born every moment as the children of *our* generation. As a liberation theologian who addresses the condition of oppressed and victimized peoples—including my ancestors who were brought to slavery in this enlightened and progressive society in which you have such confidence, Ms. Hightower—I can tell you, these anonymous figures do count morally."

"Actually, I agree with you," Stephannie acknowledged, sensing that the argument had just turned in her favor. "Our complete lack of ability to foresee the distant future is a fundamental justification for permanent geologic disposal. We will make every effort to render the radwaste irretrievable, even to the point of erecting a pyramid atop the mountain as a warning to anyone not to dig there."

"I can't see how that would help," countered Nawaraj. "It's likely that the meaning of any monumental structure eventually would be lost—in which case it might well prove to be an attractor, suggesting that something valuable lies underneath. Tombs and pyramids of ancient Egypt were looted frequently and over long periods of time. You can't assume symbolic continuity over thousands of years."

"I admit the task is difficult," Stephannie said, "but the fact remains: If we have any duty to future generations, it is to protect them from themselves with respect to our radioactive waste. Yucca Mountain is the best strategy to fulfill that duty."

"Your attitude is very paternalistic, Ms. Hightower," Carry responded.

"I'll agree to that, but only if you define 'paternalistic' to mean responsible caution and prudent action for the protection of others," Stephannie responded.

"I'm unconvinced that we have any moral duties whatsoever to future persons, or at least to those beyond the next two or three generations," David added. "They are so contingent. I mean, we can't possibly know who they will be, what their needs will be, what their values will be. How can we then take any specific action and have confidence that its consequences will benefit them?"

"Most of your concerns are specious, Mr. Earl," Carry replied. "If I'm designing a passenger airplane, I know none of these facts about the thousands of passengers who will fly in the aircraft over several decades. Nonetheless I have profound duties to design the safest plane possible. And I disagree that we can't know the needs of distant future persons. They will be the same as those of generations in the distant past, as well as our own. All persons require elemental living conditions in their physical and social environments that will enable them to flourish. In my estimate, we certainly do have duties to potential persons, and generally we can know what they need."

"We can't forget duties to the current generation," replied Stephannie. "We are in the midst of an increasing crisis—global warming. Nuclear energy is the most rational response to the urgent need to reduce the production of greenhouse gases, particularly carbon dioxide. We would be discriminating against the current generation not to take full advantage of the technology. Besides, it's obvious that the efforts we make to stem those emissions will greatly benefit future generations. It seems only fair, then, that disposal of the radioactive waste generated by this effort should be shared by all generations. It's a win-win situation, and the responsibility is distributed equitably. Wouldn't you agree?"

"I do not," Nawaraj replied forcefully. "Although it is true that the benefits will be distributed somewhat equally with respect to global warming, the *risks* will not. Future generations will be subjected to the risks of Yucca Mountain to a far greater extent than we will. Such 'temporal' inequity resembles what we might call the 'geographical' inequity suffered by the citizens of Nevada—80 percent of whom oppose Yucca Mountain. Why should they bear the burden of potential harm from long-term storage of nuclear waste just ninety miles from their largest city while everybody else in the country enjoys only the benefits?"

"The answer to that question," replied Stephannie, "was well stated by a columnist for a Washington newspaper when she wrote that 'ninety-eight senators didn't want the waste stored in their states, but only two senators didn't want it stored in Nevada.'"

"Does that make my point or yours?" asked Nawaraj.

"Actually, mine," answered Stephannie. "In a representative democracy we have ways of distributing the harms of a decision affecting everyone as fairly as possible. But this distribution is never perfect. There are costs to the option of nuclear power, but the benefits to be shared by everyone, including Nevadans, far outweigh those costs—and that's what makes the decision morally proper."

"I do recall," said Carry, "that nineteenth-century slaveholders rationalized the institution on those very same grounds. And it's just that kind of injustice that inspired the creation of my office."

"Ms. Delling," interrupted David impatiently, "I have no training in either theology or philosophy, but even my engineering mind can see that your demands for moral perfection are the enemy of the good. Permanent geologic disposal assures that the great majority of this generation will enjoy the benefits of nuclear energy, and concern for the good of the majority is always the ethical ideal."

"If that's true, you've just placed yourself in a difficult position, Mr. Earl," said Carry. "That great majority is actually all those who have not yet been born. Members of future generations upon whom the harms of the risks of this radioactive refuse will fall will vastly outnumber us. We are the minority dictating to them, the majority, how the benefits and costs of nuclear energy are to be distributed. The minority enjoys the greatest benefits, while the majority bears the greatest risks. I don't think your moral calculations allow for that."

"All right, Ms. Delling," said Stephannie, "let me introduce another possibility that may meet your objections. You are familiar, I'm sure, with the nuclear industry's offer to create a legacy trust for future generations. We will levy a tax on the electricity we generate and use the funds as compensation to future generations for any burden unjustly imposed upon them by Yucca Mountain. Would that arrangement be acceptable to your office?"

"Yes, I am familiar with that proposal," Carry replied, "and I'm of two minds about it. On one hand, it would lessen their financial burden with respect to the problems caused by storage. On the other hand, in a moral sense nothing can compensate for injustice, especially for those consequences that result in terrible suffering and loss of life."

"Do you favor reparations for the wrongs suffered by African Americans during the centuries of slavery?" Stephannie inquired.

"Yes, I do," answered Carry. "Entire generations of African Americans continue to suffer from the social, political, economic, and emotional effects of that institution, even though they were not born into slavery themselves. Being a member of that community has enabled me to feel great solidarity with future generations in this case."

"Well, isn't our offer of compensation with the legacy trust the equivalent of reparations for the unborn whom you believe will be egregiously affected by our actions at Yucca Mountain?" continued Stephannie. "Isn't it reparations paid up front?"

"Perhaps," replied Carry, "but the situation is different. Reparations are one of the few strategies that my community has to rectify the wrongs of the past. You, however, are using the fund as a tool to justify actions that may well be harmful in the future. It's a payoff to future persons in the place of giving them the power to make decisions regarding these risks for themselves."

"This is exceedingly frustrating," Stephannie exclaimed. "You tell us what you would do with the waste that would resolve all of these issues."

"I can respond to that," said Nawaraj. "To maximize the autonomy and decision processes of future generations, we would advocate a plan that would store the high-level waste in monitored retrievable storage sites located throughout the country for the indefinite future."

"Isn't that just denying the problem?" asked David.

"Not at all," continued Nawaraj. "It would allow for the development of new technologies to deal with the material in better ways than primitive burial. Most important, it would preserve the options of future generations to address the risks in their own ways. In other words, retrievable storage, perhaps in conjunction with your legacy trust, empowers future persons. Justice demands as much."

Stephannie thought for a moment before responding. "Your position shares some of the difficulties of our own," she said. "The retrievable storage cannisters could be buried by the same violent geological activity that you speculate may someday affect the integrity of Yucca Mountain, and they could be forgotten. Succeeding generations would then be no better off, and perhaps even worse off than if the cannisters were buried here in a sealed chamber. Another problem is even more interesting," she continued. "If some future generation actually exercised its power to decide on the method of disposal, then it would be put in the same position as we are in—depriving all future generations of their power of choice. Your problem is that you speak vaguely of preserving the power of decision for all future generations as if they were contemporaries, when the power actually can be used only by one generation at a time, with serious consequences for all the others that follow. How ironic!"

"Stephannie is right," said David, "and may I add that the risks of terrorism and accidents make the plan unworkable."

"Perhaps," Nawaraj admitted, "but, while the risks are there, they are no greater than the risks of radionuclide release from Yucca Mountain, and the great advantage is that our generation meets its overriding obligation of justice."

"But the risks of terrorism and accidents in exposed and vulnerable surface storage are, in our scientifically considered estimate, much greater than those of permanent underground disposal," Stephannie insisted. "The moral perfectionism David alluded to earlier creeps back into your argument again. You ignore obvious and substantial harmful consequences for the sake of satisfying an abstract and apparently unconditional obligation to justice. Your position makes you, in my view, a good person in the worst sense of the term.

"Concern for justice is one thing we have in common, Dr. Sharma, even though we disagree profoundly on how to bring it about," Stephannie said.

At that moment they were interrupted by Carry's associate, who told them that the car taking them to Yucca Mountain had arrived. The meeting was concluded cordially, with the promise to meet again the next day.

As they walked out together, Nawaraj turned to Carry.

"It's interesting how our very different religious commitments— yours to Christianity and mine to Hinduism—converge on this issue," he said.

"How do you mean?" Carry asked.

"Well, you work from a perspective derived from the community experience of oppression of your people and of African American women. So your basic moral principle concerns justice for the downtrodden and marginalized, whether they live now or in the future. Am I correct?"

"Yes," answered Carry, "and what is your perspective?"

"It's rather mixed," said Nawaraj. He hesitated for a moment, gathering his thoughts. "As a secular philosopher, I take seriously the ideas of inherent human worth and dignity and our duty to be harmless. As a Hindu, however, I take my clues from the idea of reincarnation and karma."

"You mean that your actions in this life will determine the conditions of your next life?" asked Carry.

"Yes, and intergenerational justice is achieved this way, by the operation of the law of karma," Nawaraj replied. "But with respect to issues concerning future generations, there's an added twist—a very practical one."

"Yes?" Carry asked with growing curiosity.

"You see, each of us will actually be present in each of those future generations for thousands of years. Hence, we will be the recipients of decisions made today that will affect their well-being, since we will be numbered among them," Nawaraj explained.

"So this means that if in 5,000 years nuclear waste stored at Yucca Mountain leaches into the groundwater, you and I, as our future selves, could be at risk from drinking that water," added Carry.

"Exactly," Nawaraj replied. "We are potential victims of our own actions. We harvest the harmful consequences of the seeds we sow— or, in this case, the high-level radioactive waste we bury."

"Is this your idea, Nawaraj?"

"I've seen it in several scholarly publications. I must add that because it encourages a rather selfish motivation for doing good, it does not represent the highest intentions of Hindu ethics."

"Yes," agreed Carry, "but perhaps we should share your thoughts with Ms. Hightower and Mr. Earl. It might encourage them to focus their minds admirably in our direction."

"I don't think so," Nawaraj said. "They are strongly committed to the science of deep geologic disposal. I have no doubt that they would be willing to subject themselves in their future lives to the consequences of their decisions in this life confidently and with no second thoughts."

"Well, perhaps we have provided them with those second thoughts," said Carry.

With that remark they entered the car for the trip to Yucca Mountain and a tour of its deep and cavernous tunnels.

Commentary

When the first nuclear plant came on line in 1955, commercial generation of electrical power by nuclear fission was a dream in progress. That dream included the potential of abundant and inexpensive electricity that would be, as one optimist put it, "too cheap to meter." In one sense the vision has been realized. According to the Nuclear Energy Institute (NEI)—an advocacy organization for commercial nuclear power for whom the dream continues— the 103 commercial nuclear power plants currently operating in the United States provide more than 20 percent of the nation's electrical needs. Two-thirds of Vermont's electricity, for example, is provided by nuclear power.[1] The average electricity production costs for nuclear generation are less than those for coal, oil, and gas-fired plants; nuclear power is indeed cheap.

Of increasing importance is the fact that nuclear energy generation releases no emissions products such as sulfur, particulates, or carbon dioxide (a major greenhouse gas) into the atmosphere. Widespread public concerns about the safety of nuclear plants were reinforced by the crisis at Three Mile Island in 1979 and the meltdown at Chernobyl in 1986, as well as the monumental costs of decommissioning aging plants. Nevertheless, mounting environmental concerns and increasing political and security interests in national energy independence revive the industry's hopes for an expansion of nuclear power.

At this point the dream enters its potentially nightmarish phase. The NEI claims that "the nuclear energy industry is the only industry established since the Industrial Revolution that has managed and accounted for all its waste, preventing adverse impacts on the environment."[2] Accounted for—perhaps. Managed? For many people this claim is highly questionable and is the major issue addressed by this case.

In brief, nuclear plants use uranium oxide fuel to generate electricity. Bundles of metal fuel rods containing the uranium in small ceramic pellets undergo the atom-splitting process of nuclear fission. The impressive energy released in reactors boils water, and the resulting steam drives turbine generators, producing electricity. Every year or two, depleted fuel rod assemblies are replaced. The major problem is that they have become highly radioactive and must be stored safely and securely. Typically a nuclear power plant produces twenty tons of spent fuel each year. The combined total of such high-level radioactive waste (HLRW, or "radwaste") produced by the industry over four decades is more than 40,000 metric tons. Where is it all stored? Currently each plant is responsible for managing its own HLRW. Most store it in nearby steel vaults or concrete containers. This nuclear "outhouse" arrangement cannot continue, however—primarily because of space limitations and increasing concerns for security and safety.

The Nuclear Waste Policy Act of 1982 (NWPA) was a response to this emerging crisis for the entire nuclear industry. The NWPA mandates the construction of a deep geologic repository for nuclear waste. The Act thereby eliminates consideration of any other option for long-term storage. An amendment in 1987 went even further by authorizing a detailed scientific study of a single potential site: Yucca Mountain, about 100 miles north of Las Vegas, Nevada. After three decades and $7 billion dollars, the Department of Energy (DOE) in George W. Bush's administration approved the site and ordered construction of storage facilities to begin, with the goal of making Yucca Mountain operational by 2010. In a last-gasp effort to block the project, Nevada filed an objection, forcing Congress to decide the question. The Senate overwhelmingly approved the plan. This result is not surprising because most senators have nuclear plants in their states, and their constituencies express no desire to either continue piling spent fuel rods locally or to allow their states to become dumping grounds for the nation's radwaste. The environmental acronym for this reaction is NIMBY—Not In My Back Yard.

The ethical issues in this case are localized geographically—Yucca Mountain, Nevada—but not local temporally. Spent uranium fuel is dangerously radioactive for tens of thousands of years. Other by-products of the fission process are potent for far longer—hundreds of thousands and even millions of years. The responsibilities of our generation to provide for safe and secure disposal of these dangerous materials for vast periods is a unique ethical and philosophical issue for a variety of reasons.

The initial issue often is the moral considerations of future persons. Some philosophers have serious reservations about the duties of the current generation to persons who do not yet exist and whose specific characteristics, cultural beliefs and values, and preferences cannot be known.[3] Moreover, even if we acknowledge some duties to these persons, how are we to carry them out? Anything we might do now, even with the best intentions of preventing harm to future generations, undoubtedly will change the very identity of individuals who otherwise would be born if we did nothing. This odd problem is an interesting philosophical conundrum. Nonetheless, barring some cosmic catastrophe that wipes out our species entirely, somebody—known or unknown—is likely to be around in 1,000, 5,000, or 10,000 years to be imperiled by the radioactive waste deposited by our generation as a result of benefits we enjoyed from the cheap electricity it provided. Although we cannot be certain that these same benefits will be available to persons inhabiting the future, we can be certain that the risks associated with them will be. To continue our metaphor, our dream could become their nightmare. Our geographic NIMBY could become their NIMG—Not In My Generation. This would be a cry of frustration, not resolution, because Yucca Mountain would already be a reality in their midst.

Despite this philosophical question, both sides of the issue—proponents and opponents of deep geologic disposal—generally agree that we do indeed have duties to future generations to deal with our own waste. The problem is how best to deal with it. Initially one might conclude that this issue is a question of science and technology rather than ethics, but that is not the case. The technical strategy selected to resolve the problem carries subtle philosophical and ethical presuppositions.

One of these premises is the attitude of paternalism that comes with the territory of Yucca Mountain. Stephannie and David assume that our generation is best suited to make the final decision concerning the disposal of radwaste. Although this attitude is expressed in the guise that "this is our problem, so we must solve it," the effect is to remove the autonomy and independence of future persons by preempting the decision about how best to dispose of the material through the irreversibility of permanent and irretrievable storage. Their competence is called into question without justification.

When pressed, however, our advocates seem to contradict themselves. In response to Carry's question about possible human intrusion into the storage site, Stephannie suggests that future generations may be far more advanced both technologically and morally than the present generation and hence fully capable of dealing with such intrusions. Her faith in the apparent inevitability of progress is inadequately based in reason; it is based on a highly selective and convenient reading of history, as Carry notes in her reference to the institution of slavery in morally "advanced" Western civilization. Thus, one advantage in arguing from our ignorance of the essentially unpredictable future is that one can speculate both ways with equal reliability.

The presence of subjectivity and ignorance in technical and scientific judgments cuts another way as well. For reasons we discuss below, the scientific analysis or "site characterization" of Yucca Mountain is based in utilitarian moral theory. That is, decisions are to follow a cost-benefit analysis of the consequences of the act under consideration. In the incredibly complex situation of long-term storage of nuclear waste, costs are expressed in terms of risks or probabilities of harmful or beneficial consequences occurring as a result of the massive project.

A major geological problem is leakage. Someday, some unknown amount of radioactive material might be released through corrosion of the storage canisters (whose integrity cannot be assured for more than 300 years, given present technology), resulting in pollution of underground water sources for the region. Future persons, conceivably ignorant of the danger, might drink this water and become sick. What are the chances of leachate migration into the groundwater? No one knows for sure, but scientific inquiry allows for probabilities to be assigned. Such risk analyses are prone to expression as value judgments in the face of considerable uncertainty. Do geologists really have knowledge about volcanoes, earthquakes, climate change, and hydrology in the region of Yucca Mountain that can be extrapolated confidently over thousands of years? Do experts know enough about these things to offer optimistic assessment of risks?

The troubling answer, apparently, is that only the experts know for sure— at least, they believe they know for sure. Although the findings of science are never accepted on the appeal of authority, there is a disquieting "expertise inference" at work in the attitude and claims of the proponents. It is true that only trained scientists can assign numerical values to the risks of long-term disposal, but it is not true that they alone are qualified to assess the acceptability of those risks for other affected groups. Yet Stephannie gives greater value to expert assessment of "actual risk" than to a layperson's assessment of "perceived risk," suggesting that only experts are objective. What is safe enough, and what is too risky? Experts do not enjoy privileged access to wisdom in answering questions concerning the acceptability of risks, and equity dictates that the judgments of all affected parties count equally. For example, the logic of Stephannie's assumption that "normal" risks are acceptable as a working principle for risk assessment fails when examined by Nawaraj.

Another questionable approach used by advocates of Yucca Mountain relies on negative premises grounded in ignorance to reach an affirmative conclusion. After twenty-five years and $7 billion, scientific examination of the site has revealed no reason it would be unsafe; therefore, it is safe. Having no evidence to the contrary, we conclude that the contrary is false. This approach, oddly enough, is the scientific method. A scientific hypothesis that is not falsified by repeated experiments or observations is accepted provisionally as robust and true. Note that the hypothesis is not "proven." Its success in fending off refutation simply builds confidence in its likely truth. This approach explains the odd aphorism that science progresses only when it rejects theories as quickly as possible. The hypothesis that Yucca Mountain is safe is subjected to inquiries designed to discover facts (e.g., volcanic or seismic activity in the area) that would defeat it. If none are found, confidence grows in the reliability of the hypothesis. Stephannie and David have great confidence in the thoroughness and integrity of the long scientific investigation of the site. Consequently, they are willing to accept conclusions that emphasize what the scientists and engineers did not find. Nawaraj, however, would feel more comfortable if the conclusion of the site's integrity were couched in positive findings. He may be asking for too much. Given the incredible complexity of the mountain's geology, the extremely long time period for which claims of safety and security must be made, the size of the affected population—hundreds of generations and millions of individuals—and the irreversibility of the decision, however, it seems that extreme caution would be of supreme importance. Stephannie and David believe that such caution has been exercised.

A further issue concerns the intermeshing of science with the utilitarian approach to ethical judgments. Although science is celebrated for its apparent "value neutrality" and objectivity, scientific methodology is tied so closely to utilitarian ethical theory that in cases such as Yucca Mountain, other ethical approaches are neglected.[4] Utilitarian calculations of the moral desirability of an act depend on the power to predict and assess consequences that would occur (or probably would occur) if an action were taken. In the absence of predictive power, the approach is blind. Science provides such power. Thus, when science is the only method used to gather knowledge about a morally relevant situation, the deliberations that follow, based on this predictive knowledge, are almost always utilitarian. The risks of radiotoxic substances buried at Yucca Mountain for millennia and the harms they might pose for future persons are conclusions drawn from an evaluation of the facts of geology, hydrology, climate studies, and so forth. The risks and the benefits are compared, and a decision is made on the basis of the social utility; that is, the good provided by the action for all affected persons may be assessed.

In this case, the increasing prominence of global warming weighs heavily on moral deliberations about the disposition of radioactive waste. David and Stephannie argue strongly that development of the nuclear power industry is mandatory if we are to slow the progress of global warming and mitigate its disastrous consequences. The harms potentially brought about by permanent geologic storage pale in comparison to those of increasing global temperatures. If we take no action to develop climate-friendly sources of electrical energy, the adverse consequences borne by future persons will only increase. Therefore it is our overriding responsibility to construct as many reactors as we can. That future generations will be the primary beneficiaries of these actions is a major justification for taking them.

Even if moderation of the adverse effects of global warming proves to be a substantial benefit for future generations, the transfer of risks to them still constitutes a moral problem. The moral situation defined by an unwavering commitment to permanent geologic disposal of radioactive wastes allows for a limited number of options carried out in a state of great uncertainty about the geologic future of the site and the unpredictable character of human societies hundreds of generations in the future. Stephannie and David believe they are taking every possible precaution to assure the well-being of these people. Thus, they feel justified in asking Carry and Nawaraj if they have a better plan. They do.

The preferred alternative is "negotiated, monitored, retrievable storage" (NMRS).[5] The scientific and technical advantages of NMRS are the same as its moral advantages. Storing the waste—probably in hardened canisters—in designated sites around the country where they would be maintained with heightened vigilance would provide future generations with the option of deciding for themselves the most suitable method of disposal. Although future generations would still inherit the risks of the waste, they also would inherit the power to do what they choose with it. NMRS therefore would satisfy our duty to maximize the autonomy of future persons in dealing with our legacy to them. Granting them active control rather than passive acceptance of our irrevocable decision for disposal of nuclear wastes satisfies the demand of procedural justice that everyone should be treated fairly and given their say in debating actions that may affect them adversely.

In their final conversation, Carry and Nawaraj make explicit the religious bases for their ethical positions. Carry is an African American Protestant and Nawaraj a Hindu. Carry's principle of ethical interpretation is based on the demands of justice for the poor and powerless, victims of powerful oppressors. Nawaraj's principle is found in the role of karma in determining the appropriate future consequences for one's actions. Because harms that come to individuals in a future incarnation are overwhelmingly the just results of actions taken in this life, there are no innocent victims. Despite these widely divergent religious foundations for their ethical deliberations, Carry and Nawaraj agree that future persons are not best served by deep geologic disposal of radioactive waste.

Questions for Discussion

1. Some philosophers have argued that because future generations do not yet exist, we have no moral duties toward them. Do you agree that we do not need to factor them into the long-lasting consequences of our actions? How can you argue that humans who do not yet exist count morally?

2. Many authorities conclude that alternative energy sources—including wind, geothermal, and solar—will satisfy, at best, only a small portion of our energy needs. Without adequate energy, future generations will suffer. Which is worse from a utilitarian perspective: Bequeathing to them our nuclear waste or denying them the advantages and comforts of abundant nuclear energy by hindering its development?

3. A major concern in this case is the acceptable level of risk of long-term nuclear waste deposit. Risk assessment can be made only by trained scientists. To what extent are you willing to place your trust in their judgment? To what experts, seen or unseen, do you entrust your safety and well-being on a daily basis? How can experts be held accountable by those who are most affected by their judgments?

4. This case does not address safety concerns associated with the transport of high-level nuclear waste to the Yucca Mountain storage site. Yet it is clear that the citizens of Nevada are in a situation of greater risk than the remainder of the country. How can this increased risk be justified morally—or can it?

Notes

1. Nuclear Energy Institute website, www.nei.org.
2. Ibid.
3. See Robert Heilbroner, "What Has Posterity Ever Done for Me?" *New York Magazine*, 19 January 1975, 74–76.

4. Constantine Hadjilambrinos, "Ethical Imperatives and High-Level Radioactive Waste Policy Choice: An Egalitarian Response to Utilitarian Analysis," *Environmental Ethics* 22 (January 2000): 48.

5. Ibid., 60.

For Further Reading

De-Shalit, Avner. *Why Posterity Matters: Environmental Policies and Future Generations.* New York: Routledge, 1995.

Goldberg, Jonah. "Dead and Buried." *National Review* 54 (April 8, 2002): 36–38.

Hadjilambrinos, Constantine. "Ethical Imperatives and High-Level Radioactive Waste Policy Choice: An Egalitarian Response to Utilitarian Analysis." *Environmental Ethics* 22 (January 2000): 43–62.

Nuclear Energy Institute website, www.nei.org.

Partridge, Ernest, ed. *Responsibilities to Future Generations.* New York: Prometheus Books, 1981.

Routley Richard, and Val Routley. "Nuclear Power: Some Ethical and Social Dimensions." In *And Justice for All*, ed. Tom Regan and Donald VanDeVeer. Totowa, N.J.: Rowman and Littlefield, 1982, 98–110.

Shrader-Frechette, K. S. *Nuclear Power and Public Policy.* Boston: Reidel, 1989.

————. *Burying Uncertainty.* Berkeley: University of California Press, 1993.

White, G. F. "Socioeconomic Studies of High-Level Nuclear Waste Disposal." *Proceedings of the National Academy of Sciences* 91 (November 1994): 10786–89.

II

RESTORING AND RECREATING THE ECOSYSTEM

7

Ecological Quick Fixes? Restoring Degraded Coral Reefs

"The reefs we saw at Labac and Subaki are coming back very quickly," announced Wayan, the *kelian banjar*, or village chief, of Binging, a seaside village in western Bali. "The villagers there told us stories of how destroyed the reef was, but we saw new coral and small fish. The rate of coral growth in the new 'fencing' is at least as fast as coral growth in the healthy natural reefs, and the coral has already attracted different schools of small fish that had disappeared. This is the best model for addressing coral reef destruction of Indonesia's shores; it is what we want here on our reef in Bali."

"The new fencing is a valuable tool, Wayan, but not a total answer," protested Ismail Mutalah. "Look at all the other things that also were necessary to save those reefs. The local governments policed and monitored the reef to prevent dynamite and cyanide fishing and the use of traps for ornamental fish. They prevented pesticide runoff from the fields from flowing directly into the bay. And they continue to do these things. If we only put down the fencing, and the reef regrows and the fish return, so will the dynamite and cyanide fishers, and the nets of those catching ornamental fish will wreck the new coral, and coral sellers will return and steal the new coral just as they did the old. If measures are not taken to prevent these things from happening again, the new technology cannot save the reefs."

In question was a new system of anchored fencing treated with an ionized chemical coating deployed within three reef areas among the many destroyed coral reefs off Indonesia's 13,600 islands. The fencing attracted new coral growth—even seemed to feed it for a time. International environmental groups, mostly from the United States, had developed the fencing. It was not exorbitantly expensive, though it was far beyond the ability of local villages, or even provincial governments, to afford. Wayan's village had approached the local environmental agency that Ismail headed after hearing that they had successfully installed the fencing in several other degraded reefs. A committee from the village, having seen the regeneration in two of the three reefs, was enthusiastic about joining the project and seeing their reef regenerated as well.

Over the previous fifteen years—especially since the Asian financial crisis of 1997 and the fall of the New Order government—overfishing, the use of dynamite and cyanide to kill fish, harvesting of coral to sell abroad and to tourists, and an explosion in overseas sales of ornamental fish (reef fish as well as freshwater fish) had devastated the Binging coral reef. Fishermen had to go further and further out to sea to find fish, and the few who were still trying to eke out a living by fishing were now fishing far out at sea—beyond the safety limits for their small, old boats. The coral reef had once been not only the primary source of protein for the village but also a tourist draw for scuba divers and snorkelers. Now it was bereft of fish; all that was left were clumps of broken, dead, and dying coral, often covered with silt and debris unsettled by the explosions of the dynamite fishers.

Ismail tried unsuccessfully to convince the chief that the new fencing alone was not the answer, but the chief would only insist that his was a "good" village, and he would ask the dynamite and cyanide fishers and the trappers to stop. Then he added that this wasn't really necessary because there were no fish to be gotten on the reef, so all the fishermen were gone elsewhere. Finally, in frustration, Ismail and his associate, Elma Sato, left the village to return to their office in Denpasar, Bali.

"He does understand, you know," Elma offered. "He hears you. He just doesn't want to have to deal with the conflict. Remember your country, Ismail! Even you fierce Acehnese must share some character traits with the rest of us Indonesians!"

Ismail smiled.

"Indonesians are Asians, you know," Elma continued. "They aren't like Westerners. They prefer indirectness and abhor confrontations. The way Balinese village chiefs work is that they talk with people and express a preference, and generally people will comply with that—just because everybody will know if you don't, and you will be considered disrespectful, not only of the chief but of the village as a whole. But these are not ordinary questions; you are talking about people's lives, their incomes, their food supplies. You want Wayan to confront the dynamite and cyanide fishers, tell them to quit, and threaten dire punishments if they are caught. For all we know, though, he or members of his family, may be among them! You want him to monitor the reef, even pressure the police to arrest these people. You want him to agree that trapping of ornamental fish on the new reef should be prohibited—and you haven't even told him about banning all reef fishing for three to four years while the reef is getting established."

"I know, Elma," Ismail said. "He wants a technological fix to a complex environmental problem caused largely by humans because it looks easier than dealing with the human social conditions that caused the problem in the first place. Maybe I would too, if I were he. Why wouldn't he jump at this chance? It not only looks like a magic solution, but the village wouldn't even have to pay for it; the overseas donors do. He wants a fix to the village problem without having to accept any responsibility or ownership of the problem. And that is *my* problem with him and his village. If the village has nothing invested in fixing the problem, why should they protect the fix? If it gets destroyed again, they will look for another donor with another fix. We could install the fencing, regrow the reef, and find that ten years from now the reef was just as devastated as it is now. This village just doesn't look like a good prospect for our project."

By this time they were back in the office, and they expanded their conversation to include two other staff members—Nyoman and Ketut, both of whom were Balinese. Ketut agreed with Ismail, adding that the steps required to protect coral reefs were going to continue to be more demanding; no village should be chosen that was not likely to accept the difficult work ahead. "You know we haven't seen much coral bleaching here," Ketut said, "compared to the Caribbean and Hawaii, or even the Great Barrier Reef in the heat wave of 1998. We're probably helped by a greater difference between our day and night temperatures; the shallow waters have time to cool down at night. But the latest information on global warming makes it pretty clear that coral reef news is going to get worse and worse. Remember Susan Solomon, who led the 1986–87 research expedition to Antarctica that proved that chlorofluorocarbons in aerosol sprays were accumulating at the poles, creating holes in the ozone layers? Well, she briefed the Joint Scientific Committee of the World

Climate Research Program recently, and it seems that the chemical poisoning of the stratosphere is not just causing ozone holes—it is disrupting weather patterns all over the world by deepening low-pressure centers over both poles, shrinking the vortices of the weather patterns that used to dance around the poles, distributing cool weather to mild climates. The result is that the tropics get hotter and the temperate zones get colder, with tremendous glacier melts where glaciers touch oceans whose currents come from the tropical waters. The very day she was briefing the Joint Committee the Larson B glacier formation collapsed, spawning thousands of icebergs. That put an exclamation point on her presentation!"

Nyoman grimaced at Ismail and Elma and said, "Yeah, he just made me read the report, and I have to agree it's kind of scary. Even before this development, however, most scientists were agreeing that local ocean temperatures were likely to increase by two to six degrees over the next fifty years, and that already puts a lot of reefs in danger of bleaching."

Ismail turned back to Elma. "You really think that this village—led by the quick-fix man—will have the discipline to protect the reef from themselves and from others, even when it's not feeding them? And when new measures are necessary—from bleaching, for example—you think we will get the necessary cooperation from them, and even the necessary work crews that we may need?"

"I don't know, Ismail, I just think we have to look beyond the chief. We need to meet with the rest of the committee, with the fishermen, with the people who have stalls in the fish market, with the dive boat owners and hotel owners—all of whom have a stake in the reef. Maybe we will decide that they don't have the discipline for what we need, as you say. I just don't want to give up too soon."

Ismail agreed to another meeting but added, "Make it soon. We have to decide on two more project locations by next month, and if Binging isn't one of them, we need time to find another."

They agreed to call the chief and set up a meeting of all the reef stakeholders for the following week. In conversation with Wayan, Elma tried to make it clear to the chief that a project in his village was not something he could choose but that the village had to be chosen, and the decision would be made on the basis of whether the village and its leaders were willing to take responsibility for reef protection for decades into the future. At last Elma convinced the chief that it would be a good idea to have the provincial governor's office liaison and the government environmental officer, as well as the local police chief—his cousin—in attendance as well. This way they could share the responsibility with him.

Six days later, as the four staff members bumped along in the van on the way from Denpasar to Wayan's village, Ketut was still talking about global warming and coral bleaching. "You know, we need to find out what's happening in genetic research on coral. Is anybody working to find out what kinds have the highest resistance to bleaching from high temperatures, and what their requirements are? How hard is it to engineer coral?"

"Wait a minute," Nyoman protested. "You sound like Chief Wayan now, wanting a technological fix. We need to take steps to stop the chemical poisoning of the stratosphere to stop global warming, not look for technological fixes for isolated problems it creates. Even if there is research that could make coral reefs resistant, if the weather continues to warm those species will reach their limits, too, and we will be starting all over again—as Ismail is afraid will happen if Wayan's village isn't resolved to stop the abuses that are killing the reef now. What about you, Elma? Where do you stand on this?"

"Well, I understand what Ketut is saying," Elma said. "The United States pretty much killed the Kyoto Accords—and how the richest nation in the world, with 6 percent of the world's population but 25 percent of the CO_2 emissions, has the nerve to reject relatively minor restrictions on production of CO_2 because it might undermine its economic dominance, I don't know. Now I don't see much hope for making any headway on global warming for at least a decade. It probably will be even longer before any cutbacks could actually show results. So one part of me hopes that we do have some technological fixes to stop the tremendous ecological losses that will otherwise happen until we can reverse or at least stop global warming."

The others asked no more questions; they had talked many times about their frustrations with the political impasse over global warming.

Ismail broke the silence. "Did any of you happen to see the memo on my desk from SEAREEF?" As they all shook their heads negatively, Ismail continued, "Among many other regional reefs, it lists six Indonesian reefs with some degree of bleaching this season. They aren't sure if sea-surface temperature is the only stressor on these reefs, but the bleaching corals are varieties that are sensitive to heat."

"So we need to start looking for bleaching in our areas, too, and try to determine the specific causes of the bleaching," murmured Elma woefully.

"More than that, Nyoman declared. "We need to get the data on heat-sensitive and heat-resistant coral types and start integrating it into our work. In the past we haven't distinguished different types of coral in deciding where to locate the projects. Now, as Elma says, we have to start monitoring for all known stressors. It won't do any good to concentrate fencing on reefs with higher proportions of heat-resistant types if those reefs have other stressors that the heat-resistant types are sensitive to."

"We need as much specific data as we can get," Ketut added, "both on different varieties of coral and on the conditions on the project reefs before we can incorporate bleaching into our selection or monitoring processes."

Ismail turned around from the front seat to look at the three staff members in the second row of the van. "That's good, really good. It's exactly what we need to do. Nyoman, you contact SEAREEF and the AIMS group in Australia and get as much data as you can on coral bleaching, both on heat resistance and any other environmental stressor information they have. Ketut, your job is to review all the assessment procedures, both for selection and monitoring, and suggest where we need to make modifications once we have the data. Elma, when they're finished, your job is going to be to review the materials we send to prospective villages, to the environmental officers, and to the press and see what needs to be changed to adequately represent these new concerns and procedures of ours." There was a moment of quiet in the face of this new threat and the responsibilities it brought.

Then Ismail returned to the earlier conversation. Speaking slower and more deliberately, in a softer voice, he began.

"The whole question of intervention is a puzzler for me. On one level, like Elma I want both: I want global action to protect the environment by cutting emissions, shifting from chemical pesticides that kill rivers and bays, and preventing overfishing, and I want some technological fixes, such as the ionized fencing we are using, to try to repair the damage and save what can be saved. But I know it is possible that the fixes we engineer may be ecologically disastrous in the long run. Look at the pesticide problem in Bali. Until the green revolution introduced new high-yield species, people didn't use pesticides. The new species required them, though, and the amounts required get higher all the time as the insects become resistant. But the rivers and fish are dying from the pesticides, and then the pesticides wash into the ocean and continue killing. We have tested the ionized fencing as much as we can in the limited time we had to make sure it is 'safe,' but we may well find that it is toxic to some species of reef inhabitant or that it interrupts the gestation process. Who knows what it could do, in addition to assisting coral? On the other hand, if we had waited and tested it on every possible species we could find, how many reefs would have totally died, and everything been lost? Yet I wonder where we draw the line—if it is even possible to draw a line—between where it is acceptable to interfere in the natural process to try to save it and where it is not. It seems to me that this is the practical issue we must wrestle with. Is there a rational difference between engineering heat-resistant coral and using ionized fencing to regrow coral reefs?"

"Whenever possible we need to return to safer, more traditional ways of caring for the earth," Ketut responded. "Before the trawlers came, when it was just local fishermen taking fish from the reef, there was no overfishing. We just need to go back. Things that get us back help, and things that mandate our inventing new ways of interacting with nature are dangerous."

Nyoman was shaking his head. "That's a dream. We can't go back. Population pressure alone won't let us go back. One of the reasons for the trawlers is that small-scale local fishermen couldn't catch enough to feed the increased population. Look at Bali: You can complain about the pesticide residue, but we can't go back to the old strains of rice; they didn't produce enough per acre to feed people when the demographic shift began, when the death rate dropped and population expanded. We have to find a new balance that preserves the earth, but it won't be the old balance because there are too many people for those ways to work. We are going to have to find ways of intervening in nature without screwing it up—ways that extract more food and shelter without exhausting the source."

Ketut, ever the traditionalist, continued to disagree. "But you can't introduce more and more 'engineering' without waiting to find out the results of the first interventions; you won't know what caused the changes you see. That's a pretty basic scientific principle. We have to make sure that these reefs, for example, are monitored by the locals who know them best, not only to keep out the abusive practices but to watch what comes back, at what speeds, and what doesn't, and how the differential speeds affect the different species. Isn't that why we're doing only two or three projects a year—so that we can monitor them and watch the effects?"

"Maybe there's a difference between introducing ionized fencing and engineering new coral species," Elma said. "The fencing doesn't reproduce itself. If it proves harmful to some species, and that harm is potentially more dangerous than the benefits it provides to others, we can stop introducing it—maybe even remove it, though that would be difficult. If we introduce a new species of engineered coral, though, theoretically it could reproduce itself all over the world and could never be retracted."

"Elma," Ketut said, "that is a difference, yes. But I don't think it resolves Ismail's question about where the appropriate boundaries should be. What if the ionized fencing interferes with the reproduction of some basic element of reef life, like a prominent type of algae that feeds certain kinds of fish? Then it has the potential to alter the entire reef food chain by eliminating some fishes on which other fishes depend, extinguishing some species and enlarging others—with implications for the whole coastal shelf and beyond. Rather than look at the mechanism of the intervention, whether it involves changing genetic structures or not, I think we have to look at the possible consequences of the intervention."

The van bounced as it hit a big pothole. As they settled back down, Ismail responded.

"I agree with Ketut; we need to look at the consequences. And that is the problem, isn't it? Because we are losing so many species, so many habitats, so quickly, we don't have the time to do the research that would allow us to assess the long-term consequences with any degree of certainty. We're operating blind."

Everyone was silent until Elma spoke up. "We're almost there," she said. "It's going to be a big group. Looks like we got the dive boat operators, the hotel people I wasn't sure would come, as well as the chief, the fishermen, and the fish sellers from the market. So how do we persuade them that they can't go back to the way things were before the reef died but that it's still worthwhile to save the reef?"

When they arrived at the meeting and had been introduced by Wayan to the environmental officer and the governor's liaison, Ismail and his staff joined a lively discussion among the locals. The committee had excited everyone with descriptions of the coral and fish they had seen at the project sites and the magic of the fencing. The fishermen wanted to know how long it would take to restore the reef. It quickly became clear, however, that their real question was how long it would be before fishing would be restored to past levels on the reef. They were not pleased with the news that a fishing ban would have to be enforced for three to four years. Nor were the fish sellers at the market. Both groups demanded to know how they were to live in the meantime. Ismail's temper was fraying, and he responded, "How are you living now, since you destroyed your reef?"

Even Elma reeled back in surprise at the curtness of Ismail's question, which clearly offended the Balinese at the meeting. Ismail pressed on, however. "The reef did not destroy itself. This was no accident, no natural disaster. The reef at Binging was destroyed by years of overfishing, dynamiting, and cyanide fishing; by divers pulling out coral to sell; by dragging traps across the coral to catch ornamental fish; by tourists breaking the coral with their flippers and dive boats with their anchors. You all participated in this destruction, either directly or indirectly. The fish sellers bought and sold the fish they knew had been dynamited or poisoned. The dive boat operators didn't anchor outside the reef or train their tourist-divers to protect the coral. You all saw this destruction happening over years, and you did nothing to stop it. *We* have no responsibility for fixing your reef. What we want to know is how *you* intend to fix your reef. If we decide that you have a good enough plan, and the will to carry it through, then we may have a tool that can help in the project. But this is your problem as a community. Our time is short; we have to decide in the next two or three weeks which villages to select for our projects next year. You have no plan now. Can you agree on a plan and how to implement it? Contact us when you do."

Ismail turned and began walking toward the van. Elma whispered to Nyoman and Ketut as they began following Ismail, "I think that Acehnese directness of his has been exacerbated by these years working with Americans and Europeans—the Indonesian rituals of politeness have been rubbed right out!"

Commentary

A coral is an animal that lives in colonies in a symbiotic relationship with millions of tiny algae plants. The plants use the carbon dioxide produced by the coral animal, along with sunlight, to produce oxygen and nutrients that feed the coral host. Bleaching occurs when, in response to various stressors, the coral animal begins to expel the algae that give it its brown or green color. When sufficient amounts of the algae have been expelled, the coral becomes a white skeleton, and dies. Corals can recover from some degree of bleaching if the stressors are removed, but once it has become white it cannot recover.

A coral reef is an area where the ocean floor has been built up by coral. It usually contains both living and dead coral. The waters of coral reefs usually arc relatively shallow and therefore warm, compared with deeper waters. Coral reefs are nurseries for fish and other marine life.

Southeast Asia has more than 34 percent of the world's coral reefs, as well as 600 of the world's 800 varieties of reef-building coral. According to "Reefs at Risk in Southeast Asia," a World Resources report, "it is not unusual to find a greater variety of species around a single island in this region than can be found on all the coral reefs in the Caribbean." Indonesia and the Philippines have 77 percent of Southeast Asia's coral reefs, and nearly 80 percent of them are threatened. About 65 percent of them are threatened by overfishing, 37 percent by sedimentation and pollution caused by coastal development and agriculture, and 56 percent by destructive fishing practices, such as dynamiting and poison-fishing.

Several different environmental issues are involved in the preservation of coral reefs. The two most overarching factors are global warming and population density. Of those two, population density is the most pressing present problem, though global warming has disastrous long-term potential. Population pressures are directly related to overfishing and the poverty that underlies dangerous practices such as cyanide and dynamite fishing, as well as pollution of coastal reefs by agricultural runoff (including pesticides) and by soil eroded from cleared forests. In some parts of the world, especially the Caribbean, coral bleaching from global warming already is a serious problem. As this case implies, as global warming seems to be accelerating, raising the temperature of the oceans, coral reefs and all of the species that live in the oceans begin to experience dislocation pressures.

Population Pressures

The earth is headed toward a population of 7 billion human inhabitants, having added 2 billion since the 1950s. By contrast, there were 2 billion or fewer human inhabitants on the planet in 1800. There is a direct correlation between the growing size of the human population and the fact that almost half of the world's major areas for taking saltwater fish are in some degree of decline. The species that have disappeared—or may disappear in the near future from commercial nets—are precisely those that humans have decided are tasty. Species not targeted for human tables generally are not affected, though some of these species are now being caught on a large scale as feed for fish-farms, such as those for salmon, and may suffer the same fate as table fish.

Population pressure also is one of the prime causes of global poverty today, as the increasing need for farmland pushes the poorest farmers into clearing land that should not be farmed. The least privileged farmers all over the world clear and plant hillsides that erode, filling streams with silt. Because there is not enough good land to make a living, poor farmers tear up trees and other borders between fields, which had been windbreaks and soil anchors, further encouraging erosion. They plant too often, not allowing the land to rest, and frequently plant only the crop that will pay the best, which soon wears out the soil nutrients. This process then pushes them to seek out and clear more land that is unsuitable for farming. This cycle creates massive erosion, which fills the streams and empties into the oceans.

Population pressures in rich nations also are furthering the destruction of coastal waters through clearing of coastal land, often wetland, for housing and commercial development. The result is soil erosion, as well as discharge of storm sewers—and in many places, sanitary sewers and industrial wastewaters—into the ocean.

The quest to keep food cheap and to find enough to feed everyone has led the global fishing industry to become extremely technological and mechanized: Single ships often are as large as huge factories; they use electronic and satellite technology to locate, identify, capture, and recover millions of fish, erasing whole schools at a time. In this case, and along the Indonesian coastal shelf generally, the high-tech, high-volume fishing ships are not the largest floating fish factories; but the smaller high-tech trawlers are still large enough to inhibit the ability of local fish populations to reestablish themselves. High tech by itself is not the problem here, however. Even at the local village level, population growth has meant that a single fisherman in each successive generation frequently leaves behind two or more children who grow up to be fishermen. The proportion of fishermen to farmers may be the same, but the numbers of both have risen. Yet the reef, like the land itself, is the same size.

Overfishing is a worldwide phenomenon. The current annual worldwide fishing catch is about 84 million tons of fish. This figure includes only legal catches; there is no way to adequately measure the amount of illegal fishing that occurs, though many estimates place it at around 30–35 percent of the legal catch. Assessment of global ocean fisheries has led to estimates that catches above 100 million tons per year are not sustainable. That is, when catches near or exceed 100 million tons annually, species dwindle; if the catches continue to exceed the sustainable limits, species become extinct. According to the 1999 report of the Committee on Ecosystem Management for Sustainable Marine Fisheries of the National Research Council (NRC) in Washington, D.C., about 4 percent of marine species are endangered, 30 percent are overfished, and 44 percent are being fished at or near the maximum sustainable rate.

The NRC report recommends that substantial global reductions in fishing capacity are the highest priority to help reduce overfishing. It also suggests that fishing capitalization (the amount of capital invested in fishing boats and equipment) be reduced and recommends introduction of controlled-access management of fisheries with experimental approaches to community-based fishery. That is, the numbers of fishers must be reduced, and the efficiency of fishing equipment also must be reduced.

Overpopulation and the poverty it helps to maintain are directly related to destructive fishing practices such as dynamite fishing and poison fishing. Not only are these methods mostly employed by poor, local fishermen, but poverty is the chief reason for the culture of official corruption that prevents effective enforcement of laws against such practices. Judges in Indonesia make less than $200 per month; police earn much less. A major part of the attraction of low-paying jobs in the public sector (besides simply having an income!) is the opportunity to earn bribes, which can amount to more than the salary of the job itself. Corruption is almost never prosecuted; when it is, defendants are rarely convicted because evidence disappears, witnesses are bribed not to testify or to retract testimony, or judges are bribed to acquit. Hardly a day goes by that the newspapers do not report multiple new cases of corruption at high levels of government and commerce. Corruption is not even very covert: On Bali, the site of this case (though it is by no means unusual in this regard), visitors may be stopped by police roadblocks multiple times in a single week, at which point local guides and drivers routinely hand out bribes to the police to pass the roadblocks—which have no other purpose. Little will change if enforcement of a fishing ban on the newly fenced reef and prosecution of dynamiters, cyanide-fishers, and dive boat operators who drag anchors across the reef depend on police who must take bribes so they can afford uniforms and books for their children to attend elementary school or judges who take bribes to send their children to university.

Global Warming

For almost two decades there has been acrimonious debate about global warming. Some scientists insist that human activity is accelerating warming of the global climate, and others insist that there is insufficient evidence to prove that increased warming is not simply part of a normal cycle of warming lasting hundreds of years before a cooling cycle begins. All are agreed that we are in a warming cycle; the dispute has been over whether human activity is responsible for some part of the warming that is occurring.

Over the past five to ten years there has been a consensus growing that human activity—specifically emissions of certain gases, especially carbon dioxide (CO_2)—is contributing to global warming. At the very least, research has proved that the release of chlorofluorocarbons (CFCs) and, to a lesser extent, hydrochlorofluorocarbons (HCFCs)—which are widely used in aerosols and refrigerants (in air conditioning and refrigerators, for example)—was responsible for the holes that developed in the ozone layer over the earth's poles. Agreement on this issue led to the Montreal Protocol of 1987, in which the nations of the world agreed to ban CFCs by 1996; in 1992 an amendment was added that banned HCFCs as well.

Evidence in favor of human contribution to global warming has been escalating, despite evidence that global warming is influenced by several different factors and that it has fluctuated tremendously in the past. Scientists have been able to extract a core of polar ice dating back 40,000 years ago; the layers in the core allowed scientists to test and compare the average yearly temperatures over that time span, and they found that increases in annual average temperature over the past century are significantly above the average in any comparable period of time over the past 40,000 years. Moreover, there is a direct correlation between increases in CO_2 emissions over the past 50 years and increases in temperature in those same years. Scientists believe they are close to developing a comprehensive model of the process of global warming, as evidenced in the latest report of the Joint Scientific Committee of the World Climate Research Program.

In the 1992 Kyoto Protocol, 170 nations agreed that countries producing gaseous emissions that were disproportionately larger than their population share—the industrialized nations—would cut their emissions to below their

1990 levels between 2008 and 2012. They were allowed to buy or trade emission credits from nations that did not reach their quota. One of the first decisions of the new Bush administration in January 2001 was that the president would not ask Congress to ratify the Kyoto Protocol—on the grounds that its target for the United States of 7 percent below 1990 emission levels could seriously harm the U.S. economy. This decision angered many nations—especially those in Europe, which had accepted a target of 8 percent below 1990 emissions, but also some Asian nations—some of which decided to honor the accord even without U.S. participation. Because the United States alone contributes more than one-quarter of the world's gaseous emissions, however, and some nations were encouraged by the U.S. rejection of Kyoto to ignore it as well, the possibility of meaningful reductions in the near future is remote.

Although coral bleaching from warmer sea-surface temperatures (SST) is largely a localized problem, it may well become a serious problem for all nations with coral reefs, including Indonesia. Australia's Great Barrier Reef has a significant number of areas of bleaching, some seriously devastated and some capable of recovery. Coral reacts to many different stressors by bleaching, and if the stressors do not persist too long, the coral can recover. Once it has fully bleached—expelled all of its living plants—it dies; new coral must grow to replace it. In the summer of 1998 high temperatures, few clouds, and very calm weather produced a devastating epidemic of bleaching in the Great Barrier Reef, from which many areas had not yet recovered in 2002. Moreover, there was fear that 2002 was repeating the conditions of 1998 on the Great Barrier Reef.

The Australian Institute of Marine Science has been conducting studies on coral bleaching and has found that different kinds of coral have greater and lesser degrees of resistance to bleaching when exposed to higher SST. Although this finding is good news for Indonesian reefs—they have such a large diversity of coral types that they are likely to include resistant types—it may simply mean that some reef coral may survive initial increases in SST. All types of coral seem to be sensitive to some level of high SST.

Coral has been studied relatively recently. For example, there is no comprehensive map of the world's coral reefs. Few nations in Southeast Asia can map more than half of their coral reefs, much less know what types of coral and varieties of fish and marine life are found on each reef. Although genetic manipulation of coral may be technically possible, it is not near. The symbiosis between the coral itself and the plants it hosts severely complicates any genetic modification. Lack of knowledge about the environmental contexts of the different types of coral also increases the risks involved in genetic modification.

Boundaries

The core questions about this case are essentially questions about ethical principles. The first is this: Whose responsibility is the reef? The second is Ismail's question about boundary lines: How does one decide which proposed interventions are appropriate and which are not?

Regarding boundary lines, there clearly is no single—let alone simple—principle by which we can separate appropriate and inappropriate interventions. The appropriateness of any particular intervention will always depend on what other interventions are available, the situation in which the intervention would be used, and many related factors. For example, the riskier the intervention, the more desperate must be the context in which one considers using it. A reef with only initial stages of bleaching, for example, is the wrong place to use a new and relatively untested intervention when there are others that are less risky. The same intervention may be appropriate, however, in a reef whose death is imminent and in which several previous interventions have failed.

Some technologies may be inappropriate anywhere, though there certainly are few environmental technologies in that category. Most technologies that are designed to benefit the environment require so much investment of time and knowledge and funding, with so little possibility for reaping large monetary rewards, that it would be unusual to produce technologies that are entirely inappropriate for any context. On the other hand, there certainly are scientists and environmentalists who think that some commercial, nonenvironmental technologies should be banned altogether—including floating fish factories, chemical pesticides, and clearcut logging. Although these technologies were designed to intervene in the environment, they were not, however, developed with the intention of assisting in environmental health and preservation. (Nor, of course, were they designed to destroy environmental health and preservation; their developers simply failed to adequately consider these technologies' impact on the environment.)

Elma's suggestion that the fencing was less risky because it did not procreate as genetically modified coral would reflects a common point of view within bioethics today on the difference between genetic engineering of somatic cells and germ cells. If a person has a disease gene that can be turned off in the somatic cell system, he or she can be cured of the disease but can still pass on the disease gene to his or her children, who will then have the disease if the gene is dominant. On the other hand, if the gene is turned off or replaced in the germ cell—which determines the chromosomes contributed to offspring—then the disease cannot be passed on to the affected person's descendants. Of course, if there is some problem with the engineering, that "problem"—perhaps in addition to the disease gene—can be passed on to unlimited generations into the future, which is why many bioethicists are warning that we should leave germ-cell engineering alone, at least until we have a much clearer idea of what we are doing and the risks involved.

Although Ketut dismisses Elma's suggestion as inadequate, it should be taken seriously. It may be valuable but not sufficient. The idea that whenever possible our interventions should be short term rather than self-perpetuating is a valuable insight. It is one part of the argument in the case discussion of the importance of evaluating consequences. The consequences under discussion are systemic consequences. Human interventions may be aimed at one particular species (here coral) but have direct and indirect consequences for many others within the same ecological system. Analyses of consequences must consider the entire ecosystem and all of the interrelationships within that ecosystem. When Ismail says, "We are operating blind," he means that we do not understand reef ecosystems (as well as many others) well enough to be able to predict consequences. This lack of understanding is a good reason for short-term interventions.

The argument between Ketut and Nyoman over the value of traditions also is instructive. Both have important contributions to make. Ketut is right that there usually is an ecological wisdom in the practices of traditional peoples that often can guide us toward the safest methods of intervening in nature. Yet Nyoman also is right that although such traditions may offer a great deal of wisdom about particular interventions in ecosystems, their overall life systems—including modes of production—are not competent to promote the welfare of the human community or the ecosystem. Those life systems, which once had their own internal equilibrium with the environment, already have suffered many interventions—perhaps most importantly population growth caused by reductions in infant mortality and epidemics—that leave them unable to provide for growing populations or to deal with the side effects of those interventions (e.g., garbage, emissions). Many aspects of the traditions of native peoples can be an invaluable resource for finding answers to the ecological dilemma, but as lifestyle systems they cannot provide a guide for how to reach the equilibrium we need today between a sustainable ecosystem and the well-being of the entire human community.

Perhaps the best answer to the search for boundary lines is that the question is as important as the answer. It may be better not to have a clear, obvious answer because then we might stop asking questions and reflecting on the entire issue of appropriateness. That could be dangerous. In the famous Robert Frost poem, a New England farmer is repairing the rock wall between his land and his neighbors, and he says, "Good fences make good neighbors." Later, however, upon reflection he wonders whether there isn't a price paid, a separateness, for this clarity regarding rights and possessions, and finally he questions whether good fences really do make good neighbors. In the same way, an answer that clearly and universally defines which interventions in the environment are appropriate and which are not may encourage us to ignore—to stop reflecting about—the most important issue: connection and relationship between humans and the rest of the biosphere.

Who Is Responsible for the Reef?

The conclusion of the case leaves us with the question of whose responsibility the reef is. Ismail clearly thinks responsibility for the reef belongs to the adjacent village of Binging. On the other hand, although Indonesians—as individuals and as local communities—often claim ownership for nearby natural resources, they are accustomed to understanding themselves as lacking the financial resources necessary to address many social and environmental issues. As in most nations, the people look to the national government to address many issues for them; in some areas where the technical expertise requirements or the financial outlay requirements are large, they are accustomed to their national government looking to the international community for assistance in addressing their problem.

Ismail holds the village responsible for the destruction of the reef, but the villagers regard the destruction of the reef as the result of the necessary and desperate search for food and work—for survival. They do regard their struggle for survival in terms of disaster: The financial crisis that began in 1997 had a cataclysmic effect on the lives of Indonesians. The village also understands, as poor individuals in the developing world typically do, that those who are better off have an obligation in justice to help those who are not. From this perspective, the problem of this village—the reef—is the problem of the rest of the world, too.

At the end of this case, the village and Ismail are talking at cross-purposes, and they are both partially right. Both sides recognize the need for the commitment of the other group. The difference between Ismail's agency and the village is that Ismail's agency has more options than the village does. Other villages also want the fencing project located on their reef, whereas the village of Binging has no other agency that is willing to fund and supervise the restoration of their reef. Thus, Ismail speaks with more power.

Ismail is right that the village will have to accept responsibility for the reef if the reef is to have a chance to come back. Ismail sounds almost religious in his speech. He accuses the village of a variety of sins against the reef and the common good and demands that they repent, acknowledge their failures, and commit to changing their behavior. The village, on the other hand, sees restoration of the reef in terms of its effect on the villagers' precarious, even hand-to-mouth, existence. As of 2001–2002, the Indonesian government estimated that more than one-quarter of the population was living in dire poverty, and another half of the population was living at or under the poverty line. April 2002 studies of school children showed a 47 percent incidence of malnutrition throughout various schools in various districts in numerous provinces. Although the villagers are not looking at the whole picture and may be intent, as Ismail insists, on a quick fix, their concerns point to their need to have their welfare—especially their survival—taken seriously as one part of the social planning necessary to save the reef. The reef is important, but so are the people.

Religious Resources

It is significant that this case is set in Bali—a small island off the east coast of Java whose population is predominantly Hindu. Balinese Hinduism is syncretic—a form of village Hinduism adapted to Indonesia that is oriented toward the fruitfulness of the environment. Bali has a rich ritual life that includes frequent festivals of thanksgiving commemorating people's dependence on their fields, forests, and ocean environments. On almost any day, driving through Bali one sees parades of brightly dressed women in one village or another headed for the temple carrying on their heads towers of beautifully arranged, colorful offerings of fruits and flowers. Plant and flower offerings to the gods are placed daily in small colorful shrines outside each house and often dispersed throughout the family compound as well. Balinese ritual is full of reminders of the providence of the gods in supplying people's needs through the local environment.

Thus, Balinese religion offers a tremendous potential resource for environmentalism, in that it ritually recognizes the environment as sacred and people as interdependent with it. The temples, the temple rituals and activities, and the priests and priestesses and other holy persons associated with Balinese religion together constitute an important resource for supporting the people of Binging in accepting a proportionate share of responsibility for the restoration and preservation of the coral reef. They should have been at the meeting, and they should be enlisted in the project.

If environmental preservation is to succeed, the billions of persons on the planet will need to have more than simply intellectual appreciation of human interdependence, to be faced with more than simply religious commands and civil laws. Humans do—and will continue to—need to feel connected to the environment, to feel its sacredness and to act out that sacredness in some kind of ritual, whether traditional or new.

Questions for Discussion

1. Why does Ismail doubt that Binging is an appropriate site for one of the organization's reef projects next summer?
2. What religiocultural resources in the Balinese tradition could be useful in the movement to preserve the coral reefs? Why?
3. In what way does Ismail wonder about the efficacy of his own work in this organization? Is it possible to eliminate his doubts? Why or why not?
4. Is there any evidence that the current warming of the earth is caused by humans and is not merely cycles of warming and cooling that have always occurred?
5. In which ways does the prospect of global warming affect the need for more data about coral reefs? Whose responsibility do you think it is to gather these data, and why?

For Further Reading

Burke, Lauretta, Elizabeth Selig, and Mark Spaulding. *Reefs at Risk in Southeast Asia.* Washington, D.C.: World Resources Institute, 2002.

Committee on Ecosystem Management for Sustainable Marine Fisheries. *Sustaining Marine Fisheries.* Washington, D.C.: National Academy Press, 1999.

"Creation of Artificial Coral Reefs Begins." *Jakarta Post,* 15 November 2000.

Cropley, Ed. "Global Warming Hits Tropical Species All Around the World: Study." *Jakarta Post,* 2 April 2002, 16.

Dursin, Richel. "Environment Indonesia: Coral and Fish Trade Reefs at Risk." *Environment Bulletin,* 13 March 2000.

Erdmann, Mark V. "Saving Bunaken." *Inside Indonesia* (January–March 2001); available from flotsam@manado.wasantara.net.id.

Hittenger, Kerry. "Fears of Massive Coral Bleaching." Australian Institute of Marine Science report (January 30, 2002); available at www.aims.gov.au/pages/about/communications/backgrounders/20020130-coral-bleaching.html (accessed April 9, 2003).

Moreau, Ron. "Saving the Coral Reefs." *Newsweek International* (November 12, 2001), 58.

Sandilands, Ben. "Ozone Holes Set Freak Weather." *Jakarta Post,* 2 April 2002, 16.

Stoppard, Anthony. "Environment: Saving Coral Reefs from the Marine Trade." *Environment Bulletin,* 26 October 2000.

Weber, Peter K. "Saving the Coral Reefs." *The Futurist* 27, no. 4 (July–August 1993): 28–34.

Yoong, Sean. "SE Asia's Reefs Threatened by Overfishing, Pollution." *Jakarta Post,* 2 April 2002, 15.

8

River Run or River Ruined: Hydropower or Free-Flowing Rivers?

"Move to your left so I can get more of the dam." Dale could barely hear Karen's instructions above the roar of water cascading over the sixty-foot spillway in the gorge below.

"That's perfect. Now either smile or look appropriately somber for the camera," Karen joked, as she snapped three pictures in quick succession.

Karen Henson was a writer and photographer for the *Coos Bay Courier*, a small daily newspaper whose front-page headlines usually featured local baseball teams and arts festivals. Neither she nor Dale had made the hour's drive and the twenty-minute hike to the lovely viewpoint just above the Chapman Gorge Dam on the Coquille River for any Chamber of Commerce snapshots, however. Karen was working on a series of stories on the rapidly moving plans of the Coos County Public Utility District, the dam's owner and operator, to sell the fifty-year-old structure to the electrical giant Pacificorp for rehabilitation. A major task stood in the way of the successful exchange of ownership. The dam was coming up for relicensing proceedings by the Federal Energy Regulatory Commission (FERC). In a hearing the following week before the FERC investigators, the two parties would make their case for the deal.

They would face passionate opposition from others who thought the project was little more than a bad idea.

For Karen, this was high drama and well worth several articles in the *Courier*, along with profiles of the major players—including Dale. Dale Laney was a fourth-generation citizen of Coos Bay, a city of 20,000 people in the coastal basin of southern Oregon. Dale's father, now retired, and his father before him once fished the Pacific in trawlers with large nets, taking in their share of the abundant harvest of coho and sockeye salmon. As times changed, however, the fishing and logging industries that fueled the economy gave way to agriculture and tourism. A practicing attorney in the town for more than a decade, Dale had been elected as one of the three members of the city's Board of Commissioners.

Karen completed the photo session and returned along the trail to a picnic table to tinker with her camera and remove the lenses for storage. Dale remained for a few moments, mesmerized by the rushing water. As she looked back toward the reservoir she could see the Klamath Mountains, sources of the headwaters of the Coquille River, mirrored in the lake's waters. The cold, clear streams from the mountains merged into the south and east forks of the Coquille, and the confluence of the forks formed the river's stem about five miles behind the dam.

Dale walked back toward the picnic area to join Karen, who had packed her camera and awaited her, warmed by the direct rays of the mid-morning sun on this otherwise chilly April day. Although Karen represented the media and Dale was the politician, Dale felt at ease with Karen. Karen did not have the attack personality some journalists had. No spin was necessary in her presence. In fact, given her considerable knowledge about many aspects of the town, Dale felt she could learn much from Karen.

"You seem to be enjoying yourself up there," Karen said.

"Yes, lots of good memories here. It's a beautiful place."

Dale had been here before—many times as a child with her family—so the experience was familiar. She recalled canoeing in the 2,000-acre Chapman Gorge Reservoir and hiking down the trails into the gorge below the dam, where the water rushed by—but with far less power and volume than must have been the case when the river flowed freely.

From an earlier interview Karen knew how seriously Dale took her responsibilities not only as a commissioner but also as a citizen who was genuinely concerned about the beauty of the gorge. Dale was to represent Coos Bay's interests at the hearing. She was of two minds and not a few conflicts. She would prefer to speak decisively, as attorneys do before the court. Life is not always modeled after the prosecution confronting the defense, however.

"Would Mayor Kelly agree that this is a beautiful place?" Karen asked.

Dale smiled. She knew that the question was only partly serious, but important.

"I'm not sure that Henry and I agree on much of anything—not since he was elected mayor last year and certainly not after our vote in the city commission favoring some version of a restored dam but also recommending severe restrictions on enlarging the structure. He wants to sell the dam to Pacificorp, double its size, and increase the power production to 15 megawatts. I'm afraid that beauty will be the last thing on his mind when he testifies at the FERC hearing against his own commission."

"That is, against you—correct?" asked Karen.

"I'm afraid so," said Dale. "Because I'm an attorney with considerable experience arguing in adversary proceedings, the other two members of the commission cordially compelled me to represent them at the hearing."

Dale hesitated for a moment, returning to Karen's earlier question. "I think Henry would view the gorge and lake as beautiful," she confessed, "if he could see past those dollar signs in his eyes. But you tell me, since you interviewed him yesterday and I haven't spoken with him privately in two weeks."

"Well," Karen began, "I haven't completed the article. The deadline is tomorrow afternoon, so I'll be working late tonight. He did have some interesting comments. It seems that Mayor Kelly has an informal advisor prompting him on plans for the dam. Some guy from the Northwest Hydropower Reform Coalition, Adam Toolen. Toolen isn't a big secret. Kelly gave me his phone number, and I spoke to him. He goes to Portland every year when the legislature is in session to serve as a lobbyist for the interests of Pacificorp, Oregon Edison, and others who would like to see every brook, creek, and river put to work squeezing out kilowatts. Toolen is a true believer, and his missionary zeal obviously has converted the mayor."

"No surprise there," Dale remarked. "Since this thing came up last November my mailbox has been stuffed with material from every environmental advocacy group objecting to the plan and every industry institute favoring the restoration. The packet of materials from the coalition sticks in my mind. It was the size of a mail-order catalogue."

"Then you know their slogan," Karen continued. "The mayor repeated it to me half a dozen times: Hydroelectricity is green because it is CCRP—they pronounce it 'crip': cheap, clean, renewable power." She shook her head. "These people could use a more poetic publicist."

132

"I agree with that. But money is green, too," Dale responded. "Henry wants the new business, especially from the huge new reservoir that comes with the taller dam. He has big plans for increasing tourism with new recreational facilities to be built along the expanded shoreline. In addition to fishing and boating, he sees great promise for the further development of agriculture on the coastal basin and an enlarged tax base for roads and schools."

Karen agreed. "He did emphasize irrigation as one of the major benefits of the new dam. Toolen obviously had helped him along with another point. Large reservoirs work well in what he called 'cyclic climates' of flood and drought—which southern Oregon knows only too well—by impounding water that would inundate the river's floodplain and storing it for us when rain doesn't come, and the added land can be put into crop production."

"Oh yes, how can I forget the argument for flood control discussed on page 213 of their catalogue?"

"But back to green power," Karen said, recognizing sarcasm when she heard it. "Hydroelectricity is a lot cheaper than electricity produced by fossil fuel—as much as 80 percent cheaper. The mayor had some figures from upstate oil-burning plants to back up that claim. And, of course, there is no pollution, none at all. Kelly and Toolen got real excited when they talked about that. It seems like a valid point, doesn't it? No combustion, no pollution—including even carbon dioxide, the greenhouse gas accused of collecting in the atmosphere and warming the planet. We may not get our river back, but we'll breathe cleaner air. For clean kilowatts, hydro sure beats its only other real competitor, nuclear. Dams are never in danger of meltdown, and there are no messy toxic fission products to dispose of."

"I'm sorry to persist," interrupted Dale, "but let's not forget that Pacificorp stands to make big money from its investment, given the shortage of energy and the increase in demand in the Northwest—and the whole country, for that matter. With the price of electricity today, the Coquille is a river of liquid gold."

"Strange, Toolen never mentioned that! Let's see," Karen paused as she recalled the third letter of the coalition's acronym, "'R' is for 'renewable.' That's the easy one, and fascinating, too. Driven by gravity, water from the reservoir turns the generators and then is released to flow to the ocean, where it evaporates and falls as rain to replenish the reservoir and begin the cycle again. The sun provides the energy. I don't think we're in any danger of running out of sunshine anytime soon."

"You seem to be more excited than an objective reporter should be," Dale said jokingly.

"Perhaps, but you know I'm professionally objective, especially when I write about the new church softball league or the homecoming parade! And what about you, Commissioner Henson?" Karen reached in her coat pocket and pulled out a small pad. "My notes from our interview show that you favor a new license for the dam, too."

"Aha," replied Dale with some animation. "Your notes also show that I favor only retrofitting the dam, not adding to it. New and more efficient generators to replace the old ones that were shut down by the Public Utility District back in 1989 would increase the power output by half again, with very little additional impact on the environment. We would benefit from the electricity, which would be distributed locally, and the reservoir would continue to support recreation and modest irrigation."

"Yet, isn't it true that the original construction back in 1955 had a severe impact on the environment?" Karen's voice indicated that she, too, was more argumentative, but with the intention of provoking Dale to clarify her own thoughts on the issues. "Look at what happened to the salmon runs. With no way for the fish to get over the dam to their spawning ground upstream, the salmon population collapsed. And the river downstream from the dam: no more whitewater rapids and no more lush vegetation. What about the tidal marshes at Bandon, where the Coquille meets the Pacific? They were changed permanently by the reduced flow. Then there's the reservoir, which drowned hundreds of acres of forest and displaced the Indians."

"No one can deny that all these things happened," Dale responded. "Back then dams were being built throughout the country. The good citizens of Coos Bay, including my father, didn't want to be left out of a good thing. And this gorge was the perfect place to construct a hydroelectric facility. I'm not being flippant when I say all that is water over the dam."

She paused. "Sure, we should lament the destructive consequences for the environment. But that was fifty years ago. We simply didn't know better. The dam's production was modest compared to those massive concrete arch dams—Hoover and Grand Coulee. Still, the 4 megawatts of electricity it generated were a big economic boost for the county. The environment has adjusted. You have to admit, the reservoir adds a lot to the beauty of the place."

Dale shifted topics to answer all of Karen's concerns. "And a lot of good things happened, even to the Indians. Sure, I remember how sad it was, at least for me, when I first learned about that episode in my high school social studies class. Several tribes—all small, poor, with no federal tribal status and little recognition of their reservation rights—were removed from their traditional lands, which had been broken down into small parcels anyway. The rising waters of the reservoir inundated most of it. The Coos, Coquille, and Lower Umpqua tribes eventually confederated and built a tribal hall on the six-acre reservation that was finally granted to them."

"Nevertheless, they lost a great deal, didn't they?" Karen interjected.

"That's just half the story—the worst half," Dale continued. "The Indians are survivors. They've made the best of a bad situation and actually are much better off today, with two schools on the reservation, roads, and, most of all, several successful small businesses along the lake—all made possible by development around the dam."

Dale's thoughts turned assertive. "I'm caught in the middle, and happy to be there. I oppose those who want to breach the dam, empty the reservoir, and restore the Coquille River to its historic flow. And I equally oppose those, like the mayor and his coalition advisor, who want to reconstruct the dam and enlarge the reservoir. Now *that* would really impact the environment."

"We could leave well enough alone, couldn't we?" Karen asked. "Allow the dam to play its role as a pretty waterfall in a park?"

"And miss the opportunity to help the people of Coos County?" Dale asked incredulously. "With the price of electrical power soaring and relentless pressure in Washington to rely more and more on fossil fuel, especially coal, how can we fail to act and restore what the professionals call 'a deadbeat dam'? Economically and environmentally, it's the right thing to do."

"Being in the middle means being crushed between the extremes," reflected Karen with only slight exaggeration.

"With pithy sayings like that we know that philosophy is not your calling," Dale said. "Actually, you're right. Political moderates alienate almost everybody. I take solace from the remark you made about me two years ago, though, when the commission was debating approval of a new high-rise office building down by the docks. You said I was a 'radical moderate.' I liked it then, and I like it now."

Karen smiled and looked at her watch. "It's getting late, and I know we both have work this afternoon. Besides, I'm hungry. Want to have lunch at the barbecue grill we passed on our way up?"

"Love to," Dale responded, "but only if they have moderately hot sauce!"

Several days later, as Dale walked to her office, she noticed someone waiting for her arrival. She recognized him immediately: Norman Jenson, owner of extensive cranberry bogs a few miles north of the city, a friend of her father, and one of the more dedicated environmentalists in Coos County.

"Norman, how are you?" Dale said, giving him a hug. "I'm so sorry. Have you been waiting long? Did we have an appointment?"

"No," he responded with a smile. "You know me. I don't make appointments. I just show up. Makes a bigger impression."

Dale unlocked the door, and they entered her office.

"Here, please sit down," she said. "I would offer you some coffee, but the coffeemaker broke down last week, and I just haven't replaced it yet."

"That's fine," Norman responded, "I have something more stimulating than caffeine, if you can spare a few minutes."

"Of course I can," Dale responded as she took the chair next to him.

"Have you seen today's *Courier*?" he asked, unfolding a copy of the paper he carried. "It has a big interview with the mayor. All about how he plans to endorse the sale of the Chapman Gorge Dam to Pacificorp at the relicensing hearing next week. I've known Henry a long time. That's why I never voted for him. But this is the most ill-advised scheme he's ever promoted," said Norman, obviously agitated.

Dale smiled. Few people were as forthcoming as Norman about politics—or about any topic. Yet she had always respected his opinions, however strongly expressed. He backed up his opinions with arguments, often well articulated. She credited her turn toward the legal field in part to his influence.

"I know where you stand," he continued, "and though I disagree, at least it's a lot closer to my position than the mayor's is. Maybe I can convince you to see it my way."

"You are very welcome to try," Dale said, "but you know it will be hard to change my testimony at the hearing."

"Perhaps, but you can show those regulators on the panel just how dangerous Henry's position is."

"Norman, you and I have never talked about the dam, but my guess is that you'd like to see it completely dismantled," Dale said.

"I would, indeed," Norman responded. "You don't remember what the river was like before they built the dam. There were rapids in the lower gorge; lots of deer, moss, and ferns; and small farms above the floodplains. You could fish for trout along the way, and every year salmon would push upstream by the thousands. Sure, some of the trout have returned now that water flows over the dam regularly, but nobody can eat them—too much mercury."

"Mercury?" Dale inquired.

"Yes, last year the state Department of Fisheries found high levels of mercury in the trout and other fish. They were surprised, too."

"What was the source?" Dale asked.

"According to the report, high levels of bacteria in the reservoir, especially in the silt that built up behind the dam over the years—the same silt that should be reaching the marshes at Bandon and supporting all kinds of life. They even found traces of selenium, which is such a problem further south with the dams on the San Joaquin River in California.

"And while we're talking about fish," Norman continued, "the salmon will never return until the dam is breached. There's no way any new and bigger structure can leave room for ladders to help the fish around the dam, not in that narrow gorge. And there are other kinds of pollution, too." Norman leaned toward Dale to project his point. "All that talk about clean energy is bunk. According to what I've read in the literature from that group Oregon Rivers Unlimited, the decaying vegetation in and around large reservoirs gives off greenhouse gases the same as fossil fuels. The Chapman Gorge project will triple the size of the reservoir, killing thousands of trees and massive amounts of other vegetation. Sure, it will produce lots of cheap electricity, but clean and green? That's just not true."

Dale remembered receiving material from the Oregon river group, but she had set it aside as part of an ever-growing stack of environmental promotion mail that she simply did not have time to read. She was glad that Norman had done her work for her.

"I know you have work to do, and I appreciate that you're giving me this time to have my say. I have a couple of other things to get off my chest. They won't take long, and I'll be on my way," said Norman, almost apologetically.

"Look, I don't see you very often, and mixing important business with pleasure is the best way I can think of to spend any hour of my day," Dale responded.

"I'm a member of Friends of the Bay, a group that looks out for the health of Coos Bay and the estuaries nearby. This area includes the mouth of the Coquille at Bandon. The marshlands there are very special places. They survived the damage from the original construction at Chapman Gorge, but the new plans to control the river almost entirely with a taller dam are deeply worrisome to my group. The salt water from the ocean combines with the freshwater from the river to form a very nice place that is full of nutrients and attractive to all kinds of wildlife. Choking the river will create a tremendous imbalance, beginning with saltier water and a reduction in nutrients, not to mention serious increases in chemical toxins from the silting of the reservoir we've talked about already and fertilizer and pesticide runoff from larger irrigated croplands. Chapman Gorge is only fifteen miles from the Pacific—as close to the ocean as any dam its size in the country. No one knows precisely the effects of the larger dam on these estuaries. We do know they will be destructive."

They were interrupted by someone opening the office door. It was Dale's first appointment of the day. She invited the lady to come in and take a seat, while she and Norman stepped outside.

137

"I apologize for taking up so much of your time," Norman said, "but I have one final point. All that extra electricity—where do you think it'll go? Not here; we don't need it. It'll go to Eugene, Portland, Seattle, and even, God forbid, California. The mayor seems to think that all those new tourists and the jobs they'll bring to the county are worth it, but the Coquille Confederation of Indians won't like it. They lost much of their traditional land with the first dam, and they stand to lose much more now. They've already come out against the deal. In fact, the confederation president told me that where's there's a dam, there's a tribe underneath. And the small farmers downstream—how will they compete with the big agricultural industry when so much more water is there for irrigation? It's not just a matter of clean energy to fight global warming or to save the Arctic National Wildlife Refuge from the oil companies or for cheaper potatoes and corn or to power our home computers. It's about local folks who stand to lose even as they gain, and the marshes and the river, which are declared more beautiful even as they're destroyed. I know that sounds crazy, but think about it."

"Did you ever consider running for mayor, Norman?" Dale said with some seriousness. "You're very persuasive."

"Thanks, my dear. Your dad raised a great daughter and an attorney who actually listens! But I won't know for sure if you're persuaded until you act on it. A lot of folks will be at that meeting. They need persuading, too."

They hugged again and said goodbye, and Norman walked away.

Dale hesitated before returning to her office and her waiting client, but her mind remained on Karen's article in the *Courier* and Norman's powerful arguments. A new and enlarged dam would have serious effects on the Coquille River environment. Yet despite their addiction to development and profits, the mayor and his Pacificorp lobbyist did have their points. The project would contribute to easing the larger crisis of energy, particularly in reducing pollution and generating renewable energy. She had to smile when a cherished mantra of the environmental movement jumped into her mind: "Think globally, act locally." Dale realized that she faced a conflict of both imperatives. Perhaps being in the middle was her attempt to balance the two and bring about the greatest justice for the Indians, the forests, the estuaries near Bandon, and the larger earth beyond her hometown. Or perhaps not.

Commentary

This case is an interesting mix of issues—politics, economics, ecology, consumption, and social justice—each with a range of morally significant options that carry benefits and harms. Nonetheless the case, complex as it is, can be approached by focusing on a single set of possible actions regarding the future of the Chapman Gorge Dam. Should this "deadbeat dam" provide the foundation for an ambitious enhancement of its electrical generating capacity, as the mayor of Coos Bay and his lobbyist advocate? Should it be improved but not enlarged, as Dale prefers? Or should it be razed, unleashing the Coquille River to run free again—the option preferred by Norman, the passionate environmentalist?

Before entering this fray, we should examine the larger context of the place of dams in recent history. For much of the twentieth century, the United States engaged in a concerted effort to dam as many rivers as possible. Beginning with Hoover Dam on the Colorado River, Grand Coulee on the Columbia, and the massive Tennessee Valley Project during the Great Depression, Americans sought to utilize the potential of stored water to generate electrical power, irrigate crops, control flooding, and slake the thirst of growing cities, especially in western states. Bruce Babbitt, secretary of the interior during the Clinton administration, once said, "On average, we have constructed one dam every day since the signing of the Declaration of Independence"—an amazing total of 75,000 dams of all sizes, shapes, and functions. About 2,300 of these dams are hydroelectric facilities.[1]

That age is over. Most rivers with hydroelectric potential have been dammed, and the environmental movement has raised the collective consciousness about the damaging consequences of dams on riverine systems and the surrounding natural landscape. Indeed, the trend has been reversed, with several smaller dams breached in recent years to restore natural flows in the rivers they blocked. Advocates of natural rivers now take the opportunity provided by relicensing hearings to make their case for decommissioning of larger dams. The FERC exercises this authority every thirty to fifty years for individual projects. Fifty years ago there were few complaints when the original Chapman Gorge Dam was constructed. Today, however, with the emphasis on diminishing salmon populations—caused in large part by the loss of their river runs and spawning areas and the radical alteration of the landscape—this dam probably would never have been built.

What is true for the United States is not yet true for the rest of the world. Forty percent of irrigated land worldwide relies on water provided by dams, which also generate nearly 20 percent of the world's electricity. No wonder, then, that developing nations are engaged in massive projects to conquer their rivers. About 60 percent of the Earth's large rivers have been affected. The trend is likely to continue unabated as this percentage grows much larger.[2]

The benefits of large dams are irresistible. In addition to generating cheap electricity—often in great quantities—and other benefits, such as water for expanded agriculture and domestic use and flood control, dams often create large lakes that enhance tourism and its supportive business enterprises. For people like Mayor Kelly, whose minds and values are shaped by economic concerns, these benefits are paramount. In this utilitarian attitude, a rising reservoir raises all boats in that everyone derives some material advantage from the improvement of the dam. This is true even for the Indians—although, as we shall see, the benefits they receive come with a much greater cost than those enjoyed by most of the citizens of Coos County. We should recognize that the mayor is simply carrying out the responsibilities of his office in promoting the new dam. He is charged with protecting and developing the economic well-being of Coos Bay.

The advantages of hydroelectric power also include helping the environment—or so we are told by Mr. Toolen, who represents the hydropower industry. Rushing water, impelled by gravity, powers turbines and generates electricity. Because gravity generates no pollution, the process is perfectly clean. Through the hydrologic cycle of evaporation and rainfall, the water eventually returns to the reservoir to repeat its trip through the turbines. Clean and cheap, abundant and renewable—hydroelectricity has no rival. In a vigorous and growing economy, the demand for energy also is growing, taxing the ability of energy industries to provide it in abundance. Although "alternative" energy sources—such as wind, photoelectric, geothermal, and hydrogen technologies—show considerable promise, the United States continues to rely heavily on fossil fuels, including oil, natural gas, and coal, for its generation of electricity.

Pollutants from fossil fuel combustion damage the atmosphere and cause serious health risks. They are heavily regulated by the federal government. Most people agree, as well, that the major by-product of fossil fuel combustion, carbon dioxide—released into the air in millions of tons annually—is a primary greenhouse gas. Every kilowatt generated by hydroelectric facilities, especially during periods of peak demand, saves the release of these pollutants from fossil-fueled plants, which otherwise would be stoked to their maximum production.

As Norman points out, this picture is incomplete. Certainly, *production* of hydroelectricity is pollution free, but when the larger context of the reservoir is included the picture is less cheery. Decaying vegetation is its own source of carbon dioxide and methane. A taller dam means a larger lake, and for some time following its construction the vegetation inundated by its rising waters will produce these gases. Their release into the atmosphere must be factored into the savings in fossil fuel pollutants prevented by the use of the dam's electricity.

Pacificorp is to "big electricity" as Exxon is to "big oil." Despite the green rhetoric of its representative, Mr. Toolen, one can imagine that the company's essential interests are in producing and marketing an increasingly scarce but greatly demanded product. This is not to say, of course, that the company has no environmental sensitivity but to suggest that its social responsibilities are subordinated to its profit interest, as is necessary in the competitive system. By emphasizing the "CCRP" promotion of hydropower, Pacificorp can gain additional leverage with the state legislature and the citizens of Coos Bay and be well received at the FERC hearing. This is not to claim hypocrisy on the part of Toolen or the industry he represents. It is the business of business to contribute to the greater material welfare by providing an essential service within a free-market system. By acting completely in its own self-interests, as well as those of its stockholders, the industry would defend its actions as producing consequences that benefit the larger community.

Whatever these advocates of the larger dam claim about its favorable consequences for tourism, the bottom line, and the general welfare, this kind of thinking raises serious moral questions for human and nonhuman life—questions that broadly concern justice. The Indians represent several of these issues of justice. The history of the interaction of the local tribes with the federal government is not a happy one. They struggled for decades to attain recognition as tribes, thereby receiving the legal reservation rights that accompany that status. More than 300 Native American communities in the United States enjoy tribal status, with others in various states of application. Some smaller tribal groups are legally nonexistent in the eyes of the federal government because they refused to enter into treaties with the United States in the nineteenth century. The small tribes around Coos Bay originally were marginalized by their invisibility; as a result, some of their traditional lands were parceled out, with ownership passing to farmers and others. Confederation was somewhat helpful, but it failed to give the tribes the power to have their interests fully recognized. The new dam project would result in the disappearance of yet more of their land beneath the expanded reservoir.

Although Dale grants that the predicament of the tribes and the historical treatment of them are reprehensible, she seems to emphasize the other half of the story. The Indians have done well with businesses related to the Chapman Gorge Reservoir. Economically, they have improved their condition with jobs, new roads, electrification of their community, new schools, and, one should expect, improved health care.

The ethical concerns go beyond this happy ending, however. One concern highlights a weakness in the utilitarian approach of recommending actions with consequences that bring the greatest benefits to the greatest number of person who are affected by the action—the so-called "Principal of Utility" (see chapter 1). The catch is that the "greatest number affected by the action" does not necessarily include *all* who are affected. Utilitarianism simply requires that the most preferable moral action maximize the average good for everyone who is affected. There is no obvious insistence that this good, the benefits of that action, or the costs of achieving it should be distributed equally to everyone involved. Some may receive more benefits than others for no good reason, in violation of the principle of *distributive* justice. Some may be required to bear greater costs than others, even if they also receive benefits, in violation of the principle of *contributive* justice.

With respect to the tribal federation both principles are violated, although one could argue that because the tribes received considerable economic benefits from the original dam and stand to receive additional benefits from its enlargement, the requirements of distributive justice are met. The Indians might beg to disagree, however. This is not the case with contributive justice. No other group involved in the construction of the dam paid so dearly for their benefits. The small farmers and perhaps the fishermen will join the Indians in paying further for reconstruction. The farmers will find themselves in a less-than-competitive position with the inevitable growth of agribusiness, given the abundance of irrigation water promised by the new dam. The fishermen, whose livelihood vanished with the precipitous decline in salmon stocks, will now surrender all hope of recovery if the Pacificorp purchase is approved. The tribes lost their traditional hunting lands—and with them a good part of their culture. Even the development and improvements brought by the dam as blessings contributed to this cultural impoverishment. These costs are not incurred by the non-Indian community of Coos Bay—certainly not by most others in Oregon and the Northwest who will profit from "CCRP" hydropower from Chapman Gorge.

Apart from the inequitable distribution of costs and benefits, another question of justice is to be found here, again affecting primarily Native Americans, small farmers, and fishermen. All business transactions carry some degree of risk; such is the nature of capitalism. With Pacificorp and the city of Coos Bay these risks, which appear to be minimal, are well-understood, factored into future strategies, and mitigated in various ways by good business practices. These groups are the *voluntary* risk takers. Questions of justice concern the *involuntary* risk takers: the Indians, farmers, and fishermen. These groups, which are most at risk from the plans for the dam, also have the least say in their destinies and less control over the negative possibilities that accompany the risks. Indeed, "risk" is too weak a term here because it is virtually certain that these groups will suffer from the new dam. This combination

142

of loss of control over their future combined with vulnerability brought on by the outcomes of decisions made without their contributions results, once again, in a frustration of justice.

Norman makes the additional point that the electricity generated by the new dam is not needed by Coos Bay. Instead, Pacificorp will export it to other regions. Likewise, the vast amount of produce from expanded agriculture is more likely to be consumed in Los Angeles than in southwest Oregon. Despite the economic advantages that remain in Coos Bay, these consequences of regional, national, and international corporations harvesting resources of particular areas for consumption elsewhere represent a reallocation of benefits and raise an additional question of justice. In developing nations it represents a far greater problem than in the United States because of increased poverty among greater numbers of people living around the impacted area, lack of responsible governmental oversight, willingness to put development first at all costs, and the need to pay off heavy international debts.

Dale is impressed by Norman's point and reflects on the irony of the environmentalist mantra, "Think globally, act locally." Restoring and expanding Chapman Gorge Dam will bring inevitable impacts, good and bad, upon the people and natural environment of the Coquille River watershed and the marshes at Bandon. If Toolen is to be believed, however, the "CCRP" benefits will be enjoyed by all Americans and, indeed, by peoples of the earth, as well as the earth itself as a planetary ecosystem. Considerable pollution will be avoided by the increased availability of hydroelectricity. With Chapman Gorge on line and with other alternative energy sources, perhaps even the National Arctic Wildlife Refuge would be spared the damage of invasive drilling for the extraction of oil.

Quite possibly, Norman—despite his enthusiasm for the natural environment of Coos County—feels conflicted in advocating a position that would cancel out this global good. Perhaps not. He could argue that if all our rivers ran free and the conduct of Americans reflected that value, we would not need either the oil or the hydropower in the first place. There is something to be said for this position. Americans—and, increasingly, humanity at large—define themselves largely in terms of material pursuits. We have an insatiable appetite for power sufficient to liberate us from material limitations. "Know no limits" is the bracing claim of one credit card company. Our consumption of energy and goods is fueled by overriding consumer values that often conflict with traditional values of the good citizen.

This kind of discussion can turn sermonic quickly because it is a shift from the ethics of utilitarianism and even human dignity and justice to an ethics of virtue. What counts is not what one does but who one is. Virtues have to do

143

with standards of excellence in human conduct that classically have included temperance and fortitude, or what we would call today moderation and discipline. Virtue ethics also includes a willingness to subordinate personal desires for the good of the larger community—the expression of the time-honored virtue of *civitas*. This virtue certainly is not encouraged by the prevailing philosophy of radical individualism or that of a free-market economy, with its insistence on increasing consumption of material goods as an expression of personal fulfillment. Another revealing commercial slogan: "Some things are priceless; for everything else there's MasterCard." Yet every commercial that ends with this bit of wisdom begins with a happy family or personal event that would not have been possible without the credit card. Despite the warm conclusion, it seems that one can charge even priceless experiences.

Political advocates of expanded use of fossil fuels to meet growing energy needs want to maintain the "lifestyle" of Americans. Norman and many others would recommend otherwise. A good dose of constraint and conservation would reduce levels of energy consumption and therefore the need to build thousands of additional power plants. In other words, there is a direct relation between our energy crisis and our collective character as a people.

The costs of enlarging the dam are not limited to humans. The salmon and the saltwater marshes also stand to lose. Dams in the Pacific Northwest have had a major impact on the natural production of salmon. When the fish are denied access to their natural spawning grounds upriver from the dams, the levels of their historic populations plummet. So-called fish ladders or artificial waterfalls by the dams ease the problem only slightly. Even if some fish are successful in reproducing, the smolt—immature salmon the size of minnows—depend on the river current to carry them downstream. They often lose their way in reservoirs or are killed while passing through turbines. Hatcheries offer some remedy, but biologists are concerned with the reduction of the gene pool of some species in the process of artificial reproduction. The danger, of course, is not only to the livelihood of fishermen but also to the diversity of the sea as species of salmon continue to arrive on the endangered species list.

Wetlands on the deltas of rivers affected by dams fare no better. They depend on the nutrients swept downriver and on the flushing action of the river to maintain the variety and quality of plant and animal residents. Diminished flows alter radically the makeup of the wetlands and open them to invasions by opportunistic or exotic species, as well as to accumulation of toxic pollution from nearby towns and cities.

All in all, dams are deceptively simple. They are huge concrete and earthen plugs that create lakes and generate power. Their repercussions, however, good and bad, are many. And they raise serious and complex moral questions—as the characters in this case realize only too well.

Questions for Discussion

1. Hydropower is clean, cheap, and renewable. These characteristics are economic and environmental requirements for an energy source. Why, then, are many environmentalists opposed to hydropower?
2. Local Native American tribal communities are among those who apparently would profit most from a new Chapman Gorge dam. Why do they oppose it?
3. While new dam construction is under attack in the United States, huge projects are underway in many developing countries. Through Internet research, identify three such projects. What are the moral issues with the dams in these cases?
4. Dale wants to maintain the old dam. Her position lies somewhere between removing the old dam entirely to establish a free-flowing Coquille River and constructing an even larger dam. Do you accept her arguments for the status quo? Give reasons for your opinion.

Notes

1. American Rivers website, www.americanrivers.org.
2. "Dams and Development: A New Framework for Decision-Making," World Commission on Dams report (November 16, 2000); available at www.dams.org/report (accessed February 12, 2003).

For Further Reading

American Rivers website, www.americanrivers.org.

Boyle Robert. "Can You Spare a Dam?" *Amicus Journal* 20 (fall 1998): 18–26.

"Dams and Development: A New Framework for Decision-Making." World Commission on Dams report, November 16, 2000. Available at www.dams.org/report (accessed February 12, 2003).

Lowry, William. *Dam Politics: Restoring America's Rivers.* Washington, D.C.: Georgetown University Press, 2003.

Reisner, Marc. "Coming Undammed," *Audubon* 100 (September–October, 1998): 58–66.

Robbins, Elaine. "Damning Dams." *E: The Environmental Magazine* 10 (January 1999): 14.

United States Society on Dams website, www.uscid.org/~uscold/.

9

Nature Creates Deserts, Too:
Addressing Desertification in China

As Lin Xu walked out of the provincial office building to start his long bus ride home, he was preoccupied with worry. At the next meeting he and others would discuss a proposed government plan for addressing desertification in the Sanjiangyuan. Two years earlier he had left his job as assistant manager of a small factory outside Beijing to move back to his native Qinghai Province because his parents were old and needed him. His father was a herder on the Tibetan plateau and could no longer travel the long distances required to find winter forage for his herd. Neither of his parents wanted to leave Qinghai, and he was the only son, so it was his job to take care of them. He had not even tried to convince them to come live with him; his two-room apartment in the city was too small for them and Lin's own family, and they would have been miserable in the middle of the industrial area. So he had moved his wife and son to his parents' village and again become a herder, as he had been before he left home.

Last year he had been chosen to represent a group of local villages at a meeting that was part of the government's attempt to assess the agricultural environment in northwestern China. At that meeting Lin had described the desertification as racing, not creeping, across his area of Qinghai. This rapid desertification forced the herders to leave their contracted allotments in the wintertime—because the allotments no longer had enough grasses to support the herds—and move the herds into other counties; there had even been sporadic violence. He recognized that this process only advanced the desertification, both by overgrazing of the areas not yet desertified and by allowing the rats to multiply and further degenerate the abandoned grassland, but he insisted that the herders had no alternatives. They lived at subsistence level already. Population levels had been dropping for more than a decade as young people left to find work elsewhere. Now the desertification had become so severe that many of the lakes, rivers, and wells had dried up. For the past two summers Lin's own village had had to buy water trucked in from a spring five kilometers away.

As a result of Lin's participation in that meeting, he had been appointed to another committee composed of government officials in agriculture and environment from all of the provinces that were part of the Sanjiangyuan, the three-rivers area of northwestern China—the area that formed the headwaters of the Yangtze, Yellow, and Lancang (further south called the Mekong) rivers. One-quarter of the water in the Yangtze, half of the water in the Yellow, and 15 percent of the water in the Lancang originated in the Sanjiangyuan area—at least it had, until the intensification of desertification in the 1990s.

As Lin participated in the work of the Sanjiangyuan environmental planning committee, he learned that desertification was a massive problem in China. Deserts occupy one-third of Chinese territory and grow by 2,400 square kilometers per year. More than 110 million people live in areas affected by desertification, and people in other areas are increasingly affected as well by the vicious sandstorms that blow off the desert areas. A desert dubbed "the heavenly desert" is now only 70 kilometers from Beijing—and moving closer. The rate of desertification in China, the experts said, is eighteen times the world average.

In these meetings Lin learned about several ways in which the people of his village were increasing the local desertification. When their contracted grazing lands were no longer sufficient for their herds, most were forced to reduce the size of their herds. To make up for the lost income, many became facai diggers. Facai is a black moss that grows in the barren hills and is a popular food in south China. They also dug up the grassland for licorice root—a basic ingredient in many Chinese folk medicines. With land cover already sparse, such digging, he was told, accelerates desertification, though without it half the local populations would starve in the winters. Until the water ran out, some of them also were cultivating small gardens, even expanding them as other income sources dried up. Abandoned

147

cultivated areas also contributed to desertification because there was no longer anything to hold the topsoil in place.

What now had Lin worried was the plan that the experts were devising for the Sanjiangyuan area. Although many of the experts agreed on what should be done for specific areas, they disagreed on general goals. One of the problems was that desertification seemed to have many different causes, and one of them seemed to be climate change.

Some of the environmental officials from the State Environmental Protection Agency had argued that nothing should be attempted to reverse the general pattern of desertification caused by climate or climate change, both because such efforts were largely doomed to failure and because attempts to reclaim these lands would eat up China's limited resources, which were better saved for reclamation efforts that had a chance of success. Instead, they argued, efforts should be channeled into reversing the desertification that was caused or accelerated by human activities. The environmental officials emphasized sustainability: Efforts should go toward restoring land that could then be self-sustaining without additional inputs to continually restore it.

Agricultural officials, on the other hand, emphasized China's need to reclaim as much usable land as possible—not only farmland and pasture but forests as well. They pointed out again and again that China has one-quarter of the world's population but only 7 percent of the world's arable land and that since 1949 one-fifth of that arable land had been lost to desertification and erosion. China's forest coverage is only 13.9 percent—about half the world average—and rapid deforestation, which had been halted by government decree only the previous year, had contributed to desertification. One-third of China is now desert—more than twice its amount of arable land. For these officials, sustainability could not focus only on sustaining resources and animal habitat; it also had to include sustaining the entire population—as well as sustaining economic growth.

The environmental officials objected that such thinking had been responsible for the "reclamation" in the northern province of Heilongjiang, in which thousands of young soldiers and revolutionaries between the 1950s and 1970s had turned the wetlands of Heilongjiang into farms to produce food for China's masses. The aggressive agricultural development turned millions of hectares of swamps, marshes, and forests into farms, but by the 1990s the devastating consequences were clear: The area, which once had served as a sponge to hold and slowly release water that otherwise would cause floods, became subject to tremendous erosion that silted up the rivers and caused the most destructive flooding ever recorded. The weather changed, hailstorms battered the area, and native bird and animal

148

populations disappeared. Now large parts of Heilongjiang were being reclaimed again—this time back to wetland—at a cost of billions of yuan. Land use, they concluded, must be based first not on the needs of the human population but on the soil, climate, and natural contours of the land.

Lin and the two other representatives of local populations in the Sanjiangyuan area thought that sustainability also should include sustaining the local population. Lin did not think that the needs or desires of the human population were the only criteria for resource planning, and he accepted the need for state regulation. In fact, he had argued with many of his neighbors, who thought that the government plan should focus on restoring the local herding economy. His parents' friends had insisted that the local culture was based on herding and spoke of the large herds that they and their parents had maintained over many years; these herds had provided an adequate income for whole families.

"When the herds were large," Lin's old neighbor, Hui, had repeated, "only a few children left for the cities. Most stayed here and took over their parents' herds."

Lin did not think such times would return soon. He was afraid that if government efforts to improve the pastureland were successful, the local people would simply increase herd size until the land was once again degraded, and then supplement their income from smaller herds by digging up the facai and licorice root—and the cycle would repeat itself. Yet he also was afraid that although the plan might be good for the land and good for the future of China, it might not provide for the present and future welfare of the peoples who lived in the Sanjiangyuan.

Both of the other two Qinghai village representatives were Muslim, and they felt this fear even more strongly. They spoke of greater suffering among their people, extending over generations. They told stories of the great famine of 1929—in which their grandparents had seen cannibalism—and the famine of 1960, in which they had been forced to eat tree bark and seeds to survive. If the new plan called for enforcement of bans on herding and grass digging, many villagers would be forced to starve. Muslim residents of Qinghai had even less trusting relations with the government than the rest and would not easily accept such regulations.

The night before Lin was to leave for the next meeting, he confided his worries to his wife, Mu, as she prepared a herbal tea for his father's persistent cough. "I don't understand how the committee can hope to draw the lines accurately between the different areas," he said. "The experts are clear that a few areas have been desert for many generations and that climate change has been expanding those

149

areas. For most of the areas, however, we have no idea when they became desert or whether they became desert because of climate change or human activities, so how can we know what parts are reclaimable and which not?"

"But surely the people who live there know how the state of the land has changed between their own time and that of their parents and grandparents," Mu suggested.

"Not really. They focus on a bad weather year or famines—dramatic events that stick out in their memories or in the stories of the elders. They can tell how the size of their herds decreased from generation to generation, but the degeneration of the land is so gradual that they only know the year that there was so little grass that they had to slaughter much of their herds. Many of the allotments were deliberately cut up to include both dry and grassy areas; it was easy to miss the gradual shrinking of the grassy areas. And they weren't aware that as the grass gradually decreased, they failed to reduce herd size, so they overgrazed the land. It seems almost impossible to distinguish the natural from the human causes of desertification. So how can the experts making this plan possibly know where it can be reversed and where not?"

Mu sighed. "Why are you so anxious about this? You are not responsible for the plan. It will not be you who will be judged on whether it succeeds or not. It is up to the experts to decide."

"But what they decide will determine whether there are any people left in this region of Qinghai when our son is grown," he said. Mu was silent, unwilling to upset Lin by reopening their disagreement over returning to Beijing after his parents died, as she preferred. She wanted to resume her work as a pharmacist's assistant and to send their son to the better schools that were available in the city.

When Lin arrived at the meeting the following afternoon, he saw a huge map of Qinghai on the wall, with vivid colors demarcating the new proposed sectors of the environmental plan. As the vice-governor explained, the center of the new proposal was a nature reserve of 31.8 million hectares, covering parts of sixteen counties in southern Qinghai. Twenty-five closed areas, totaling 6.2 million hectares, were to be protected areas for the endangered wildlife that live there, which included thirty species of birds and twelve animal species. No logging or other human activities were to be allowed in the closed areas. Lin noted that this area included the reserve patrolled by the famous game warden Zhaba Duojie. Zhaba had worked to stop gangs of armed men in four-wheel-drive pickup trucks from hunting the endangered chiru antelope for the soft fur under its chin that is used to make shahtoosh shawls. Trade in the shawls is outlawed globally, but on the black market such shawls sell for as much as $10,000. On

November 8, 1999, local officials announced that Zhaba had committed suicide by shooting himself in the head. Environmental experts in the capital became suspicious, especially after they learned that there were three bullets in Zhaba's head, and the case became infamous throughout China.

The vice-governor continued, explaining that the closed area of the nature reserve also contained several sectors that had been logged and required immediate replanting of trees, as well as degraded grasslands that required action to control the rat population and then would be seeded with native grasses. The plan included the building of an ecological research and monitoring station in the reserve and enforcement of the ban on human activities.

Circling this closed center zone of nature preserve would be a 5 million hectare buffer zone, designed to be half open and half closed. The open areas would be available to herders for grazing of sheep and cattle in limited numbers that would be monitored and adjusted annually. Outside this second zone was to be a 20.6 million hectare multifunction test zone to be used for scientific experiments and tourism.

All three of the village representatives immediately checked to see in which sector their own areas were located. They all discovered that that their villages were in the multifunction test zone, and their questions to the planners focused on these zones.

"What does multifunction test zone mean?" Lin asked. "Will we be allowed to herd as in the past? What about our grazing allotments?"

The answers from the officials were neither clear nor reassuring.

"It depends," they said, "on the condition of the land in specific areas of the allotments. Most of the allotments were able to sustain herding in recent decades, so they probably can be restored relatively quickly with a temporary herding ban of only a couple of years—if funding is available to plant trees as windbreaks, for rat control, and for reseeding large barren areas. While the bans are in place, families will receive maintenance food supplies. But it all depends on the level of funding; we may have to concentrate the funding on a few areas for a few years, and then move the funding to other areas. Local officials will have to decide if herding is to be allowed in areas that are designated for reclamation for which funds are not yet available, but if there is herding the numbers will be strictly controlled. And, needless to say, all grassland digging will be forbidden, and herd size will continue to be controlled on the basis of the condition of the land after it is restored."

At the end of the meeting, Lin waited for his bus with the two Muslim village delegates. All were upset at the news they had to take back to their villages. The Muslims especially were distrustful of the promise that the government would send food supplies to sustain the people while the ban on herding lasted. "We know what will happen," said one. "The first shipment will arrive late, the second later, and the third not at all. It will enrich some bureaucrat."

Lin acknowledged that this scenario was possible. He was even more concerned about whether his local land would continue to support the present reduced population, much less the former levels of population that his people hoped for. If the number of sheep and cattle that could graze on each allotment must decrease to stop the cycle of overgrazing, the allotment sizes would have to increase for people to be able to earn enough to support their families, especially with a ban on digging. That meant that there would be fewer allotments—perhaps many fewer, if not all the previous allotments were restorable. Fewer allotments meant fewer families.

Lin wondered how the officials—those who would decide which sections of allotment could be reclaimed and which couldn't—would make that decision. In his former factory, such decisions about productivity had always required a baseline for comparison, but here he saw no useable baseline. Each of the farmers in his village knew his own allotment and could have selected without much trouble the parts that until recently had been among the most fertile, even if the borders of such areas were unclear. Would the bureaucrats who were drawing up the rules choose to reclaim these parts that had been lost only recently? Would they even have any idea which parts had been fertile until recently—or could be again? Nothing was said at the meeting about conferring with the allotment holders before working out the rules of the local plans. As he climbed on the bus for the long ride home, he wished that he had more faith in the experts or in the wisdom of the government. Instead, he reassured himself that if worst came to worst, he and Mu were educated and employable, and they could pack up his parents and take them back with them to Beijing if they had to.

Commentary

Global analysts are clear that China has made tremendous strides in industrialization in the past quarter-century. Yet this progress—which has raised the standard of living throughout China and eliminated the massive famines that, until recently, killed millions of people every few years—came at a high environmental price. Eight of the ten international cities with the most polluted air are in China. Much of south China is faced with a massive water shortage, and before most logging was halted in 2000, China had lost millions of hectares of forest. This synopsis of environmental concerns does not even mention problems with garbage, toxic waste, and endangered animal and plant populations. Not until the mid-1990s did China begin to face the extent of its environmental quagmire. The first step was to seek funding to research the extent of the problem and begin monitoring. By 2000 several projects had begun.

Urban issues, not desertification, generally take top priority in China. To the extent that the government does need to satisfy the peasantry, it looks primarily at the more densely settled rural areas. The Sanjiangyuan probably got the attention that it did because of concern over China's rivers. Not only were the major river systems increasingly given to silting and flooding; long stretches of major rivers were actually drying up. The Sanjiangyuan was a likely place to begin addressing the silting and the loss of water. Environmentalists pointed out that restoring forests and grasslands would not only hold the soil in place so that it did not erode and silt up the rivers, causing flooding; it also would help to attract rain clouds and restore the original rainfall cycle.

Unclear Origin of the Problem

The Sanjiangyuan project is distinct from many of the current environmental projects in China today precisely for the reason that Lin points out: The problem is not simply one of human destruction or pollution; it is a complex web involving the interaction of natural destruction with human destruction, without any clear line of demarcation. For example, we know that although geography and weather patterns can aggravate pollution, human activities create the pollution, and we can test to detect which human activities in particular produce the problem. Faced with desertification, we have evidence of climate change that seems to have begun long ago, as well as overgrazing, logging, and widespread grass digging. We cannot even be sure that the desertification that began hundreds of years ago in the Sanjiangyuan was not itself initiated by overgrazing. We simply do not know. This lack of knowledge is very worrisome for Lin, who was trained in a scientific mind set. He wants a baseline—a constant to which all the subsequent experimental results can be compared. The case exposes what some people might regard as the soft underbelly of environmentalism: the fact that it is not entirely science-driven. Yes, ecologists use experimentation, measure results, and make comparisons. As we saw in the case of the Indonesian coral reefs, however (chapter 8), we cannot always take the time to do all the experiments that would be ideal. In the coral reefs case, the new fencing had not been tested for its effects on all elements of the coral reef habitat. In this case, the project had drawn the specific boundaries of the three zones arbitrarily, without a baseline study or historical data.

153

Precautionary Principle versus "Sound Science"

The reason for haste in both situations is the acuteness of the destructive processes, which could be seriously advanced in the years such studies would take. In many ways, this haste is an application of the precautionary principle—which calls us, in situations of serious risk in which there is not yet great clarity about the exact destructive process, to act in ways that are most likely to protect the biosphere. It may later turn out that some measures taken on the basis of the precautionary principle were unnecessary. This outcome is considered to be better, however, than refraining from action until the causes of an environmental problem are clear, only to find that it is too late to save the threatened parts of nature.

In many situations around the world, the precautionary principle has become the rallying cry of environmentalists, whereas "sound science" has been the slogan of those who favor economic development. Both sides agree that when an environmentally dangerous activity is identified and confirmed, it should be stopped. The differences arise when a destructive *consequence* has been identified but the *activity* that causes it has not been identified definitively. Environmentalists use the precautionary principle to argue that initial steps must be taken on the basis of the present state of scientific knowledge, without waiting for definitive results. Advocates of sound science insist that until definitive results are in, there are only guesses and that these guesses are too unreliable to be the basis of social decisions that affect the welfare of large numbers of people.

In this particular case, it is not clear how the committee could even go about obtaining the data that would be necessary for "sound science" to render a definitive result. Some of the most important missing data is historical: When did desertification begin in the Sanjiangyuan, and under what conditions? Was it being overgrazed? Were there any human activities that could have contributed to desertification at the time? In the decades since, what human activities have been present, at what levels, and did any of these activities correlate with increasing levels of desertification? There is simply no way to obtain this information from the past.

In fact, Lin has failed to note—and the committee has failed to explain—what will occur in the multifunction test zone. The intention for this huge zone is that different sections of it will be monitored for different kinds of interventions. For example, the initial condition of several sections will be assessed; then one of those sections will remain unchanged as the control, a second will have one type of experimental intervention, a third yet another type of intervention, and so on. Within five to ten years, scientists should have some clearer ideas about the different elements in the destructive processes. They can test to discover the level of herding at which grassland deteriorates; under what conditions rats multiply fastest; under what conditions, if any, digging for roots is not destructive.

Some kinds of experiments will be more difficult because they require a huge scale. Testing to discover what size replanted forest one needs to restore rainfall patterns to an area requires beginning with many thousands of hectares of replanted areas. This criterion represents a huge expenditure, given the possibility that it may turn out to be impossible to restore previous rainfall patterns. Lin is worried that his village may be prohibited from digging and may be forced to drastically reduce herd size—at great cost to individual families and the village community in general—when it is not clear that such measures will prove effective in restoring land. The cost of such measures is evident not only in individual and local sacrifice, however; such measures also can cost the nation of China millions of yuan that could be used to provide food, schools, and health care for Chinese who now lack these basics. Yet what is the alternative? Can China allow desertification to continue to destroy thousands of square miles of land every year?

Environmentalism in China

Environmentalism has been one of the most interesting new movements in China in the past decade; compared to other nations, China had a late start. At the level of government, environmental concerns long took a back seat to the drive to industrialize, to modernize, to export. Given China's history and the global political system, this dynamic is understandable. It also is typical of the governments of developing nations. China's involvement with environmentalism, however, is different from the experience of other developing nations with regard to nongovernmental organizations (NGOs) and religion.

The Chinese government continues to be largely intolerant of NGOs and religion. No foreign NGOs are allowed to operate in China, and native groups that in other nations would have set up as NGOs have been forced to find other organizational frameworks. Given China's recent openness—even warm invitation—to capitalist ventures, most fledgling environmental organizations have incorporated as for-profit agencies even though they never make any profit. Some have remained informal research groups that feed their findings to news media outside China. Others have made use of the increased freedom of the Chinese media to focus on specific environmental problems and have had great success at prompting government officials to intervene to protect specific animals and habitats, to deal with corruption that prevented implementation of environmental laws, and to institute new research.

The Chinese government's lack of tolerance for NGOs is related to its intolerance for religion. The government has never particularly enforced atheism and has been especially tolerant of native Chinese religions—as long as they are private, largely domestic, religions, without public or institutional aspects. The arrest, conviction, and imprisonment of thousands of Falun Gong members since the late 1990s is believed to be prompted by their organized challenge to the monopoly of the Chinese government in terms of social control. The government will not tolerate other organizations mediating between the government and its citizens. People can believe in their god(s) and worship as individuals or in their families, but religion must stay out of the public forum.

The treatment of NGOs in China stems from this same policy of unchecked government control. In many developing nations, NGOs wield tremendous power, especially when they are networked and can present a united front to the government. The fact that many NGOs in developing nations are funded by different institutions—often from a variety of different developed nations—and implement the policies and reporting rules of their funders tends to undermine effective networking, though exemplary networks exist in some areas of the world (e.g., South America). The reason NGOs wield such power within developing nations is that in many cases they have come to exercise some of the normal functions of government, which the local government is too poor or weak to carry out. In much of the developing world, for example, NGOs are the primary source of health care, especially in the areas of infant and maternal health, family planning, and HIV/AIDS prevention and treatment programs. Many NGOs have consistently better demographic data for their urban districts than does the government. In many nations NGOs are much more knowledgeable about the needs and status of the majority poor than are government agencies. In fact, many government agencies are largely dependent on NGOs for funding, supplies (e.g., government family planning programs), and data. Education is another area in which NGOs play essential roles in developing nations, especially religious schools.

The typical pattern is for environmental NGOs to take the same general shape as NGOs that have been working on health, nutrition, human rights, family planning, job creation, and housing in developing nations. Most are funded, at least in part, by foreign—sometimes international—agencies. This outside funding helps cover not only operating costs but also project costs. This is one reason for the influence that environmental NGOs wield: They can go to the governments of developing nations and say, "We have this plan for restoring this 25,000 hectare area of grassland so that it will again support thousands of people and animals, and we can supply 75 percent of the funds necessary, if you will agree to continue monitoring the area to see that it is not overgrazed again." China, however, has not tolerated other groups influencing public policy, so it has banned NGOs.

Chinese hostility to religion and NGOs has eliminated two of the most potent pillars that environmentalism has had in much of the developing world. At the grassroots level, religion has been the single most important impetus to environmental activism around the world. Among indigenous peoples, traditional religious mythology and rituals support attitudes of reverence for and connection to nature—which, in the context of varied environmental crises, easily translate into environmental activism. In the United States, Native American tribes and the Environmental Protection Agency (EPA) have been partners in a long list of lawsuits seeking redress of environmental destruction. One of the best known was the 1996 *Isleta Pueblo v. City of Albuquerque* decision, in which the federal district court agreed with the Pueblo tribe and the EPA that the city of Albuquerque, six miles upstream from the Pueblo reservation, could not pollute the water to such a degree that the Pueblo could not use it for religious ritual purposes or farming; instead, the city had to spend $300 million to upgrade its water purification system to ensure that the water downstream from Albuquerque was as clean as the water upstream from Albuquerque.[1] The tree-hugging women of South India, the Gikuyu Green Belt movement in Kenya, and the Amazon tribes fighting against botanical piracy and oil exploration there are only a few of the many examples of indigenous religion, with its sacred connection of a particular god, a particular people, with a particular habitat, supporting the protection of the biosphere.

In China, both Buddhism and Taoism could offer significant support to environmentalism if they were allowed to have a public role. Forests play a major role in Buddhism. Buddha himself retreated to the forest for meditation, he achieved enlightenment under a Bo tree, and he ordered his monks to spend the rainy season months in forest retreats. Buddhist monasteries frequently sit amid forest, and the forest is understood as conducive to meditation. Although this understanding of nature as useful for the human task of meditation grants nature only limited standing, the Buddhist principle of codependent origination reflects the basic environmental principle: the interconnectedness and interdependence of all creation.

In many ways Taoism is a nature religion. Its basic tenet urges humans to imitate nature and its harmony. In Taoism nature is more than simply a support for human spiritual awareness; nature is understood as enspirited—as having a reality of its own with which humans can commune and from whom they can learn. The folk elements of Taoism are especially imbued with this sense of nature as alive and communicative. Although the different elements of the biosphere are distinguished, there are no sharp divisions between humans (living and dead), animals, plants, streams, and oceans. Reverence for the whole and for all the elements that make up the whole is necessary.

For China's many peasants, folk Taoism meshes well with the awareness of and respect for nature that is common among farmers. But the lack of organization in Taoism—the lack of any centralized system for training Taoist priests or for affecting the Taoist traditions passed down in families—makes it difficult to bring the environmentalism that is implicit in Taoism to the foreground. This resource remains largely untapped.

The Confucian tradition works against environmentalism in a variety of ways, perhaps most centrally by supporting what has been a traditional Chinese characteristic: accepting the government's authority in many areas of life that in other societies are considered private or under the authority of other bodies. One important way this acceptance of governmental authority in "private," even familial, life has benefited the environmental movement involves the success of the one-child policy in China. Few other governments in the world could have successfully imposed a limit of one child on their urban population and two children on their rural population. Yet the Chinese people accepted both the necessity of the limitation and the authority of the government to impose it. If the one-child policy (which began in 1979) had not been implemented, the world would now have an additional billion people or more, and the environmental situation in China would be much worse than it is now. In other areas of environmental policy, however, the combination of the breadth of authority entrusted to the government and the enforced absence of other social institutions in China means that environmental protection there must rely almost exclusively on the government: Either the government must take the initiative in environmental protection or the government must be carefully prompted to implement environmental protection.

This is not to say that there are no individual initiatives regarding the environment. Some government agencies (e.g., health and family planning clinics) have encouraged local environmental actions such as litter collection, tree planting, and composting. In some places there are the beginnings of neighborhood recycling programs. The general citizen tendency, however, is to wait until the government has given some directions for action. Lin's wife, Mu, is typical in this regard. She does not understand why Lin is so worried. After all, the plan is the government's responsibility, not his, and government officials will be held responsible for any failures. Given this attitude among many Chinese, it is a good thing that in the past decade the Chinese government has shown greatly increased interest in its environment and in serious efforts to preserve and restore it.

Questions for Discussion

1. Why is desertification a serious issue for China?
2. How had the local herders added to the problem of desertification?

3. Compare the impacts of desertification with the impact of the new plan for addressing desertification for the local herders of Qinghai Province. Which does Lin Xu prefer, and why?
4. What is the role of the government in environmentalism in China, and how is it unusual compared to the government role in other nations?
5. Why is Lin Xu worried about the potential efficacy of the plan to restore the Sanjiangyuan? What does he think is its vulnerable point?

Note

1. When the Supreme Court declined to hear the case in 1998, the lower court decision stood. See D. D. Ford, "State and Tribal Water Quality Standards under the Clean Water Act: A Case Study," *Natural Resources Journal* 35, no. 4 (1995): 771–802.

For Further Reading

Bezlova, Antoaneta. "Environment—China: Desertification Eats Into Productive Land." *Environment Bulletin* (May 31, 2000); available at www.oneworld.net/ip52/may00/07-29-003.htm or IAC Expanded Academic Index 1998–.

"China Tackles Environment-Damaged Longest Inland River." Xinhua News Agency (July 25, 2000); available at IAC Expanded Academic Index 1998–.

"China's Ecological Environment Is Worsening." *Asiainfo Daily China News* (December 4, 2001); available at IAC Expanded Academic Index 1998–.

Jing, Zhang. "Environment-China: Province Curbs 'Aggressive' Agriculture." *Environment Bulletin* (May 12, 2000); available at IAC Expanded Academic Index 1998–.

Li, Changsheng. "China's Environment: A Special Report." *EPA Journal* 15, no. 3 (May–June 1989): 44–47.

Ng, Isabella, and Mia Turner. "Toxic China." *Time International* 153, no. 8 (March 1, 1999): 16–17.

Qi, Wu. "Environment-China: Sources of Great Rivers Under Threat." *Environment Bulletin* (October 15, 2000); available at IAC Expanded Academic Index 1998–.

Wang, Chenggang. "China's Environment in the Balance." *The World and I* 14, no. 10 (October 1999): 176*ff.*

10

Rewilding: Restoration of Degraded Ecosystems

"But Professor Wu, my father says that the restoration of the parcel will be beautiful, like a golf course, and his company will pay for it," Jenny exclaimed, without even raising her hand to be recognized by her biology teacher.

"Yes, yes," said Richard Wu. "I know what the Carson Corporation is proposing to do to make the prairie pretty once they've finished extracting the ore. For a moment, however, consider the project from the point of view of a budding ecologist: Is that what we want as the fate of a pristine and original grassland ecosystem?"

Richard—known as "Rick" to most of the citizens of Bentonville, a small college town in the middle of the northern Great Plains—was a popular young biology professor on the state university extension campus. Since joining the faculty four years earlier, all he had wanted was to teach. His popularity and expertise, however, had pushed him to the center of a controversy he would rather have avoided. Jenny's father, a senior corporate vice president for an international mining company, was on the other side.

"But think about it, Mr. Wu," Jenny persisted. "The company owns the mineral rights to all that land outside of town, including the Omaha parcel. They've been mining in this part of the state for two

160

generations. That's why Bentonville prospers so much. Until now nobody has complained."

"Your logic probably would earn you an A if this were a class in corporate public relations," Rick responded, "but we're studying environmental science, and for the next few weeks we'll be looking at prairie ecology. Now, once again, what would an ecologist say about a plan that would destroy one of the last remnants of a historical prairie grassland by digging up the zinc ore underneath and then replacing the surface with a carpet of fairway grass?"

"But Professor Wu . . . ," Jenny protested plaintively before she was interrupted.

Elaine, sitting behind Jenny, also forgot classroom etiquette and blurted, "The ecologist would see nothing but a green desert."

"Ah," Rick responded. "That answer is right, so your sin of interruption is forgiven—if, of course, you apologize to Ms. Ritchner."

"Sorry, Jen. Last Saturday the four of us on my class project team assigned to survey the biodiversity of the Omaha parcel counted fifteen species of tall and short prairie grasses. We haven't identified all of them, but the ones we recognize are all native. If the mining takes place, they'll be gone, replaced with one kind of turf."

"And what would that mean?" prompted Rick.

"It would mean that the variety of grasses would be zero, and what's worse, all the life that depends on these native species would vanish, too. What a loss!" Elaine exclaimed.

"Yes, scientifically your prediction is correct, but to call it a 'loss'— well, that's a moral and political judgment. Although I'd prefer to stick to the science, it's hard to avoid the politics." Rick sighed and confessed, "That's why I reluctantly agreed to head up the citizen's committee opposing the mining project." Then he added humorously, "Why did I drop that course in public speaking while I was at UCLA?"

After class, Jenny approached Rick in the hall. "I still think that mining that land is good for everybody, but this course has taught me that the prairie we never pay much attention to is, as you said, a rich and diverse community of thousands of species of plants and animals. It seems wrong to destroy it. I think Dad and I are going to have a talk," she said with the smile of a young woman who knows that she can easily get the loving attention of her father for her opinions.

Rick held out little hope that anything would come of the Ritchner family dinner conversation. He focused instead on the long list of parties he had to call over the next several days as he marshaled opposition to the Carson Corporation plan to mine 500 acres of prairie outside of Bentonville. The area included the fifty-acre plot of original grassland—the Omaha parcel—that had been deeded to the city several years back by a cattle rancher who had preserved it from grazing because he thought it was special, too. Rick knew that

Carson had the law on its side, but he also knew that many of the good and prominent citizens of Bentonville were opposed. He also was in contact with several major environmental groups whose response was very encouraging. Rick hated controversy and dreaded the prospect of going to court as the plaintiff in a suit to halt the project. He would, though, if it meant preserving the Omaha parcel.

So he was surprised when the phone in his office rang two days later. "Professor Wu, this is Harry Ritchner. My daughter is in your biology class. Do you have a moment? I think you'll be interested in what I have to say."

"Of course," said Rick, bracing himself slightly for the contentious conversation he was certain was about to follow.

"Jenny can be quite persuasive. I hope she pursues a career in law." Ritchner began. "She set me to thinking about those grasslands in the middle of our proposed mining site. I hadn't realized how strongly people like you felt. Carson has tried to be a good citizen and neighbor throughout the state and here in Bentonville. We want to continue that tradition. I've spoken to the central office. We agree that the environment is important and that we have some responsibility for it. So we intend to go further than simply reclaiming the land following the mining operations. Carson will pay for the restoration of the Omaha parcel. I mean by that completely reconstructing the area so that it resembles the original as closely as possible. We want you to advise us on it, and it seems to me that it will make a wonderful long-term project for your classes for some time to come. Carson thinks this is a fair, even generous, offer—a real win-win situation for us, the community, and the grasslands."

Rick sat back in his chair—stunned, relieved, and confused. He realized that Ritchner was waiting for his response, which initially was a spontaneous "Wow." Recovering his composure he continued, "You're right, sir, Carson's offer is generous. We can talk again, but I feel the responsibility to report back to people in the community who have expressed concern."

"Of course," Ritchner agreed. "I'm confident that their response will be as positive as yours. In any case, this is what Carson intends to do. Keep me informed, and have a good day."

Rick's day was very good—until he walked into his biology class and shared the news with his students. Then he learned why he had felt that earlier confusion when Ritchner called.

"Yes, Jose, you have a comment?"

"God made the Creation, and we've destroyed most of it. We don't have the decency even to preserve fifty little acres as God made them. That's wrong."

"Terry?"

"Look, it took thousands, even millions, of years to make the grasslands through evolution. Now we want to do it all over again in three or four years. Sure, the new system will look and act like the old one, but it'll be a fake, a forgery—like a copy of a masterpiece of art."

"Jose, you want to conclude your comment?"

"Terry's right on. Isn't actually making something and calling it 'wild' a contradiction? I mean, being wild means *not* being created or managed by humans. How can you have a wild artifact? Let's face it, we would be doing this for ourselves, not for nature. You can't respect nature by destroying it. No area can be wild unless it's left alone. We have no right to disturb, much less destroy, any more wilderness."

Rick hadn't expected this. "Okay, one more comment," he said reluctantly, in recognition of the rising debate.

"Robert."

"I really disagree. I'm not worried about God or evolution, Professor Wu. This is a great opportunity to restore nature. And, more importantly, even to improve it."

Robert held up his copy of Aldo Leopold's famous book of essays, *A Sand County Almanac*. "You told us this was a wonderful book, and it is. Leopold says that we have a duty to protect what he called the 'integrity, stability, and beauty' of ecosystems. He also believes that humans have a duty to restore, manage, and even improve on ecosystems."

"Improve! How do you improve on nature?" Jose exclaimed loudly, throwing up his hands.

"Let's calm down," ordered Rick. "It's becoming a little 'wild' in here. Continue, Robert."

"Why can't we take the Omaha parcel and make it richer and more abundant than the original? Let's put in thirty species of grasses. As long as Carson foots the bill, let's add some sand hills and wet depressions and divert a creek or two to flow through it. These features will attract all kinds of wildlife that aren't in the parcel now."

Jennifer waved both arms, seeking permission to speak. Rick couldn't deny her. After all, she had started all of this with her candid talk with her father.

"Robert's right. All we've talked about in class is biodiversity as the single most important feature for the health of an ecosystem—Leopold's integrity, stability, and beauty. If biodiversity is a good thing, then more biodiversity is even better. I think God would approve. After all, the Bible says that Adam and Eve were placed in the Garden of Eden to till and keep it. The Omaha parcel is our garden. Who's to say that we can't improve on evolution? We're not producing a counterfeit; we're making a new ecosystem in the style of the old one. I think you're wrong, Terry. One day the parcel will be wild again because it will be a healthy ecosystem functioning in the way God or nature intended. What else could 'wild' mean?"

Rick left his class that day more confused than ever. Out of the mouths of babes, he thought, recognizing the irony of a situation in which his students were teaching their instructor. For a course in environmental science, the discussions were becoming decidedly philosophical and theological—and, because of their consequences for the future of the parcel, very political as well.

Rick walked over to the Prairie Resources Institute, a research center on campus funded primarily by the state agricultural commission. He was working closely with Ben Gilman, the institute's director—the only real ecologist in town and Rick's expert confidante on the Omaha parcel. Now was the time to have a talk.

"Ben, do you have a few minutes?" asked Rick, leaning through the doorway to Gilman's office.

"Rick. Hi!" said Ben with obvious pleasure as he swiveled his chair away from the desktop computer and its screen filled with data from a current project. "I got your message about Ritchner's offer. Been meaning to return your call, but we're pushing a deadline to get a report to the ag commission for a legislative subcommittee, and I've had no time. No time, that is, until now. Come on in."

"Thanks," Rick said as he sat down. "Ben," he started, "I'm confused. Initially, I was tremendously elated with Ritchner's offer for Carson, and, frankly, I still think it's the best—perhaps the only—way to go. But I'm not as sure as I'd like to be. Politics is a lot messier than science—and I'm a scientist, not a politician."

"I know exactly how you feel; I feel that way almost every day as I write these reports for the commission," Ben said with a sympathetic grimace. "But you're not here for confession or therapy, right?"

"Right," Rick replied. "I'm here to learn what you think about the offer."

"Well," Ben said, "I don't like it, for several reasons. One concerns the Carson Corporation and another the loss of an original and irreplaceable—that's right irreplaceable—patch of wilderness."

"This sounds familiar," Rick said. "About an hour ago I heard something like that from my students."

"Then you may hear it again from me," Ben said. "First, Carson's offer. As an international mining company, they're good at destroying things. Their operations in metallic ore extraction—zinc, copper, and bauxite—in North and South America are notorious for the mess they leave behind. Look at what happened in central Arkansas. For fifty years Carson strip-mined vast areas of pine and hardwood

164

forestland for bauxite. Sure, after the ore was depleted and they left they made an effort to carpet the area with grass—much of which died because of the pollutants dumped in the soil from on-site chemical conversion of ore into alumina. The place now resembles a patchy green-and-brown moonscape, complete with craters. The fact is, the Carson Corporation is a massive and efficient machine dedicated to the destruction of the land. Its promise to restore the Omaha parcel is part of that mentality. Fifty acres out of 500—hardly a costly gift to the good people of Bentonville."

"Well, perhaps I'm an innocent romantic," Rick said, "but I believe that Ritchner's intentions are true. He sincerely has the best interests of the parcel, the school, and the town in mind."

"Sure, Ritchner's heart is in the right place," Ben agreed. "But the corporate headquarters? You can bet that their generosity is derived from the bottom line. They want the publicity, and I guess that's okay. But I'm concerned that they will use this project to green their public image and reputation as an environmentally sensitive company and to blunt criticism the next time they gouge out a wild place anywhere in the world. I think that corporations use restoration as a way to ease their conscience and an excuse to destroy wilderness."

Ben clasped his hands just below his chin in a pose of concentration and continued. "The real bottom line for us is that by accepting his offer and all the advantages it brings to the parcel and the college, we're partners in this destruction."

"Everything you say is true," agreed Rick, "but look at it pragmatically. Apart from accepting Carson's offer, our only other alternative is to go to court to stop the project. Let's say we win. Carson would surely appeal. If the judgment were reversed, Ritchner would be forced to withdraw the offer to restore the parcel. The law doesn't require restoration. At best we'd likely get the green carpet treatment, in the worst sense of the term. If they didn't win on appeal, the legal precedent would slow similar projects in the United States. But how many Omaha parcels are out there? My guess would be very few. The decision would have little or no effect in South America or Africa, which welcome investment and jobs. We'd have our fifty original acres, and that's about all."

"Original? Yes, and that's pretty important," said Ben, "and this leads to my second point. 'Restoration' is not an accurate term. It suggests restoring the original by healing the damage, just as a physician would restore the lost function of a patient's arm or leg. After Carson does its thing, though, the parcel won't have the equivalent of an arm or a leg. The mining operation will require local shafts, so the topsoil and subsoil may survive, but the company's roads and buildings will certainly degrade the ecosystem beyond recovery. So restoration really means re-creation or complete reconstruction of the ecosystem, literally from the ground up. The original Omaha parcel will be gone forever, and in its place we will see, at best, a similar but brand-new system. You may as well allow them to bulldoze the parcel and completely start over on some other part of the prairie that's more convenient and closer to the university."

Rick frowned and then launched his counterpoint. "I agree that the loss of the original is tragic, but look at the opportunity we have to give it rebirth. Not perfectly, I know. A precise replica is impossible because we have no catalogue of the bacteria, fungi, soil invertebrates, insects, and spiders that prosper in the parcel. Some won't return, and new ones will move in to take their place. With Carson's money, however, we can enhance the system by adding to the variety of species and make it richer, more robust, and a wonderful laboratory and educational resource for the college. We can even introduce endangered species of grasses and animal and give them sanctuary."

"Rick," Ben responded with some frustration in his voice, "you're like those people at NASA who would 'terraform' the planet Mars by giving it an atmosphere and introducing oceans and plant and animal life. They see it as an improvement on the original barren red planet. Isn't Mars good enough? Can't we leave well enough alone? Good or not, nature is nature. Our attempts to reconstruct nature are not only unnatural—nature, almost by definition, is self-composing and goes on its own—they also are acts of domination. Humans are creatures, not lords. Domination is, well, tacky."

Here we go, Rick thought, wishing that he also had stuck with that course on environmental ethics at UCLA. "Why is it unnatural for us humans to change the natural landscape? Don't we count as natural, too?"

Rick glanced up at a framed painting on Ben's wall depicting several Indians riding on horseback in a buffalo hunt. The scene triggered another thought. "For thousands of years, our predecessors here on the Great Plains would burn the grasses regularly to drive the buffalo or antelope closer in the hunt or to flush out rabbits and other animals. As nomads they unwittingly transported seeds that were indigenous to one part of the Plains to another part, where they established themselves as exotics, perhaps driving out less competitive local species. Maybe some of the grasses we want to save in the Omaha parcel were introduced by the Indians. Does that make them less than 'natural'? My point is this: We've been changing nature for millennia—not as alien invaders intent on domination but as an indigenous species doing its natural thing."

"I agree," said Ben. "The Indians were limited in what they could do, however, and even limited themselves because of their spiritual sense of respect for natural beings. We're not limited, and Carson certainly sees the land very unspiritually—as a commodity. Some self-restraint would be a virtue, don't you think? And some respect for this rare jewel of a remnant of the original Great Plains would help, too."

"Okay, okay," Rick sighed. "I came here for enlightenment, but you hand me a dilemma. Do we pursue preservation of the original parcel, taking Carson to court if necessary, and possibly lose the offer of restoration? Or do we accept the offer and try to restore—excuse me, re-create—the ecosystem, using Carson's big money to improve on the original?"

Ben leaned back in his chair. "Which horn of that dilemma do you choose to impale yourself on?" he asked.

Rick smiled and continued. "I'm inclined to believe that accepting the generous grant is the best decision. But your arguments are powerful, Ben. I remember what my grandmother, who came to California from China in the early 1900s, told me as a child about the traditional principle of *wu-wei*. This phrase translates into something like 'take no unnecessary action' in an intrusive or invasive sense. 'Let a sleeping dog lie' is probably how we'd put it. Here it would mean, 'Leave the Omaha parcel alone.' That tradition is almost gone, even in China, but I wonder if it remains valid in a larger and perennial sense. Does it apply here?"

Rick excused himself from the conversation with Ben, saying he had to return to his office to pick up a set of papers to grade that evening and return the next day. When he arrived, another message from Ritchner was waiting. He played it back. "I wanted to let you know that the corporate headquarters informed me today that the mining project will begin as soon as possible, even as early as next month. Our offer still stands. How would you like to come to dinner here at my home this evening? We—and I mean the three of us, including Jenny—can work out some further details on the restoration of the Omaha parcel. We need to submit a budget quickly."

Rick didn't return the call immediately. He needed to think during his walk home from his office. As he walked across the campus he ran into five of his students from the biology class on their way to the parcel to count species—this time arachnids. They were very excited about the research. Soon he would have to report to them his decision for or against Carson's offer. He knew he had all the scientific information he needed; no list of species of spiders would help. Unfortunately for this biologist, the issues went far beyond the mere collection and analysis of data. Ritchner had to have a decision soon. Rick could certainly use his grandmother's counsel now.

Commentary

The origin of the restoration ecology, as the science of rehabilitating or re-constructing degraded landscapes has come to be known, is relatively recent. Some historians have traced its beginnings to the efforts of Aldo Leopold more than forty years ago to restore a natural prairie and pineland community on his farm in Wisconsin, which he and his family lovingly called "the Shack." In recent decades environmentalists, recognizing that we were diminishing natural landscapes at an alarming rate, have turned their attention to healing the land as well as preserving it.

Although restoration ecology is a science, it shares many features with the profession of engineering, including functions of design and construction (or reconstruction) of broken landscapes. Indeed, early efforts were attempts by civil engineers to reconstruct the likeness of degraded landscapes—especially those deeply scarred by strip mining—by using the same bulldozers and backhoes that had been used in the original acts of destruction. Restoration is not merely surface reconstruction, however; in addition to returning the cosmetic appearance of the landscape, it also seeks to re-create, to the greatest extent possible, the dynamic functional relationship between the living and geologic components of the original. Thus, restoration ecology is a true basic science as well as an applied science. There is much to be learned about the essential character of landscapes in the effort to return them to their natural states.

There also is much to be learned in ethical reflections on such projects. Experience from the medical sciences has shown that many advances are accompanied by novel moral quandaries. This dynamic also is true of restoration ecology. Although environmental ethicists have long debated the morality of radically altering pristine landscapes for human benefit, there is little debate concerning the desirability of restoring them once they have suffered degradation. Fundamental and often novel issues do arise, however, with regard to the motives and goals of these efforts. They begin with an examination of the very words we use to analyze issues in restoration ecology and to argue positions concerning them.

Americans have a well-deserved reputation for being pragmatic and action-oriented; we value results over reflection. We derisively liken abstract philosophical analysis to the mythical pugilist who reflected so much on the theory of boxing that he never threw the first punch. Arguments about words are dismissed as useless semantics. This impatience with analysis itself often is a vice rather than a virtue, however, because pragmatically, confusion about the meaning of ideas can lead to muddled thinking, wrongheaded decisions, and, ultimately, poor results. This case in restoration ecology is an example of the power of words and their meaning in scientific and political discourse. Discussions revolve around several ideas—particularly *nature* and *wilderness*—and the values associated with them. The positions of the participants often are dictated by their understanding of these fundamental terms. They demonstrate that confusion, even about everyday words, is a persistent danger because even the most innocent of terms carries the weight of numerous definitions. For example, any good dictionary has at least a dozen meanings for the word *nature*, many of which are shared with the entries for *wilderness*. *Natural* has more than twenty.

The moral desirability of the restoration of disturbed or destroyed natural areas is determined, in part, by the understanding of these concepts of *wilderness* and *nature* in the debate. No one in our case argues from purely pragmatic or ecological terms that the Omaha parcel should be mined and then restored because we have the means to do so or that it should remain untouched because we do not have the capability to restore it. Both sides seem to agree that a viable prairie ecosystem that resembles the original and perhaps even improves upon it in some ways can be rebuilt. The primary disagreement is about the "natural" or "unnatural" restoration and whether it is suitable and proper with regard to what those words mean.

We note here, by way of disclaimer, that this case, like all idealized cases, is constructed as an educational device. The two positions—preservationist and restorationist—are represented by purists who present their arguments in unambiguous terms. Admittedly, one does not often find such purity in the real world. Many restorationists sympathize with preservationists and make every effort to protect the historical continuity of a natural community even as they restore it, and many preservationists applaud the good intentions of those who rebuild degraded landscapes. For all of his ambivalence, at least Professor Wu is well informed by the highly tidy positions of each camp; like the reader, he must deliberate the merits of each side and arrive at some decision. Fictionalized cases offer ideal situations that encourage the use of critical thinking skills; such skills will prove useful in muddled real-world situations. In this sense they are "deceivers yet true," to proof-text our point with a biblical phrase.

The preservationists—those who want to save the parcel from the Carson Corporation's bulldozers—subscribe to specific values to be found in an account of "nature" and the "natural" that emphasizes the autonomy of ecosystems. In a truly natural state, an ecosystem is the result of a long period of unbroken historical development or evolution. It also is spontaneous or wild; it goes on its own, influenced minimally, if at all, by human intrusion. Jose and Terry represent the preservationist position. They argue that even the best intentions at restoration are wrongheaded because nature, by definition,

169

cannot result from acts of human fabrication. Where is the wildness in that? A restored Omaha parcel might resemble the original, but it would be a manufactured replica—or worse, a forgery. Only the historical original can be truly wild and natural. If the essence of nature is pristine or virgin independence and if the continued existence of natural places is our moral duty, then we should fight for the preservation of the parcel.

The preservationist position is dualist. It assumes that human culture and wilderness are entirely separate and incompatible realities. Thus, the irresistible expansion of human civilization into nature (e.g., the American frontier experience) is cause for lamentation because it portends the "end of nature" as a region free from human incursion. Many thinkers have argued that this understanding of nature itself is a social construct—an idea that raises numerous problems, especially because it promotes the notion that most human activity is unnatural and that culture, with all its problems and crises, is inferior to nature, a blight on creation.

In this case, Ben is a preservationist and a dualist, but his emphasis is based on a deep suspicion of the motives of the Carson Corporation to act in a virtuous way. Perhaps if he were pushed to reflect further on the matter, Ben would confess that he harbors reservations about the inherent good we often attribute to persons. Individuals, he might concede, can be good in their interpersonal relationships; Ritchner is an example. But institutions? Not so. They tend to be exploitive and self-serving, perhaps as representative of the prideful human tendency to see ourselves as superior and dominant. The ghost of Murray Bookchin, whose perspective of social ecology is introduced in chapter 1, looks over Ben's shoulder and whispers into his ear. For Ben the questions have to do with institutional arrogance and dominance and personal virtue and character.

The other side—the restorationist position—is represented by Robert, Jenny, and, to some extent, a conflicted Professor Wu. They define "natural" and "wild" in entirely different ways that allow for Carson's offer of reconstructing the parcel after the zinc ore has been extracted to be a realistic option. For the restorationist, that which is natural *functions* naturally—that is, just like the original. An ecosystem is a dynamic, self-contained, and integrated community of many living and nonliving components. The history and evolution of the system are immaterial. Its origins and whether it was constructed or self-evolved matter less than its richness and healthy functioning. This process definition of the natural allows not only for restoration but also for improvement. Robert's enthusiasm for adding new species to the parcel and modifying its geologic layout is inconceivable for the preservationists but consistent with the restorationist notion of complex natural order.

Note that the perspective is ecocentric and not biocentric. The restorationists do not argue that the components of the system are themselves reconstructed. The species of wild grasses, other plants and animals, and soil—the good citizens of the prairie community—are not assembled by human hands. They are reintroduced into the degraded site and encouraged to come together to reproduce the original functional integrity of the ecosystem. Therefore, the restored Omaha parcel is properly described as natural in that it is not artificial but synthetic, and synthetic nature is true nature, to be valued for its own sake.

Restorationists see no difficulty with human involvement in nature. Anthropogenic activity—that is, change brought about by human action—is not illicit intrusion into wilderness. It is itself natural. In expressing his position to Ben, Rick makes the point that the Plains Indians altered the ecology of the prairie for thousands of years. Homo sapiens, a primate species, may be more ingenious, constructive, and collectively powerful than any other (although some scientists claim that bacteria, not primates, rule the world), but it is no less natural for its evolutionary success. Indeed, lest we declare ourselves secure in triumph over Darwinian natural selection, we should acknowledge that our foolish fouling of the global ecosystem eventually may result in reducing us to an endangered species. In any case, restorationists dismiss the dualist position by erasing the distinction between nature and culture.

This continuity between nature and culture does not mean that there are no important distinctions to be made between other creatures and ourselves. Nature is spontaneous; humans are reflective. Nature is nonmoral. Humans are decidedly and inescapably moral. That is, our species is responsible for its actions in ways that do not apply to the rest of nature. This sense of duty, of right and wrong, simply comes with the territory of living in culture. It is as natural to us as speed is to the cheetah. Ben's preservationist position is sensitive to this dimension of human life. He questions the intentions of the Carson Corporation and sees in the restorationist project an expression of the universal human tendency to impose our preferences on nature wherever possible. How prideful and presumptuous we are to believe that we alone know better and can do better. In Ben's eyes, this assumption of dominion and the inherent right of humans to interfere whenever they please is, ironically, at the core of even the restorationist position.

Finally, to return to the pragmatic role that the understanding of words plays in arguments and judgments with which we began, we note the important place of metaphors. A metaphor is a figure of speech in which a comparison is made or implied between two unlike things. Metaphors are powerful expressions in thought. They shape discussion and disclose new insights that

171

are otherwise unavailable. Several metaphors are central in this case. Terry describes the act of restoration as a "forgery"—a very negative characterization. In this metaphor, nature or evolution is the artist, and our restorative efforts are suspect in that they intend to replace the original parcel with a copy and pass it off as somehow equal to the original. The implication is that this is a deceptive act and hence less than virtuous.

Jenny counters with the image of the garden. The Omaha parcel is a garden, and we are responsible gardeners who plant and till. Gardens imply gardeners. Within this perspective, humans have a logical connection with nature. The garden has the additional advantage of being a biblical image from which the three monotheistic religions that take the Bible seriously (Judaism, Christianity, and Islam) derive their common doctrine of humans' God-given responsibility as stewards of nature. We were put here to mind the garden, deputized by God as stewards or custodians of the creation.

Ben argues from the metaphor of medicine when he likens the process of restoration to the reparative technology of the surgeon and draws conclusions that are unfavorable to restorationists. In the case of the Omaha parcel, the patient dies (the parcel is destroyed by the mining). In this medical model, restoration therefore is impossible.

The seriousness with which we take our metaphors indicates the power of the verbal and social construction of nature. Thinking and, consequently, the actions that arise from thoughts are shaped and directed by language and other aspects of culture. Nature has an independence from culture such that, when left alone, it goes on its own. Not so for human attitudes and perceptions of nature. We construct a vision of nature, objectify that vision, and build part of our world on it. When visions clash, debates begin.

In chapter 1 we quote Aldo Leopold's famous dictum, "A thing is right if it tends to preserve the integrity, stability, and beauty of the biotic community. It is wrong if it tends otherwise." In the case presented in this chapter, Robert notes the ambiguity of this duty. Preserving those features of the Omaha parcel would mean fighting all efforts to plow it under. Yet these three values also can be recovered and even enhanced through the opportunities offered in the restoration of the parcel. As noted above, Leopold himself approved of managing the land with active efforts to improve it. One wonders what his council to Professor Wu's class would be.

Questions for Discussion

1. This case pits restorationists against preservationists. Does this opposition always arise in environmental issues? Is it possible to be both a restorationist and a preservationist and be consistent in your position?

(Hint: Recall Brian Norton's pragmatic environmental ethics in chapter 1.)

2. Using a good dictionary, find the entry for "nature." Which of the numerous definitions of "nature" best fits the restorationist's position? The preservationist's?

3. What role does history play in the development of an ecosystem? In your judgment, is it necessary for an ecosystem to have a history to be authentic?

4. What is wrong with terraforming the planet Mars?

For Further Reading

Callicott, J. Baird. *Beyond the Land Ethic: More Essays in Environmental Philosophy.* Albany, N.Y.: State University of New York Press, 1999.

Cronon, William, ed. *Uncommon Ground: Toward Reinventing Nature.* New York: W. W. Norton, 1995.

Eliot, Robert. "Faking Nature." *Inquiry* 25 (March 1982): 91–93. Reprinted in Louis J. Pojman, ed. *Environmental Ethics: Readings in Theory and Application.* Belmont, Calif.: Wadsworth, 1995, 81–85.

Katz, Eric. "The Ethical Significance of Human Intervention in Nature." *Restoration and Management Notes* 9 (1990): 235–47.

Oelschlaeger, Max. *The Idea of Wilderness from Prehistory to the Age of Ecology.* New Haven, Conn.: Yale University Press, 1991.

Peterson Anna. "Environmental Ethics and the Social Construction of Nature." *Environmental Ethics* 21 (winter 1999): 339–57.

Pojman, Louis P. *Global Environmental Ethics.* Mountain View, Calif.: Mayfield Publishing Co., 2000.

Scherer, Donald. "Evolution, Human Living, and the Practice of Ecological Restoration." *Environmental Ethics* 17 (winter 1995): 359–80.

Soule, Michael and Gary Lease, eds. *Reinventing Nature.* Washington, D.C.: Island Press, 1995.

Stone, Christopher. *Should Trees Have Standing?* Los Altos, Calif.: Kaufmann Publishing, 1974.

III

ECOSYSTEM INTERVENTIONS AIMED AT INNOVATION

11

Improving on Natural Variation?
Genetically Modified Foods

"But Dad, think of the long run!" Kyle Deaver protested to his father
as they sat in the cab of their 1984 pickup on the way to the feed and
grain. "Even if you don't care about the principle of biodiversity, you
must care about the birds and the butterflies! There are studies that
already show a decline in bird and butterfly populations from using
genetically modified seed." Kyle was a fourth-generation farmer in
Midland, Missouri, home from agricultural school for a few weeks of
summer vacation.

"So you've told me, son," Jack Deaver replied. "But you admit
that the findings are very preliminary, that long-term studies haven't
been done yet. What I do know for sure is that if I use this, or some
other GMO, I don't have to worry about the insects eating the corn
crop. Because as soon as they chew a leaf, or an ear, they die before
reproducing. And with a GMO crop, I can use less herbicide and apply it any time the weeds begin sprouting. I don't have to time it so
it doesn't damage a particular stage of crop growth. That means the
GMO corn is easier to take care of and less expensive to grow.
You've been against heavy pesticide and herbicide use; I thought
you'd applaud these GMO crops."

"No, Dad," Kyle said. "The results of our experimental fields at school point to high potential for reducing both plant and animal diversity as a direct result of these GMOs. Ours were initial experiments; more controlled comparative studies will be done next year. But ours are not the only studies—there are studies in England, on the Continent, and lots in the United States. It's the same issue as the animal predators, Dad; it's wrong to destroy everything that eats, or crowds, or could eat, our crops or stock."

The year before, Kyle had managed to persuade his father to support the forest service's reintroduction of wolves and foxes into neighboring areas of Missouri. Kyle tried to explain: "It's the other end of the same food ladder, Dad. If we kill all the predator animals, then there are no controls on the numbers of deer, rabbits, raccoons, and other small animals. And if all the weeds that grow in our fields are killed, then key foods for invertebrates and birds disappear. If all the insects that eat our crop die, then the birds that need insects to feed to their chicks will die out."

"But son, from my side it's *not* the same thing," Jack replied. "I may lose a calf every year or so if we have wolves in the area, and I can take that if it's so important to you. But you're telling me I should share my crop with the weeds and the insects. With prices so low, I don't have much choice—lowering the cost of herbicide and pesticide by planting genetically modified corn may be the only way to make anything at all from some of these fields. I sure won't make a profit if I let the weeds and the bugs get them or if I pay through the nose for pesticide and herbicide to kill them."

"No, you need to *control* the bugs and the weeds, not eliminate them," Kyle argued. "It's the same idea as the field boundaries. You didn't cut down all the trees between the fields to make one huge field without borders; you kept the tree lines, the fences, and the hedges. That was the right thing to do; it left places for the birds, the squirrels, the field mice, and the insects, and it acted as a windbreak, protecting topsoil. You did it for the long-term health of the land. GMOs don't support the long-term health of the land."

"Kyle, I encouraged you to go to ag school, and I want to use some of the fancy stuff they teach you there. This farm will be all yours in another six or seven years. But I have to think about how to make it support us for these next few years. This fall your sister is getting married, and that'll be some expense. We'll be lucky if the baler gets through to fall, and the price of gas is expected to get over $2.50 a gallon this summer. So if you want to persuade me, tell me how I can make a profit on this crop by using some other regime. Okay?"

Jack stopped speaking as they drove into the parking lot of the feed and grain. Kyle followed his dad into the store, swearing softly.

After taking out their list and getting their order filled, Jack and Kyle turned to leave and were stopped by a neighbor, Lee Martin. Lee greeted Jack, asked Kyle about his school year and what he was learning, and then brought up his reason for accosting them.

"I heard last night that you're going to use some of that GMO corn seed in your fields along SR 13. That true?" Lee asked.

"Yeah, Kyle here's trying to talk me out of it, but I can't see my way clear to making a go of it any other way," Jack replied.

"Well, that'd be a real problem for me," Lee said, "because you know I got the thirty-five acres on the other side of that road. You know I stopped raising feeder pigs last winter; prices were just too unstable. But I just got certified organic and got a contract to sell all my corn, beans, and tomatoes to a supplier of organic groceries to Midwest cities. If you plant GMO corn, there's no way to keep your pollen from contaminating my organic corn. If your corn pollinates some of mine, I'll have put all the work into growing organic—all the extra weeding, especially—and it'll still test hybrid, so it'll only command the same prices you get, not the higher organic prices. You and I been good neighbors for a lot of years now. But I can't let you ruin me. Don't force me to go to the law over this, Jack."

"Lord, Lee, I never had any idea this could affect you!" Jack said. "I sure don't want to cause you any trouble. We heard a rumor that you were looking into organic farming, but I never really thought about what that would mean."

Jack turned to his son. "Kyle, you know this stuff; does this really mean that Lee and I could never grow the same crop, part organic, part GMO? That could be a real problem, seeing as how this is corn country."

"Lee's right, Dad," he said. "He'll get a hybrid result if you grow GMO corn across the road. Corn pollen is heavy and doesn't travel nearly as far as some other pollen, but it will certainly move 500–1,000 yards. High winds and bees will carry some of it even farther. The only way for you to use GMO and Lee to be organic is if you never plant the same crop in any proximity."

Jack looked at Lee: "Can't you put the beans or the tomatoes in that field, and the corn in your field over by the creek? That way it would be too far away for my pollen to get to it—and it would be generally upwind from my corn anyway."

"No," Lee replied, "I have to put the tomatoes by the creek—not just for the water but because there are three neighbors raising different kinds of GMO tomatoes, and to keep mine away from them I have to put the tomatoes on the field in the center. I can't put every-thing in my center field—something's got to go on the perimeter."

"Yeah, I got the same kind of problem. Not every piece of land will do for any crop," Jack said ruefully. "I need to think about this some, Lee, and talk with the boy. We got a couple weeks to work this out. I'll get back to you soon. And our greetings to Sally and the kids." Lee said he'd drop over during the next week, and all three left the store.

On the way back to the farm, however, Jack complained loudly that the pollen should be Lee's problem, not his, and that if Lee wanted to experiment with some newfangled fad, he should take re-sponsibility for making it work and not expect his neighbors to take on that burden.

"Who does he think he is, threatening to sue me for raising corn?" Jack said. "Anyway, those organic crops bring in lots higher prices than regular crops; Lee will be able to afford to take some losses."

Kyle interrupted his father as they were turning into the lane to-ward the barn. "Dad, I bet his margin isn't any better than yours. The suppliers who distribute organic foods take a much bigger cut than even our processors do—they claim it's because the costs are higher to cultivate a new market. Whatever the reason, you can't as-sume he's making much more than you are, once you figure in his higher costs." His father merely grunted, as he opened the pickup door and stalked into the house to eat lunch. Kyle followed more slowly, mulling over the problem in his head.

That evening at dinner Jack related the encounter with Lee at the feed store to Lucie, his wife, and his two daughters, Millie and Susan. Lucie taught seventh grade at the local middle school, and Millie was a high school senior celebrating her last month of the school year. Susan was about to graduate from the local community college and be married in late July. All three listened intently as Jack complained that it should not be his responsibility to protect his neighbor's ex-perimental crop from damage that occurred because of the normal operations of nature.

"But Dad," Millie interjected, "that's not what you said last year when Bill Perkins started raising pit bull pups next door to the mid-dle school recess yard. Then you said that because it was the nature of pit bulls to attack strangers, nobody had the right to raise them near a public area, especially one with kids. Remember?"

"That's not the same thing, Millie," Jack snapped. "I'm not rais-ing anything that is dangerous in itself." Kyle softly snorted, but said nothing.

"Jack," Lucie said, "are these genetically modified crops safe? I know the corn is feed corn, not for humans, but we eat the meat from the animals that eat the corn. Just a month or so ago there was a big news story about how one of the processing plants had to recall a whole lot of taco shells because they had been mistakenly contaminated with GMO corn that was being milled for some other use. If GMO corn is so safe, why did they have to recall those tacos?"

"The simplest explanation is that food products for humans are monitored under food and drug laws, which are the strictest product controls on anything," Jack said. "If that particular GMO crop had been approved for animal feed but got accidentally mixed with corn meant for humans, then of course they had to recall the tacos. GMO corn might be approved for human consumption in the future—the process takes longer for human food."

"But Dad, if we eat the animals that eat the GMO corn, don't we get whatever is dangerous in it?" Susan asked.

"No," Jack replied, "not if they are eliminated in the digestive processes of the animal."

"But you don't know for sure that they are, Dad," Kyle said. "You know that virtually all of the GMO crops that you're considering use the antibiotic ampicillin as a marker for the genetic modification on the DNA strand. There are a lot of questions even about the effect of the antibiotic marker: What does it do to a herd of cows or pigs to have antibiotics in their feed constantly? They almost certainly will develop resistance to that whole family of antibiotics—and it's the most common kind. What happens when those animals get sick? And that problem is only with the marker, not even with the modification itself."

Lucie looked disturbed by this information.

"Doctors have been trying to stop giving people so many antibiotics because germs have developed resistance to many antibiotics, which means they don't work well when you need them," she said. "This seems to work in the opposite direction—flooding healthy animal bodies with antibiotics!"

"Lucie," Jack explained, "I hear you, but you have to be careful. Even if a cow does develop resistance to a family of antibiotics— and we don't even know that they will from GMO feed—that still wouldn't mean that eating the beef will pass on that resistance to people. Resistance isn't a substance that accumulates in the food chain."

"Says you, Pop, but there's no proof of that, either," Kyle insisted. "You actually think that this Novartis Maximiser GM corn can ever pass the safety tests for human consumption? I'd be very surprised. Besides the ampicillin marker, it's been modified for all sorts of production reasons that have nothing to do with consumer health or nutrition reasons. It includes a gene that is poisonous to the corn borer, it's tolerant of the toxic herbicide glufosinate, and it has the ampicillin in it. Does that sound like a good prospect for human food? That's besides all the problems it causes for other farmers and the environment."

"So you all tell me," Jack said, "if you're so sure I shouldn't plant the Novartis Maximiser GM corn, what should I plant in those fields that will allow us to eat next winter, to pay for Susan's wedding, Kyle's tuition, and Millie's driving lessons? Are you really so concerned about this seed—seed that has been approved by the government and that no existing studies show is dangerous for domestic animals and the people who eat them—that I should buck the central trend in U.S. agriculture and risk our livelihoods to do it?"

Commentary

This case does not demand that we completely accept or reject the entire technology of genetically modified crops or even genetically modified foods. The decision to be made is whether to plant this particular kind of genetically modified corn on these particular fields this year. Kyle is concerned that early tests of the first genetically modified crops, among them this type of corn, have shown some deleterious effects on butterfly populations—implying the possibility of effects on other insects and birds. Lucie is concerned about the possible effects of inserting antibiotics into feed corn, which may cause a resistance to antibiotics that could move through the food chain through animals to people. Their neighbor is concerned that his organic corn will be cross-pollinated with their genetically modified corn and then will not test organic. In that case, he wastes all the extra labor organic crops require and must sell his crop at the lower price that nonorganic corn receives. Application of the precautionary principle in this case clearly would lead to at least postponing, for a season or two, a decision to plant GMO corn. On the other hand, as Jack points out, the dominant model of agriculture, supported by corporate research and U.S. government regulatory bodies, has adopted GMO crops and insists that there is no evidence of danger in their use.

Genetically modified food today involves new methods of modifying the genetics of a crop or animal. All domesticated seeds and animals have genetic modifications; they have been selectively bred, generation after generation, to produce some uniform characteristics and to suppress others. This was traditional genetic modification. Today when we speak of genetically modified food we are talking about food that has been modified in the laboratory within a single generation of that food, generally by gene splicing—taking a gene from one strand of DNA and inserting it into the DNA of another species. Many of the goals of traditional methods of genetic modification remain as goals of the new technologies as well. Scientists seek modifications that allow crops to resist drought and pests, grow larger, be easier to harvest, pack and transport without damage, and resist spoilage.

At the same time, there are some aspects of the new technology for altering food strains that are entirely new. With gene splicing scientists can take a characteristic of one plant that could not be either cross-pollinated or grafted onto another species of plant and include it in the genetic makeup of that plant, in a single generation. Many scientists regard this new technology as a tool, for example, for reclaiming desertified land through new drought-resistant, ground-cover plants that resist erosion or for developing new fast-growing trees for logging that can save old growth forests. The possibilities seem limitless. Interestingly, on the issue of genetically modified plant and animal species, environmental motives propel both proponents and opponents.

Health Concerns

Most though not all of the opposition to genetically modified crops today emerges from health concerns. Many people note that for a variety of reasons, many not yet clear, allergic reactions to various foods—some potentially fatal—are on the rise in the human population. Many persons are allergic to substances such as nuts, shellfish, eggs, milk, certain families of fruits or vegetables, and untold individual foods. However, a person who knows that he or she is allergic to nuts, for example, does not know what part—which gene or gene complex—in nuts triggers the allergic reaction. If every different food producer can move genes from one food to another, the gene in nuts to which I am allergic also may turn up in strawberries, broccoli, or potatoes. We cannot prevent widespread health dangers from such allergies because there is no practical way to test the entire world population for all possible genes that could cause allergic reactions in them. Labeling modified foods with the names of added genes cannot be effective because people do not know which particular genes might affect them. Thus, the effect on human health is incalculable, especially if some scientists are correct that the rise in food allergies is a response to exposure of specific populations to new varieties of foods through globalization. In that case, an increase in the genetic variation of foods would not only complicate safety for people with food allergies but actually increase the number of persons who have food allergies.

The issue of antibiotics as markers in the GMO crops is related to regulations proposed in September 2002 by the U.S. Food and Drug Administration (FDA) for the use of antibiotics in animals that are used for human food. The deputy director of the FDA's Center for Veterinary Medicine reported, "We have substantial evidence now that resistant pathogens do form in treated animals and can be transmitted to humans through the food supply. From a public health perspective, that risk has to be minimized."[1]

Most of the health concerns about genetically modified foods focus on the precautionary principle. We simply do not know what the health effects of any of the modifications are, even in the relatively short run, and we know even less about the long-term effects. In the past, when selective breeding introduced new varieties of food, the new foods were eaten by the relatively small local populations who bred them. It usually took generations for new varieties to spread to other peoples in the same region or to other regions. The slowness of this process allowed for communities to test the new foods and discover any deleterious effects not only for human health but for the land, local animals, and surrounding plant life. In some cases, this slowness also may have allowed for gradual adaptation of the human digestive tract to the new food.

Scale and Speed of Genetic Modifications

In contrast, genetically modified food today is introduced by huge multinational seed companies for planting on millions of acres of land at the same time. The high cost of developing new seeds dictates a company's interest in widespread distribution as quickly as possible to recover research costs. Because the new seed has been developed by corporations with an eye to the market, it usually offers advantages that appeal to broad numbers—as in this case: Jack is attracted to the pest-resistance bred into the seed and in the seed's imperviousness to herbicide at all stages of growth. Thus, the research and marketing system of GMO crops today ensures that modifications are introduced on a massive scale with maximum effects.

Although the dilemma Jack faces at an individual level—how to make sufficient profit on his crops to afford tuition, driving lessons, and a wedding, in addition to regular expenses—is both difficult and yet easy to identify with, this is not the only level at which this issue of GMO foods can be considered. After all, Jack does not say that he has been losing money; presumably he can still make a go of his farm by continuing the methods that have served him in the past. He can observe how his neighbor, Lee, does with organic farming and perhaps convert one of his adjacent fields and crops to organic the following year, in conjunction with Lee. Jack clearly is under long-term pressure, but there does not seem to be any immediate crisis.

Capitalism and Environmentalism: Food Subsidies

A longer-range issue in agriculture without which it is impossible to consider GMO foods or the situation of American family farmers concerns farm subsidies in developed nations. Almost all developed nations give farmers subsidies for growing crops. Without them, virtually no farmers could make a living in farming in the developed world because they must compete on the world's food market with farmers from Ghana, Peru, Vietnam, Madagascar, the Philippines, and other poor nations—all of whose farmers earn only a pittance for their crops. In the European Union and the United States, for example, it is not unusual for a farmer to earn more in subsidies than he does for selling his crop on the market. The U.S. farm bill that passed in July 2002 included increased farm subsidies for a larger number of crops. Developed nations pay these subsidies because they do not want to be dependent on other nations for basic foods. In cases of war, natural disaster, or other disruption of world trade, food dependency can be very dangerous, even for rich nations.

Yet food subsidies violate the free-trade policy that has dominated U.S. and European foreign policy for decades. Nations are not supposed to protect vulnerable producers within their borders, regardless of the type of production. Within the capitalist theory that rules world markets, the only nations that should be food producers are those with comparative advantage—that is, those that can produce food most cheaply. Under comparative advantage, all products should be produced by those who can produce them most efficiently. Because rich countries cannot produce food efficiently, they should buy their food from those that can and instead produce goods and services in which they have comparative advantage. Rich nations refuse to accept food dependence, however.

Poor nations tend to be unindustrialized and export raw materials such as food. They resent the food subsidy policies of rich nations because those policies keep food sales from poor nations to rich nations relatively small (because the subsidies keep farmers producing food in rich nations) and depress the price of food by keeping the demand from rich nations out of the world market. Yet as many economists, the secretary general of the United Nations, and many politicians from developing nations have pointed out, poor nations are not allowed to protect their own vulnerable businesses (usually young industries) in similar ways. When they attempt to do so they are accused of violating free trade standards and are refused access to markets in rich nations, as well as loans and other financial necessities by the rich nations and multinational institutions controlled by the rich nations (the International Monetary Fund, the World Bank, and others).

In terms of environmentalism, the issues of food subsidies and comparative advantage are important for the concept of sustainability. An important question within environmentalism is the following: What is the size of the unit that should be sustainable? When we say that practices must be sustainable, do we mean sustainable for the earth as a whole or do we mean for smaller units—local communities, nations, regions, continents? Capitalist economic theory—for example, the concept of comparative advantage—assumes that every area has one or at most a few economic products in which it

185

can successfully compete against all other producers in the world and will concentrate on producing that product or products and that corporations continue to grow by swallowing up smaller, less competitive corporations until they are few, huge, and global. We see this process in agriculture: Some areas of the Midwest grow little besides corn and hogs; some nations of Southeast Asia and East Asia concentrate on wet rice production. In some areas known for a predominant crop, the produce nevertheless may be sufficiently varied and sufficiently keyed to the local diet that the region is self-sufficient in food and still able to export some food. In other areas—especially where monoculture patterns involve nonfood crops such as cocoa, tobacco, coffee, rubber, cotton, tea, or flowers—monoculture for export may not only make impossible a balanced ecosystem and food self-sufficiency, which is key to sustainability, but also may cause significant levels of hunger.

Most environmental analysis has focused not on a single global ecosystem but on regional ecosystems. For example, the groundbreaking book by Herman Daly and John Cobb, *For the Common Good: Redirecting the Economy toward Community, the Environment and a Sustainable Future*, lays out the case for regional units that are both environmentally sustainable ecosystems and human communities that are self-sufficient in the basic requirements of life.[2] The authors are clear that every local ecosystem should be sustainable; that is the only way to assure that the global ecosystem is sustainable. Furthermore, the distribution of agriculture around the globe generally is considered to promote plant biodiversity—though that is not automatic and requires ongoing attention and protection.

Thus, environmentalism weighs into the debate on farm subsidies on the side of the subsidies, at least in the short run. Humans are a part of the ecosystem—one species among many—and if their local ecosystem is to be sustainable it must be able to satisfy their basic needs for food and shelter, energy, health care, and education without compromising the existence of the habitats and species that share that ecosystem. Agriculture, industry, mining, and other productive forces—along with all of the disproportionate human impacts on the world—must be both minimized and widely distributed throughout the world. No single area can afford the environmental impact of all of the industry, all of the mining, all of the agriculture, even if the processes for these activities are made less destructive. Of course, another critical factor in this equation is the size of the human population. Many scientists believe that the carrying capacity of the earth has been reached, if not exceeded, and that sustainability must include maintaining if not decreasing the size of the human community.

Environmentalists' support for food self-sufficiency as a part of regional sustainability therefore legitimates Jack's concern that his farm continue to be economically sustainable. There *should* continue to be U.S. farmers, even if some food can be more cheaply produced elsewhere. Justice and the sustainability of other regional ecosystems demand, however, that subsidized farmers in rich nations reduce their crop size to the size of their domestic market, so they do not flood the world market with food that is priced below the cost of producing it. For example, in spring 2002 Indonesian poultry farmers staged protests all over the nation, demanding that Indonesia ban imports of U.S. chicken legs. In fact, Indonesia was unable to ban U.S. chicken leg imports without risking serious retaliation from the United States and international market forces. The problem was that chicken breasts in the United States were selling for more than $2.50 per pound, but there was considerably less demand for chicken legs, so producers were "dumping" the legs abroad for $.10 per pound. Indonesian chicken farmers, who typically earn less than $350 per year, produced chicken at about $.67 per pound (considerably less than the $2.50 that white meat chicken was selling for in the States) and could not compete with the "dumped" chicken price of $.10 per pound. These producers were being displaced from their own chicken market by U.S. poultry farmers, who were selling chicken at considerably less than their cost to produce it. If all the Indonesian farmers stop growing chickens, who will feed Indonesia when U.S. tastes change or shipping costs make these sales impractical?

Present world prices for many types of food are at or below the cost of producing it even in the poorest nations of the world. Thus, farmers in poor nations give up farming or turn to nonfood crops such as tobacco, coca, and poppies. The world's food supply becomes unstable.

GMO crops have the potential to offer poor farmers and poor nations great benefits, but within the present system of agriculture the likelihood is that they actually will produce great disadvantages. The modifications introduced into seed will be those that benefit the producers of the seed who control the modification process. The modifications introduced in the green revolution of the 1970s–1980s illustrated this dynamic very clearly. Seed companies introduced new seed that offered higher yields as well as greater resistance to pests and blight, as well as some varieties that required less water and were more resistant to drought.

These advantages were real for farmers everywhere. Yet poor farmers could not benefit to the same extent, and in the end they often were forced out of farming. As yields rose land became more valuable, and tenant farmers were forced off of lands their families had worked for generations. Because the new seed was hybrid and therefore sterile, seed had to be bought for every planting; the seed from the previous harvest was not capable of sprouting. Besides buying seed, poor farmers were obliged to buy fertilizer because the new seed required much heavier doses of fertilizer than the old seed. Many farmers were forced into debt to buy seed and fertilizer, and some lost their farms to debt. In most areas of the world the green revolution was of principal benefit to farmers with capital; it forced many of the poorest farmers out of farming. Many people question whether GMO modifications to seed portend similar consequences.

Other aspects of the green revolution may be relevant to the consequences of GMO crops as well. In many nations the green revolution led to drastic decreases in biodiversity, with serious potential dangers for the human food supply. The use of hybrid seed virtually eliminates possibilities for mutation— that is, for new "accidental" variations in seed; at the same time, companies have developed and patented relatively few new varieties that are planted in millions of acres. All of the crops that use the same seed will have the same vulnerabilities to pests, drought, temperature change, and other variables.

If GMO crops are to be planted, it will be important to develop many different varieties and to ensure that no single type of seed predominates in any given area. Such a policy would not only protect the human food supply from local devastation; it also could protect the local environment from too great an impact from any one type of seed. If one type of GMO corn is toxic to monarch butterflies, another type inhibits ovulation in swallows, and another type shortens the life span of earthworms, then even if it is decided that these destructive consequences are warranted by the situation (a very questionable assumption), none of these seed types should be planted in more than a few fields in any one area, so that no individual species is threatened. The effects should be monitored, and if earthworms appear to be losing ground in one area, the type of seed that threatens them should be discontinued in the region, at least until the earthworm population reestablishes itself.

As is so often the case with new technologies, the technology itself may be morally neutral. There may be genetic modifications of plants that ultimately are beneficial at all levels. Our problem is identifying which genetic modifications they would be and ensuring that only those modifications are introduced into the environment. The task of discrimination seems so immense that many people are tempted to draw the line at genetic modification itself, labeling "naturally" occurring plants as good and "artificially" produced plants as evil. Such a division seems not only simplistic but ahistorical, in that it ignores the major environmental intervention that humans made in domesticating plants and animals—a process that continues today all over the world, of which the new GMO products are but one small part. Instead of focusing on the method, perhaps the more important questions to ask are those that examine not only the consequences of specific uses of the technology but the desired ends to which those technologies are put. For example, some of the objections to

GMO food in Europe, where objections are almost universal and very strong, are that GMO food is "American" food—which is understood to be poor-quality food, low in taste and nutrition and produced to meet yield, cost, and transportability criteria rather than taste and nutrition criteria.

Some commentators have suggested that what needs to happen around this issue is social decision making. Food is a very personal thing in the lives of human beings, important not only for sustaining individual human life but also for linking human beings together in webs of production, exchange, and consumption (e.g., family dinners). Just as all persons have a responsibility to protect the biosphere, all persons have a right to be included in decisions about their food supply—decisions about trade-offs between cost, taste, variety, safety and environmental impact.

Questions for Discussion

1. Why is Kyle opposed to his father planting genetically modified (GMO) crops?
2. How will Jack's planting GMO crops affect his neighbor's organic farming?
3. The use of antibiotics in animal feed to prevent the diseases that accompany contemporary intensive farming methods has been shown to have what consequences? How does the debate over GMO feeds relate to this question?
4. Jack probably would be surprised to hear that his farming helps deprive hungry farmers in poor countries. What legal/political/economic mechanisms connect Jack's farming with the hunger of poor farmers in developing nations?

Notes

1. Marc Kaufman, "FDA Seeks to Limit New Antibiotics Used in Farm Animals," *Miami Herald*, 16 September 2002, 14A.
2. Herman E. Daly and John B. Cobb, Jr., *For the Common Good: Redirecting the Economy toward Community, the Environment and a Sustainable Future*. Boston: Beacon, 1989.

For Further Reading

Barling, David. "GM Crops, Biodiversity, and the European Agri-Environment: Regulatory Regime Lacunae and Revision." *European Environment* 10, no. 4 (2000): 167–77.

Daly, Herman E., and John B. Cobb, Jr. *For the Common Good: Redirecting the Economy toward Community, the Environment and a Sustainable Future*. Boston: Beacon, 1989.

Firbank, Les G., and Frank Forcella. "Genetically Modified Crops and Farmland Biodiversity." *Science* 289, no. 5484 (2000):1481–82.

Hart, Kathleen. *Eating in the Dark: America's Experiment with Genetically Engineered Food.* New York: Pantheon Books, 2002.

Hunt, Stephen, and Lynn Brewer. "Impact of BSE on Attitudes to GM Food." *Risk Decision and Policy* 6, no. 2 (June 2001): 91–103.

Isaac, Grant. *Agricultural Biotechnology and Transatlantic Trade: Regulatory Barriers to GM Crops.* Wallingford, Oxon, U.K., and New York: CABI Publications, 2002.

Jauhar, Prem P. "Genetic Engineering and Accelerated Plant Improvement: Opportunities and Challenges." *Plant Cell, Tissue and Organ Culture* 64, nos. 2–3 (2001): 87–91.

Jordon, Carl F. "Genetic Engineering, the Farm Crisis, and World Hunger." *Bioscience* 52, no. 6 (2002): 523–29.

Kaufman, Marc. "FDA Seeks to Limit New Antibiotics Used in Farm Animals." *Miami Herald*, 16 September 2002, 14A.

Martens, M. A. "Safety Evaluation of Genetically Modified Foods." *International Archives of Occupational and Environmental Health* 73, no. 9 (2000): 14–18.

Matthews, J. H., and M. Campbell. "The Advantages and Disadvantages of the Application of Genetic Engineering to Forest Trees: A Discussion." *Forestry* 73, no. 4 (2000): 371–80.

Peters, Christian. "Genetic Engineering in Agriculture: Who Stands to Benefit?" *Journal of Agricultural and Environmental Ethics* 13, no. 4 (2000): 313–27.

Pinstrup-Andersen, Per, and Ebbe Schioler. *Seeds of Contention: World Hunger and the Global Controversy over GM Crops.* Baltimore: Johns Hopkins University Press, 2001.

Poitras, Manuel. "Globalization and the Social Control of Genetic Engineering." *Peace Review* 12, no. 4 (2000): 587–93.

Uzogara, Stella G. "The Impact of Genetic Modification of Human Foods in the 21st Century: A Review." *Biotechnology Advances* 18, no. 3 (May 2000): 179–206.

Watkinson, A. R., R. P. Freckleton, R. A. Robinson, and W. J. Sutherland. "Predictions of Biodiversity Response to Genetically Modified Herbicide-Tolerant Crops." *Science* 289, no. 5448 (2000): 1554–57.

Willis, Lynn. "Who Regulates Genetically Modified Crops?" *Today's Chemist at Work* 9, no. 6 (June 2000): 59–66.

12

Nature Red in Tooth, Claw, and Bullet: Hunting and Human Presence in Nature

"And this is the classic western rifle—the Winchester lever-action 30-30," Earl said as he lifted the rifle from the rack of more than ten hunting pieces. "Over here is a Belgian-made 12-gauge shotgun, for wing shooting, and right next to it are the Tikka 'Whitetail Hunter,' 338 caliber, good for pronghorn antelope, too, and a Ruger 17, perfect for varmints."

"I assume by wing shooting you mean birds. 'Whitetail' are deer, and 'varmints'—what are varmints?" Janet asked, more from curiosity than real interest.

"Varmints are undesirable animals: crows, coyotes, prairie dogs, and the like. They don't do anybody any good. Because of their growing numbers and nuisance habits, whitetail deer will soon qualify, in my opinion," Earl answered.

Janet turned and caught the eye of Alex, her fiancé, who was standing next to her on this tour of the ranch household. The two had flown out to this ranch near Kiowa in the high plains of eastern Colorado at the invitation of Miriam and Earl Gleason, Janet's aunt and uncle, for a family gathering and celebration of their upcoming marriage. The Gleasons ran a large ranch—2,000 acres and 400 head of cattle, with a few sheep. It was an enchanting place, with rolling hills and meandering creeks lined with lush grass and majestic cottonwood trees. Except for the fact that the ranch's 'hired hands'—real cowboys—negotiated the prairie on mechanized off-road vehicles rather than horses, the ranch would have felt like home to Teddy Roosevelt a century ago. It also was rich with wildlife, including birds, deer, and those varmints Earl pursued with his passion for hunting.

Alex was not a hunter. He was born, raised, and educated in Philadelphia, where his father taught veterinary medicine at Temple University. Alex was not smiling.

"Keep your cool, dear," Janet whispered as she grasped his arm. "Remember, we agreed not to push the issue."

Restraint, however, was not the commanding strength of Alex's character. So he pushed the issue. "You kill a lot of these animals, Earl?" he asked.

"I prefer 'taking' to 'killing,'" said Earl. "I take a couple of whitetail each fall season, dozens of doves, and as many coyotes and prairie dogs as time permits."

"Do you sometimes think of the pain and suffering your 'taking' inflicts on these individuals?" Alex continued.

Earl was silent for a moment. Earlier Janet had mentioned her fiancé's sensibilities, for which her uncle had little appreciation. He had heard that people from Philadelphia often were this way. Restraint was not his strong suit either, but the wisdom of his sixty years tempered any inclination to a hasty response. "A couple of things, Alex. I'm an ethical hunter, and my aim is quite good. Most of the animals I take don't know what hit them. Without my intervention, they would die of predation, disease, injury, and starvation anyway. Given their great numbers, the few I take actually are the lucky ones."

"Perhaps that is true for you," Alex responded, "but it's surely not true for a great majority of hunters, especially those who pursue their prey in woods where a clear shot is difficult. I understand that up to 30 percent of animals are injured and flee, only to die in great suffering and anguish."

"Well then, those hunters—back in Pennsylvania, I presume—ought to do better and try harder," Earl said. "Here, let me show you something."

Earl picked up a small book from a coffee table as the three sat down for what each knew would be an extended conversation. Janet hoped for the best. "This little book—*Beyond Fair Chase*, by Jim Posewitz—says it all. It's the bible of ethical hunting. I understand that more than 200,000 copies have been sold. He writes that an ethical hunter is "a person who knows and respects the animals hunted. . . ." Good hunters won't put themselves in a position where they are likely to cripple an animal, and if they do, they'll track it down as quickly as possible. That kind of consideration is the very meaning of ethical hunting.

"Besides—and this is an important point to me," Earl continued, "when in doubt, I always give the animal the advantage. Without such challenge, hunting would be a worthless pursuit. I'm an avid bow hunter." He gestured to the imposing bow next to the rifles on the rack. "The difficulty increases tremendously with archery hunting. When the hunter has to get within forty yards for a shot, the advantage lies with the animal."

"But that is my point exactly," said Alex. "Although the chances for escape are greater than with high-powered rifles with telescopic sights and ranges of a half-mile, the chances of crippling are much greater with a bow."

"Well, of course a great deal depends on the expertise of the bow hunter. But look closely at my bow. It is a compound bow with pulleys, wheels, and wires to multiply its propelling power. A good clean hit is always lethal, and, as I said, I'm a good marksman."

"Whatever the weapon of choice, crippling happens often," Alex insisted. "Ethical or not, the end result doesn't change: if not injury and slow death, then sudden death—but death just the same."

"Okay, suffering is sometimes involved, and obviously dying," Earl agreed. "But offsetting that is the great pleasure and profound satisfaction hunters get from hunting—and believe me, it's greater than any urbanite can appreciate."

Earl realized that he was getting personal by evoking this stereotype and changed the thrust of his argument. "Janet tells me that you're an environmentalist; you belong to the Sierra Club, Wilderness Society, and all that. You must understand the roles various species play in an ecosystem and the havoc that overpopulation of any one species can bring to the natural order."

"Sure. But the species that is bringing the most havoc through overpopulation is the human species," said Janet, overcoming her reluctance to speak for fear of souring the mood of the family celebration.

"Perhaps, but let's stay on the subject—hunting," replied Earl. "The numbers of deer, elk, and other animals have always been kept in check by predators. Those predators—including wolves, cougars, and grizzly bears—are gone or nearly gone from much of North America. Our species must respond by replacing them. We are the new 'apex predator.' Without hunters in the field, can you imagine the destruction of habitat?"

"Of course, these predators are missing in action because we first wiped them out as competitors to our own predatory behavior," said

Alex. "In the early part of the twentieth century the Forest Service encouraged the elimination of wolves in New Mexico for the sake of more abundant deer for hunters. It succeeded; now the wolves are entirely gone. The result, of course, is that our sins against the wolves were visited upon the deer. Their population exploded. They depleted their habitat and died in great numbers. This is hardly ethical hunting with respect for the animals."

"Deer can be culprits, too," responded Earl. "I've read where the whitetail deer in Virginia have become so numerous that they are reengineering the woodlands environment. Through browsing, they clear the understory, making survival difficult for many songbirds that nest in grass and bushes. It works both ways.

"Besides," Earl continued with another thought, "wolf reintroduction results in the killing not only of pesky deer but also elk, moose, and, of course, domestic animals. My own cattle and sheep are at risk. Who's best suited to control the deer or elk and rescue the songbirds in Virginia or Colorado? My guess is that most folks out here would prefer hunters. They buy licenses, shop at outdoor stores, and otherwise help the economy. Hunters also can be regulated. Free-ranging wolves cannot—unless, of course, one hunts or traps them."

"I'm sorry, Uncle Earl, but this apex hunter image is so, well, macho," Janet said. "Once again, our species—or the male portion of it—first conquers nature by wiping out its natural managers, the large predators, and then uses those empty ecological niches as an excuse for human control. Women have seen this routine over and over, but in other contexts."

"Women are hunters, too, Janet," said Earl, coolly.

"Your niece also grew up in Philly. She's a feminist," said Alex breaking a small smile. "A major problem with your position of top predator is that wolves and the like prey on the individuals of a herd that are easy to catch—the sick, weak, and slow. That process is the very essence of Darwin's natural selection. Hunters turn this process upside down, though, by killing the largest and most majestic animals—the 'trophy' animals whose genes are important to keep the population viable and robust. There's something very unnatural and unhelpful about this kind of selection."

"That might be true for elk and moose," Earl said, "but it's not true for deer because their massive numbers assure the survival of a very large gene pool. Anyway, it's obvious that even the numbers of elk are burgeoning. The situation has changed so much that natural selection is no longer exerting effective restraint."

"What about doves, quail, pheasant?" Alex countered. "These species are mostly without the overpopulation tendencies of the large herbivores, and none of the resulting problems. Yet I see that you enjoy hunting them as well. That impressive Belgian shotgun you showed us for wing shooting is quite an investment."

"True," Earl said, "but there are hundreds of millions of doves. Their species is in no danger. And I do eat those I take. Nothing goes to waste. So take your energy and passion to all those fast-food places that serve up tens of millions of chickens that are massively produced with great suffering in factory farms like those in Arkansas, where the refuse from the production plants fouls the rivers of the Ozarks. Then we can talk about the doves and quail.

"Look," Earl continued, "the most important benefit—far more important than any of these—that hunting brings is the preservation of habitat. Sport hunters like to point out that they have never contributed to the extinction of a species, but they do contribute to the preservation of many species."

"How can that be true?" interrupted Alex. "You know the story of the passenger pigeons—how they were probably the most abundant bird on earth in the 1800s until they were wiped out by hunters. Perhaps 'harvested' would be the better word. And the buffalo: killed by the millions by hunters with nothing more in mind than to make a few bucks selling the hides. They're not extinct, but they were close to it."

"Before you become too agitated, young man, recall that I used the term *sport* hunter. You're talking about market or commercial hunters. Today we refer to them as poachers and hold them in great contempt. Don't confuse what I do with what they did." Earl made his point powerfully without raising his voice. Then he continued.

"I belong to several hunting organizations and, yes, the National Rifle Association too. They all work for the preservation of habitat. Wetlands are a good example. They are vanishing rapidly, thanks to drainage and development. Populations of game birds for whom the marshes, bogs, and estuaries are home are declining in numbers at an alarming rate. Hunters have political and financial clout. They fight for the preservation of these places right along with the Sierra Club and the Audubon Society."

"That's admirable, sir," said Alex, "but environmentalists try to save habitat for the sake of their inhabitants. You do it for the sake of killing those inhabitants."

"'Taking,' son, 'taking,'" corrected Earl. "Besides, what's the difference if the resulting benefits are not only to the species of game animals but also to species hunters have no interest in? If the habitat remains intact, all the plants and animals in it profit. How can a mere difference in intentions make any difference at all when so much good comes from our actions? Actually, these habitats often contain endangered species of plants and animals, so actions that preserve

195

habitat for common game animals may avoid the extinction of these other species. In other words, sport hunters have not caused the extinction of any species, and they may prevent the extinction of many species. That's a trade-off even the most avid environmentalist can live with."

"Excuse me for interrupting," said Miriam as she entered the room. "Lyndon's out front. He has something to show you."

Janet and Alex exchanged glances again. They knew that Lyndon, the foreman of the ranch, had ridden out in the early morning to round up some strays that had wondered through a breach in the fence. As they left the house and walked up to the flatbed truck used for heavy hauling parked in the driveway, they saw the carcass of a large pronghorn antelope and Lyndon with a smile on his face and a rifle in his hand.

"He's a big buck," said Lyndon. "Caught him by surprise drinking from the cistern at the north fence. I'd taken my 30-06 along just in case, and I got real lucky. He was too big to carry on horseback, so I took the truck out to get him. Now, I need some help with the cleaning."

Lyndon was a true cowboy. He viewed the off-road vehicles with contempt and rode a horse instead. Teddy Roosevelt would have celebrated his self-reliant, free-ranging spirit. He even wore chaps, boots, and spurs. They were not for show; they functioned admirably in the prairie environment. He was skilled with the rifle, branding iron, and lasso. Yet his complete characterization of the American cowboy belied his education—an advanced degree in history from Colorado State. He wrote a thesis on the impact of the Great Plains on American culture. That was thirty years ago, however, and for the past twenty-five he had lived out the results of his own academic research.

Overwhelmed by this scene, Alex and Janet would have preferred to exchange the subject of hunting for a discussion of the family celebration of their engagement. For Earl, however, and for Lyndon, flushed with excitement, that was not to be. After dinner the conversation turned once again to hunting.

"Lyndon, not far back you and I were talking about why we hunt and what we get out of it," Earl said. "You made some insightful points that might be worth sharing with our young guests."

"Which ones in particular?" Lyndon asked.

"Well, you said that taking a large game animal is a 'peak experience,'" Earl prompted. "What did you mean by that?"

"It's hard to explain—and deeply spiritual. That moment of taking is magic for me. There's exhilaration, to be sure, and a sense of accomplishment, but it goes way beyond that—way beyond winning the lottery or a major sports event. I can't point to any comparable experience, not in my life," Lyndon said.

"This is that 'soulful' part of hunting I've always heard about," Janet said, "and please excuse me if I'm skeptical. Hunting is an expression of a primal bloodlust. It satisfies the instinct of aggression so that we can all live together without bringing violence to one another. We don't need that outlet now, though, and even if we did there are other, more preferable, ways of satisfying it. Killing animals and calling the pursuit 'sport hunting' suggests to me that all claims to peak or spiritual experiences are pretenses."

"I think your term 'primal' is important here, Janet," Lyndon responded. "You're familiar with the claims of the emerging science of sociobiology—or evolutionary psychology, as it's sometimes called. For thousands of years we were hunters. The feelings and behavior that made hunters successful became coded in our genes. Indeed, one could argue that certain emotions and even our intellect are evolutionary adaptations of the successful hunter in those primal times."

"Funny, I don't sense those emotions," Alex said.

"Ever hunted?" Earl asked.

"Um, no," Alex admitted.

"Then you wouldn't recognize the hunting instincts, would you?" Earl said.

"I recognize them as bloodlust," Alex responded. "And the animal—the antelope you shot? It never had any say in the matter. True spirituality doesn't require victims."

"Actually, the more appropriate term, in my opinion, is blood sacrifice," Lyndon said. "Only a true urbanite could miss the deeper significance of the hunt. Out here we call the 99 percent of Americans who never get more than fifty feet from their car in a wilderness setting 'ninety-nine fiftiers.' Hikers, seeking the serene beauty of some majestic landscape, never notice the constant perishing that drives all life and its presence in all natural settings. We deny death in human society, so we are forced to deny it in nature. It's the urbanite, not the hunter, who lives under false pretenses.

"And the antelope I took today," Lyndon continued, "is special— a gift to me for which I am deeply indebted and appreciative. It's not about me. I'm just a part of the puzzle or a larger performance or ritual in nature that I can't explain."

"This discussion is far too romantic for me," said Janet. "Let me put the question another way. What's the difference between animals killing animals and humans killing animals?"

"Whoa," responded Lyndon. "Your question is very biased. Humans don't kill animals. Humans kill *other* animals."

"Why is that change important?" Janet asked.

"Because our urge to hunt and our meat-eating preferences are part of our animal—not cultural—nature," said Lyndon. "There is no difference between animals killing animals and humans killing animals. We're animals, too."

"Does that fact justify hunting, or make it right?" Janet asked.

"Morally speaking, that question doesn't make sense," answered Lyndon. "Moral principles do not apply to nature. Nature is nonmoral. It would be absurd to hold any animal responsible for its actions. What is done in nature is natural—it just is. No moral judgment can be made about it. That includes our behavior when we are acting in nature according to our place as animals."

"Lyndon," Janet continued, "your argument is, in fact, a justification for hunting and killing. What you're saying is that it is reasonable for humans to imitate the behavior of animals and thereby escape the moral realm altogether."

"Yes," said Alex, echoing his fiancée. "If nothing is right or wrong in nature, then hunting is in some funny way permissible. In fact, anything is permissible."

"I don't believe that," Lyndon said, "and I don't know any thoughtful hunter who does. All animals—and plants, too—live by the strict laws built into their instinctive natures by evolution. Hunters abide by those same laws. Abuse of game animals is a violation of those laws."

"Back to emotions," Alex said. "Do you feel any sadness when you stand over the antelope you just killed?"

"I'd be lying if I said no," Lyndon answered candidly. "There is a sense of guilt. I wouldn't be fully human if I didn't feel that. Within the natural context, though, guilt may be out of place. Anyway, it helps me appreciate the animal and respect it."

"How can that respect mean anything?" asked Alex incredulously.

"We bring the animal home and eat it. That's how we honor it. Letting the carcass go to waste is the greatest disrespect," Lyndon said. "And it's far more respect than urbanites show cattle, chickens, and other domestic animals slaughtered by the millions for their ovens and grills."

Alex decided prudently to pursue another line of argument.

"Back to your point about following our animal natures. That seems absurd. We don't base our moral principles of honesty or justice or loyalty on what animals do or on what we could do when we act like animals, so why should we imitate predatory animal behavior in hunting and killing game?" he asked.

"They're not the same thing," Lyndon replied, a bit frustrated with his back-East acquaintances. "Those principles are part of our human culture and make up our moral lives in relation to one another. Animals have nothing quite like it."

"I hear you saying that humans are the same as animals in nature and yet different. Is that right?" Janet asked.

"That's right," Lyndon answered, "and wisdom is being able to tell the difference and conduct ourselves accordingly."

With that remark, both sides of the debate silently decided to call it a draw. The hour was late, and tomorrow friends and family would appear early for the all-day celebration.

As Janet passed the rack of rifles and bows, she reflected on Lyndon's remark. "You know," she said to Alex, " if killing and dying are so much a part of nature, perhaps we should refuse to participate in it at all. Is that possible? We certainly can't redesign nature and rid it of its violence, though our zoos and parks try to do just that. Still, we want to affirm nature—but does that mean affirming stalking and killing like Uncle Earl and Lyndon do? Are we above nature when we object to hunting, or only above ourselves?"

Alex looked at her with a hint of surprise and smiled. "Well, if those are your thoughts, we'll have a lot to talk about on our honeymoon."

Commentary

Only a small proportion of Americans—about 10 percent—ever hunt.[1] Yet hunting introduces issues that go beyond mere numbers. The sport is an American tradition. It is associated politically and culturally with the gun culture in America, as well as with the country's celebrated roots in rugged independence and self-reliance. In his great work of poetry, *Leaves of Grass*, Walt Whitman credits the advance of the frontier in the nineteenth century to the broad-axe, not the rifle.[2] Many hunting enthusiasts today would beg to differ, however. In their memory and imagination it was the musket, the Sharpes repeating rifle, and the lever-action Winchester that truly won the West. Hunters are a powerful minority. The relentless lobbying of the influential, ideologically entrenched, and sometimes embattled National Rifle Association reflects their power. Even the 10 percent minority who hunt translate into more than 20 million hunters—a significant special-interest constituency and a sizable population added to the woods and fields during hunting season.

The animals these millions kill—or, as Earl prefers, "take"—also number in the millions: 200 million animals each year. About half are birds—mainly doves (50 million), quail (25 million), and pheasant (20 million). Small animals, such as squirrel and rabbits, account for 25 million killed.[3] The larger animals command the most attention from opponents and the public, probably because they *are* large. Their deaths by rifle and by bow and arrow are visually more violent than those of doves instantly shot out of the sky. Moreover, we relate to our mammalian relatives more easily than to our avian relatives. The sheer numbers are unnerving as well: Four million deer are taken annually, along with 20,000 black bears.[4] Yet hunting advocates are quick to point out, as Earl does, that these numbers do not tell the whole story. Thirty million deer forage in the woodlands and open meadows of America, many in sprawling suburban communities, and as many as 8 million black bear share their habitat.[5] Both species are doing quite well—their numbers growing despite the ubiquitous seasonal presence of their potent enemy, the human hunter.

Opponents of hunting are quick to point out that these numbers miss the point entirely. For them, hunting is a morally suspect and unnecessary sport. The death of even a single dove, whitetail deer, or black bear is one too many. Their arguments are many. The inherent violence of the sport is a major objection. If hunting is a sport, it is a blood sport akin to the slaughter of the Roman circus or gladiatorial combat. If it were a true sport, both sides would be evenly matched. As the one pursued (hunting, by definition, means to pursue), the animal is always on the defensive. The roles of hunter and hunted are seldom reversed.

The object of the hunter is to stalk and then use a weapon, usually a rifle, to take the life of a helpless animal. The fact that guns are the weapons of choice in crime and violence in American cities is not lost on opponents of hunting. What pleasure and satisfaction can come from such activity? Tracking and shooting a deer with a high-powered rifle must be in its essence cruel and sadistic, associated with some primal joy of inflicting pain. Or it is an ego trip in which the hunter is bent on domination and conquest, and the trophy head hung on the wall instructs all who see it that the hunter is superior and powerful. How can hunting be considered a sport?

Closely related to the perceived sadistic pleasure of the hunter are the pain and suffering inflicted on the prey. Even if it escapes the bullet the animal will experience fear and terror. More important is the high rate of crippling noted by Alex. Crippling occurs when an animal is injured in the hunt and successfully evades the hunter, only to die a slow and painful death from its wounds, starvation, or predators. Estimates of the rate of unretrieved animals vary considerably but sometimes approach 30 percent. "Ethical hunters" strive to reduce or eliminate crippling by taking only clear shots and maintaining their marksmanship skills. Ammunition is expensive, however. Few hunters can afford to hone their skills on a target range before entering the woods for the real thing, and the average hunter is in the field only five to seven days each year—hardly ample experience to determine a clear shot. Many novices, bent on achieving their legal limit, often "shoot from the hip" and injure rather than kill their target.

Another argument sometimes voiced by opponents of hunting is that hunters, a small portion of the citizenry, are unfairly subsidized by public funds. *The Animal Rights Handbook*,[6] for example, claims that federal and state wildlife agencies, aided by our tax dollars, maintain artificial habitats where deer and other animals are encouraged to overpopulate to provide targets for the benefit of hunters. The very name—state "fish and *game* commissions"—betrays their purpose. This practice, opponents claim, is an abuse of public funds.

It is no surprise that few of the philosophers discussed in chapter 1 who argue for the moral value and considerability of animals approve of hunting. Peter Singer objects on the basis of the unnecessary suffering that hunting brings to sentient animals, although he does approve of hunting within subsistence cultures—the Inuit, for example. Paul Taylor opposes hunting because it violates several principles that derive from his biocentric ethic. Two of these principles are noninterference and fidelity. Noninterference means that humans should let natural systems and individual animals alone whenever possible to pursue their own fulfillment. Fidelity entails the duty—framed in negative terms, as a prohibition—not to deceive animals in the wild. Fishing, trapping, and hunting violate both of these duties in that they interfere with and betray the animal.[7]

Hunting advocates are quick to respond to each of these charges and characterizations as distorted and unjust. Hunters do not seek to inflict pain and suffering on game animals. Second only to a successful kill is the avoidance of such suffering. The ideal is instant death. To achieve this goal, so-called ethical hunters will train and sharpen their skills in preparation for going into the field. The problem of crippling remains difficult. Hunters argue that the more powerful rifles—those that fire high-velocity projectiles accurately over long distances—reduce the incidence of crippling dramatically. Ironically, however, the use of these rifles also reduces any advantages the animal might have to detect the hunter and escape successfully. Earl seems to be caught in this dilemma when he promotes bow-and-arrow hunting. Although this primitive weapon gives the animal a fighting chance, its use may result in frequent incidences of crippling.

Several points can be made with respect to the expression "sport hunting." Agreeing with their opponents, apologists for hunting have reservations about the word "sport" as well. Although many sports have fervent devotees or fans, "sport" suggests recreation or pastime—a leisure activity that passes time in the absence of more serious or pressing pursuits or work. Unlike many sports, advocates argue, hunting is not a trivial pursuit intended to satisfy trivial interests. Dedicated and thoughtful hunters do not regard themselves this way. Characterizing themselves as sport hunters places them on the defensive and at a disadvantage with their critics.

Moreover, the very foundation of hunting lies in the challenge of the pursuit. Ethical hunters hold in contempt those who bait deer and bear to approach for an easy shot. Nothing, however, tarnishes the image of the hunter like artificial hunting. Private game ranches with fences and exotic animals and birds released from pens so that paying customers can shoot them at will are offensive to most hunters. Every advantage should be given to the animal. Even with its disadvantages, bow hunting is intended to do just that.

Hunting advocates respond to the accusation that public monies subsidize their activities with figures of their own. They point out that of the millions of people who enjoy wildlife-related outdoor activities, only hunters pay for the privilege. Hunting and fishing licenses, duck stamps, and excise taxes on the purchase of hunting equipment fund as much as 75 percent of the annual income of government wildlife agencies, according to some estimates.[8]

Other contributions of hunters include protection of habitat. Earl points out that environmentalists and hunters have a powerful common interest in the preservation of wild areas as habitat. Politically influential and wealthy hunting organizations recognize the importance of protecting natural areas as habitat for game animals. Because nongame species—such as plants, frogs, and birds—benefit from the same habitat, environmentalists stand to gain from the hunters' advocacy. The unusual coalition between two groups whose philosophies are irreducibly incompatible is possible because they agree to set aside their differences at the practical and political levels to achieve a common purpose. Earl's comments on this alliance represent the pragmatic approach of Bryan Norton discussed in chapter 1. Anthropocentrists, biocentrists, and ecocentrists can work together to achieve real-world interests in a common goal or project.

Nevertheless, the choice to work closely with one's sworn enemies is difficult, especially for some biocentrists for whom animal suffering and death at the hands of recreational hunters is cruel and indefensible. Norton's pragmatic approach is a win-win situation only if such sacrifices are accepted. The ecocentrist and especially the biocentrist must agree to pursue their purpose within the rules of utilitarian calculations. To preserve the great diversity of species in a hunting refuge as well as the lives of many individual animals, other animals—game animals—must bear the cost. Harm brought to deer and ducks by hunters pays off in the benefits of a healthy habitat—a marsh or woodland—for thousands of other resident species.

Other philosophical issues play a powerful role in the justification of hunting. Anthropocentrists have no difficulty offering such a justification: Humans are superior. We have a right to lord it over other species and to kill them at our pleasure, with no duties to the animal save those to ourselves (e.g., preserving a species of animal from overhunting for the sake of future game). Religious reasons sometimes are offered. Chapter 9 of the biblical book of Genesis makes this attitude clear. "The fear of you and dread of you shall be upon every beast of the earth . . . into your hand they shall be delivered (9:2)," and "Every living thing that moves shall be food for you" (9:3).

Several contemporary apologists for hunting prefer to argue, however, from a position that includes the hunter within rather than beyond nature. Earl follows this line of reasoning when he identifies with the "apex predator." This is the "king of beasts," whose role is to patrol the ecosystem of which he is an integral part—preventing overpopulation; taking the weak, sickly, and slow; and otherwise managing the system and sustaining its well-being with Darwinian efficiency. Alex quickly recognizes the contradiction entailed in this account of the hunting vocation. Hunters, he says, stalk the biggest and best of a species: the trophy animals—those favored by natural selection. This "unnatural selection" hardly works to the benefit of the natural system. Hunting advocates respond to this embarrassing insight by drawing attention to the fact that those millions of game animals taken annually do hold down populations. Without hunters as a limiting force, many disastrous consequences would follow, including decimation of crops, increased incidences of disease in animals as well as between animals and humans, habitat destruction, and massive die-offs. If this were to happen, the new managing predators probably would be feral dogs and cats whose growing numbers already put birds and small animals at risk—in addition to the increased dangers of rabies and other zoonotic diseases they would bring.

The apex predator argument does not get to heart of the matter, which Janet characterizes as "soulful." Advocates of hunting ultimately turn to atavism in the justification of their pursuit. Hunting, the argument goes, must be experienced to be understood. Its opponents do not know what they are talking about when they condemn the activity as arbitrary and capricious, cruel and sadistic, a psychopathological distortion of the healthy individual psyche. Urbanites—Earl's "ninety-nine fiftiers"—have no experience with animals in the wild, only with pets or zoos. They have lost touch with primal instincts and virtues that are revived in the stalking and taking of game. Our ancestors were not born near supermarkets. Hunting was a fundamental pursuit of humans for tens of thousands of years. Those drives still lie deep within us, aroused when we take to the woods with rifle and bow.

Opponents of hunting often wonder if nonlethal means could be used to stalk and take the prey. Perhaps a camera could provide a different kind of shot for the hunter—one just as satisfying. It would not be the same thing, however. Killing is integral to hunting. The killing of an animal may trigger a fundamentally mystical peak experience of unity with the world of nature and result in self-fulfillment. Unlike the urbanite, whose abstract vision is of nature without death, the hunter understands that nature cannot be truly experienced without encountering death. Hunting affirms the mortality of all creatures and participates in the prey-predator relationship that drives evolution. Certainly, the experience is not without some unease and even guilt. Guilt was not absent in primal subsistence hunters. They atoned with ceremonies honoring the animal—perhaps processing its soul into the womb of the maternal earth, to be born into another body. The modern hunter atones by consuming his take. Deer becomes venison when served at the table, where it is more than merely meat. Eating the animal gives meaning to its death and avoids the mortal sin of waste. Indeed, eating animals that we kill is an act of respect for all of nature and its good order.

Hunting advocates point to hunting as an expression of virtue, not vice. Discipline is involved, as are patience, courage, and respect. Of course, there are exceptions. Some hunters are insensitive slobs whose intentions are domination and slaughter. Many hunters, however, describe the hunt as an event requiring great honesty and personal integrity. Because hunting is mostly a solitary endeavor, the expression of these virtues is impelled not extrinsically by reward, recognition, or praise from others but intrinsically, as the spontaneous expression of a person's character.

Holmes Rolston III is an environmental philosopher who has wrestled with these philosophical and spiritual claims for hunting. His thoughts are represented by Earl and Lyndon. The human species lives both within culture and within nature. Our cultural life consists of our personal and social relations with others and the moral obligations that follow from those relations. Human institutions reflect these distinctly human principles and values. Yet we are animals as well, and some of our activities, including eating, belong to our animal nature. Why should we follow the dietary habits of animals in nature, however, when we don't model our other social and moral values— marriage, honesty, justice—on animal behavior? Because, Rolston argues, these are cultural values, unique to us. Eating is different. It is "omnipresent" in nature and applies equally to all omnivores. We have no duty to remake the order of nature. We may continue as omnivores. Nor do we have any obligation to remake our own animal natures—the product of eons of evolution—

when it is appropriate to express them. Stalking and killing prey is an expression of that nature. Not only is it mostly outside the realm of moral value because nature is nonmoral; it also is an act expressing the essential character of our species. Rolston senses the dialectic and even the contradiction of hunting. The exhilaration and the guilt are both present. The former derives from our place in the ecosystem, the latter from our place in culture. To affirm both as legitimate responses to killing is to embrace the tragic contradiction built into the world.[9]

Questions for Discussion

1. Many ecocentrists, including Aldo Leopold, condone hunting. Are they consistent in their position?
2. Peter Singer, the famous advocate of animal liberation discussed in chapter 1, focuses his attention on the suffering of domestic and factory-produced animals. Can his arguments for the moral value of animals be applied without modification to animals in the wild? What would Singer say about saving a deer from a stalking cougar? Are the balance of nature and maintenance of the food chain additional factors that must be considered? Explain.
3. Nature is driven by predator-prey relationships. The human species evolved in nature and satisfies the requirements for survival by adaptation, just as any other species does. If hunting therefore is a natural human predatory activity in nature, how can it be criticized or condemned?
4. Tens of millions of animals are struck and killed by vehicles on highways each year. These roadkill numbers approach the numbers of animals killed by hunters. Is it logical to oppose hunting but not oppose automobile transportation?

Notes

1. James A. Swan, *In Defense of Hunting* (San Francisco: HarperCollins, 1995), 3.
2. Walt Whitman, "Song of the Broad-Axe," in *Leaves of Grass* (New York: Literary Classics of the United States, 1982), 330–31.
3. Swan, *In Defense of Hunting*, 8.
4. Ibid., 8.
5. Ibid., 266.
6. *The Animal Rights Handbook* (Venice, Calif.: Living Planet Press, 1990), 83.
7. Paul Taylor, *Respect for Life* (Princeton, N.J.: Princeton University Press, 1986), 174.
8. Swan, *In Defense of Hunting*, 159.

9. Holmes Rolston III, *Environmental Ethics: Duties and Values in the Natural World* (Philadelphia: Temple University Press, 1988), 78–93.

For Further Reading

Leopold, Aldo. "The Varmint Question." In *The River of the Mother of God and Other Essays by Aldo Leopold*, ed. Susan Flader and J. Baird Callicott. Madison: University of Wisconsin Press, 1991, 101–12.

Lofton, Robert. "The Morality of Hunting." *Environmental Ethics* 6 (fall 1984): 241–49.

Posewitz, Jim. *Fair Chase, The Ethic and Tradition of Hunting.* Helena, Mont.: Falcon Press, 1994.

Regan, Tom. *The Case for Animal Rights.* Berkeley: University of California Press, 1983.

Rolston, Holmes III. *Environmental Ethics: Duties and Values in the Natural World.* Philadelphia: Temple University Press, 1988.

Swan, James A. *In Defense of Hunting.* San Francisco: HarperCollins, 1995.

Taylor, Paul. *Respect for Life.* Princeton, N.J.: Princeton University Press, 1986.

Western, Samuel. "Fair Game." *E: The Environmental Magazine* 10 (July/August 1999): 16.

13

Understanding Xenotransplants: Cross-Breeding Humans or Advanced Domestication of Animals?

"I'm just not convinced," Hassan said to his friends. Liz, Jason, Nirad, and Hassan were all first- or second-year residents who had met for lunch across the street from the university hospital, where they had all just completed rounds on the kidney transplant floor. They had been discussing Liz's announcement that she was planning to specialize in urology—specifically, kidney transplant surgery.

"But Has," Liz protested, "you've seen the stats on transplant life expectancy—especially with kidneys. Life expectancies are constantly rising, along with quality of life. How many thousands of people who had end-stage renal disease, or even hearts barely pumping, are now living almost fully normal lives ten and even twenty years post-transplant? And heart and liver success rates are continuing to rise. Like kidney transplant patients, they have fewer and fewer complications as the steroid dosages continue to decrease. There's no reason to doubt that in another five to ten years the success rates of heart, lung, liver, and pancreas transplants—and even these new intestinal transplants—

will have improved beyond all recognition. What kind of reservations can you possibly have when you compare that to the deaths these patients would otherwise experience?"

Hassan had just begun the first surgical rotation of his residency; he was working in the transplant clinic under Dr. Ross, under whom Liz was beginning her second year of residency.

"One of my cousins had a kidney transplant five years ago because of a birth defect," Hassan confided. "Within two weeks she had a rare and raging staph infection, and she spent six weeks in the hospital to get it under control. In these five years she has spent about a third of her time in the hospital. The prospects don't look any better for the rest of her life, basically because with the immunosuppressant drugs they can't fully eliminate that infection. I don't have all the details; I have tried to stay away from the medical side as well as I could after checking that her surgical staff was reputable. If I got involved, my whole family would expect me to pull off a miracle and save her. But I do visit Suha. She's now a fourteen-year-old ghost. She has no hope that she will ever be well; even in weeks when she feels well, she expects the infection to recur. She has no plans for the future. She has virtually no friends left because she takes no interest in their plans or activities. She doesn't think she will ever marry or have a home or career. A few weeks ago, the staff told the family that the treatment for the infection had damaged the transplant kidney and that she will be back on dialysis waiting for a second transplant within the year. When I visited that night, Suha blurted out to me that she wishes she would die because then she wouldn't have to worry about what will happen to her when her parents die and there is nobody to take care of her. Her social circle is her parents, the staff at the transplant clinic, and the nurses and aides at the hospital.

"You know we have lots more like her. You saw Mrs. Morrow this morning—the same story in a middle-aged woman two years post-transplant. Her husband had to quit his job, just like my aunt did with Suha, to take care of her, to take her for the doctor appointments, for labs, to secure and supervise her drug supply—the whole routine. In Suha's case, my aunt was working for college funds for the other three daughters, who will now have to work and go part-time to community colleges because it is all the family can do to pay for Suha's bills that insurance doesn't cover. Or what about that baseball player at the university? Right after his transplant he got Guillain-Barré, spent six months totally paralyzed on a respirator in ICU, six months in rehab, will never have more than partial use of his hands and feet again, and still faces a second transplant. These people can live for decades in this half-life, destroying the lives of everyone who cares for them. My aunt and uncle have no life other than caring for Suha."

There was silence for a moment, and then Jason spoke up.

"Well, yes," he said, "there is a small group of transplant patients who succumb to serious diseases from immunosuppression, but you know cases like your cousin's are rare, and people who are not immunosuppressed also can contract these same diseases. Remember that big cop in ICU last year who came down with Guillain-Barré after a bout with the flu that weakened his immune system?"

"Of course nontransplant patients also succumb," Liz responded, "but these diseases are a lot easier to treat successfully if the patient is not immunosuppressed. On the other hand, I've only met three or four patients who, given a choice between dying without the transplant and taking these risks with one, chose not to transplant—and those were all kidney patients who were doing well on peritoneal dialysis, on which they could hope to live out a pretty normal life span."

"That's right," Hassan said, "but that's right to my point. Why don't we put more people on peritoneal, and keep them there, instead of steering everyone to transplantation? Nine hours a night hooked up to a machine, with comparatively few drugs to alter body chemistry or damage other organs. I know that lots of our patients wouldn't have the discipline, couldn't handle the responsibility of peritoneal, but my point is that we don't even support, much less encourage, the ones who could. We shunt them into the high-tech hemodialysis and transplant list path."

Nirad, the quietest one in the group, chimed in.

"I agree with you, Liz, but I think I see Has's point, too. Organ transplantation is like the HIV cocktail in that it's not a cure, just a way to maybe survive a fatal disease for longer, without curing it—and the treatment creates problems of its own. For myself, I wish that mechanical organs like that new grapefruit-sized implantable heart with the external battery pack that Dr. Sacks is testing works out and could be the first mechanical organs. Then we could avoid immunosuppressants."

"That's a great hope," Jason said, "but as you well know, it's not likely. The heart, like all the other organs, performs many different functions in the body; many of them we don't fully understand. Just because we can get a machine to mimic the pumping action of the heart, or even a few others, doesn't mean it will replace all the other functions of the heart. We'll still be medicating the hell out of those patients. That's why the mechanicals are being treated as stopgap measures to keep people alive until we have transplants for them."

Liz smiled and reminded them of Dr. Grenville's lecture about the future of xenotransplants, which they had heard the week before.

"Imagine yourself ordering kidneys and hearts from pigs genetically designed to share some human DNA so they don't acute-reject!" she exclaimed. "I had no idea that pigs were so close to the human genotype, though I suppose we must have learned that in genetics. Grenville seems to think that pig organs would not only solve the problem of insufficient transplant organs; he also reported that animal research indicates that the amount of immunosuppression can be reduced drastically by prepping the organ recipient with the donor pig's bone marrow. By the time we all complete our various residencies, these xenografts may be the center of transplant surgery, instead of just stopgap experiments on dying patients with no other options, like that baby Faye who got the baboon heart in the early 1980s."

Hassan made a face. "Among all the mammals," he said, "why did it have to be pigs that were most suitable? None of my people would ever accept pig organs. If it's too dirty to eat, we certainly can't make it part of our bodies."

Nirad laughed along with the others. He and Hassan were American-born Hindu and Muslim, respectively, and frequently had been forced to explain particular beliefs and practices of their traditions to the others. Then he got serious.

"I can appreciate the irony, Has, but there's a deeper problem. Many millions of people in India—virtually all the higher Hindu castes—are vegetarian, and that vegetarianism is based on *ahimsa*, the principle of not harming any living thing. When you add the Jains, as well as the many Buddhists who refuse to eat animals for the same reason, to Muslims and Orthodox Jews who object to pork, you have a significant portion of the world's population that almost certainly will not accept these xenografts for religious reasons. If we are really researching a solution to diseased organs, its ethics shouldn't offend the religious sensibilities of half the world. This isn't just a problem in other nations, or with religion. Even in the States many people have a problem with using parts of any other species in the human body, whether by ingestion, testing, or grafts. It seems to me that it's crossing a dangerous boundary that is not meant to be crossed."

"But Nirad," Jason responded, "hasn't that point been made against every major advance in medicine, including all surgery, blood transfusions, up through radiation and chemotherapy and human organ transplants? Opponents of all those procedures have demanded that we not cross some boundary—usually one they felt that God himself had deliberately instituted. I really can't take that argument seriously anymore."

"Nirad," Liz teased, "I had no idea that you were an animal rights defender. How did we miss that about you? Is it related to Hindu reverence for cows? Is that it?"

"No," Nirad snorted, "I'm not traditional enough to be against xenotransplants because of the injury done to any individual pig—or even cow! I know some people would be, but if I have to kill an animal to save a human I can do that without a qualm. It seems to me, though, that crossing human and nonhuman species is dangerous stuff at a bunch of different levels. Who decides how much human DNA in a pig makes that pig human? Could we be creating 'semihumans'? Remember *The Island of Dr. Moreau*? Even if standards were set, we have seen how researchers' constant need to push the envelope eventually leads somebody to ignore the standards. It's perfectly clear to me that the reason research has turned to animals is that researchers think there are too many ethical problems in securing human organs to accommodate the need for them, and they hope to avoid these ethical problems by turning to animals. But when they give human genes or DNA to these animals, or vice versa, they create another whole set of problems. The ethical issue of how we distinguish human from animal once we start mixing them is only one of the problems."

"I have a hard time taking the Dr. Moreau tableau seriously," Jason said. "It was just fantastic fiction."

Liz responded with a chuckle. "Oh, I don't know, Jason, it seems to me that that's what they said a hundred years ago about Jules Verne's *Nautilus*, which prowled the bottom of the sea! Yesterday's science fiction really has been a pretty good predictor of our world in lots of ways."

Hassan spoke up. "But seriously, guys, look at all the things we are constantly finding that go wrong in human transplants, things we thought we understood; some of them we didn't have a clue about until thirty years after we started doing transplants. Like that new research about kidney patients who constantly reject one donor organ after another. Only now is it discovered that the scar tissue that causes the rejection is not part of the rejection response to the donor organ but a part of the patient's body's response to surgery! We know a lot more about the human body than about any other mammal—what unknown reactions would we be importing with the organ, reactions we know nothing about?"

"But we've learned about these occasional but real problems in humans," Liz said, "and we would learn about new ones from animals and find out how to treat them, too, in time. I know it sounds like a cliché, but it's true."

"Yes, science will solve all problems, including the ones it creates," Hassan mocked.

Nirad responded to Liz more seriously: "All right, we've learned how to deal with importing human viruses like cytomegalovirus in transplants. We now know that about 40 percent of the population is CMV+, and the rest CMV−, and when the CMV status of the donor and the recipient don't match we have a prophylactic drug treatment that prevents CMV disease while the positive body or organ converts the other to positive. A lot of people lost their lives, or were left disabled by conditions like blindness, before we learned that one. But animal organs carry a whole new world of viruses and infections that we don't even recognize, much less know how to test for or treat. Inevitably we would import these viruses into transplant patients, even if these donor pigs are raised in sterile conditions.

"After all," he continued, "look at hospitals, which have the most rigorous conventions on cleanliness and sterility—and remain some of the easiest places in the world to become ill. Some of these pig diseases will certainly produce mortal complications; others might not threaten the lives of the patients, but if those patients have kids, do they pass on these diseases to their kids? Then they are out there in the gene pool. Or do we sterilize transplant patients to make sure they don't reproduce? Wouldn't *that* be wonderful!" he concluded sarcastically.

"That's a scary thought," Liz admitted. "We could be introducing whole new diseases, even epidemics, into the human population. We already know that humans are susceptible to many animal diseases, like HIV and mad cow disease. Sometimes the diseases that cross over are more dangerous to humans than they are to the animals from which they come."

"That's a big one to consider," Hassan said, stroking his chin. "What about cloning and stem cell research? Don't I remember hearing a series of reports last year touting them both as potential sources of hope?"

"Yeah, but by comparison with animal xenografts, both of them are pretty far off in the future," Liz answered. "Stem cell research has some big political problems . . . "

". . . that are based on moral problems," Jason interrupted. Everyone knew that he came from a family involved in the Right-to-Life movement. "The stem cells are taken from fetuses that are aborted, and now there are researchers deliberately creating embryos with the intention of destroying them by removing the stem cells. How can that not be murder?"

"If it's not murder to have, or perform, an abortion, then it isn't murder to create and destroy embryos, however unfortunate—not to mention politically dangerous right now—it is," Liz retorted. She and Jason had gone head to head on the abortion issue several times before.

"We can argue the morality of abortion until Nirad's cows come home," Hassan said, "but in terms of the politics it's clear that there are serious objections to funding research that creates and destroys embryos to obtain stem cells—and maybe there should be." Hassan looked to Jason, who was ready to jump in on the point. "Regardless of those objections, on the science alone, do you think cloning and stem cell research are a long way from answering the need for organs, Liz?"

"Further off this month than before," she responded. "Anybody read the latest research on cloning?" At the lack of reply, she explained, "We all know that the rates of success in animal cloning are low, but the latest report says that in the animal species where researchers have had the most success, the success rate is between one and three in a hundred live births, depending on the species—and that many of the live births are short-lived and not healthy, either. Interestingly, one of the biggest problems seems to be anomalies in various types of tissue, especially organs, that soon cause death. Growth and development usually don't occur normally; the researchers suspect the problem is that the programming of the adult cell by the egg takes place in minutes or hours, instead of the months that sperm take to develop or the years that eggs take to mature. In the speed, they think, mistakes are made, and those mistakes don't always show up till later."

"Guys, you can't seriously be thinking about cloning whole people as a source for organs!" sputtered Jason. "Regardless of these technical problems, you know the size that a fetus would have to be before any of its organs would be usable for transplant—it would have to be virtually full-term, and even then many organs would not be large enough for adults. You can't be talking about creating people who are identical to living human beings and treating them like cars in a junkyard, raided for spare parts!"

"I didn't mean to imply that I approved of this use," Liz said defensively. "Of course it would be impossible to use intelligent sentient clones for parts. But who knows, maybe they can find a way to create anacephalic clones."

"Nope, I'm with Jason here," Hassan said. "Anyone who looks just like me and has all my DNA should be treated with the same respect I am, even if he is born without a higher brain. It's too damn dangerous. Brain death is one thing in comatose patients. I don't want anything to do with taking hearts out of conscious, sentient beings with fully human DNA. How big a step is that from raiding mentally retarded or even mentally ill people for organs?"

Liz shrugged. "I didn't say it was a good idea," she said, "and I do have some qualms about cloning whole humans, too, although some researchers have been successful in cloning just parts of mice—an ear, a stomach. If that technology could be perfected, we could just clone the organ we need. On the other hand, stem cell research isn't really so much about replacing worn-out organs. Instead, it offers hope of reducing the number of damaged organs that need replacing. The use of stem cells, if applied early enough in the disease process, could cure or at least retard organ deterioration in several specific diseases. Imagine what a cure for diabetes—or even a way to retard kidney disease in diabetic patients—could do to reduce the need for kidneys! The present supply of stem cells is very limited, though, so it's hard to imagine any widespread impact on the general population in the near future even if stem cell treatment is proved successful in these new applications."

"The supply is limited because they come from aborted fetuses," Jason said. "Tell it like it is. To increase the supply to treatment levels rather than just experimental levels, it wouldn't be enough to salvage more stem cells from dead fetuses; we also would have to abort more fetuses. Gruesome, huh?"

"Okay, Jason, we get the point," Hassan said. "We probably would need artificial sources of stem cells. That's why the xenotransplants look so attractive to those of us who like pigs."

"I don't know how I feel about xenotransplants," Nirad said. "I don't think I'm uneasy because my culture reveres cows, though maybe I have absorbed the *ahimsa* principle of no harm to any living thing so deeply that I'm not conscious of it. I am uncomfortable using anything living as if it were merely a thing that we humans can transform or manipulate in major ways. If it would be wrong to eliminate the whole species, then isn't it also wrong to transform the species in a fundamental way to meet our desires?"

"Do you mean to say that I can take a kidney from the eighteen-year-old brother of a dialysis patient to save the patient's life, but it would be wrong to take a kidney from a pig to save that same life?" Liz asked. "That makes no sense to me. If we are relatives of the pigs in evolutionary terms, and human relatives exchange organs for the good of the whole society, then why is it wrong to take organs from our animal relatives? Don't many native peoples understand themselves as descended from their totem animals? Wouldn't we just be acknowledging that kind of relationship?"

"I don't think that one will wash, Liz," Jason said, "because the way I remember totems, the totemic animal could not be eaten or killed by the member of the totemic group as a way of honoring the ancestral animal. In the totemic system, we are the descendants who owe reverence to the ancestral animal."

"But lots of indigenous peoples have hunted and eaten animals, even though they understand them as related to humans, haven't they?" Liz demanded.

"Yes. You know," Nirad remarked with a glance at her plate, "if you really did understand pigs as relatives, I think you would feel differently about ordering pork ribs for lunch." Hassan chuckled, and Liz acknowledged the hit. Nirad continued, "But people in India, for example, would explain eating animals in the past by saying that primitives saw no other way to sustain their lives—but that more civilized peoples realized that the relationship between species forbids using other species when we have other means of sustaining our lives."

"But we don't have other means!" Liz insisted. "These patients die without transplants."

"I don't know, Liz. I'm not much for animal rights," said Jason, "but I do think there is a difference between hunting animals when you are hungry and creating animal factories, either the ones we already have to produce veal, chicken, salmon, and so forth or the new factories that xenotransplants are creating. The hunter takes only one deer out of the herd that runs free and asks for its forgiveness for the necessity of killing it to feed his people. They revere the animals. The scale that our society works on has already taken many animals out of their natural habitats to domesticate them and bred desired genetic changes into them, reducing and controlling genetic diversity within species. Now we've moved them into factory farms and laboratories, making the animals we eat even more invisible. We don't think of the chicken breast in the grocery as an animal; we ignore the conditions under which they are produced, and the result is that animals don't have the sacredness they have had for the native hunters. We would be self-consciously further changing who the animals are and in the end making them just things—in the same way that embryos and fetuses have become, to a lot of people, just things to be used.

"And you know, I have to wonder if animals really are the answer to the organ shortage. The technologies involved here are all patented, and the companies that own the patents plan to earn billions. Did you know that the majority of investors in these xenotransplant companies are the drug companies that make immunosuppressants? They plan on charging thousands of dollars—most accounts say about $10,000 apiece—for these pig organs. That's in addition to the $15,000–$20,000 a year transplant patients already spend on labs and drugs. Even if U.S. insurance companies eventually cover these xenotransplants, most of the people in the world will be shut out by the cost."

Liz was clearly frustrated. She paused, then began.

"I don't understand how you can take that position, Jason," she said. "Vaccinations were too expensive for much of the world in the beginning, but now we have global immunization for lots of diseases. The fact that companies want to make back their research costs plus some profit should not condemn the technology. Of all of us, you are the most broken up when you watch patients die waiting for transplants, and you oppose both stem cell research and cloning for religious reasons. Now you want to reject xenotransplants as well? Are you telling me that all three of you would rather abandon promising research and just let people die? You could sit down by patients' bedsides, with their families all around, and tell them that you prefer to preserve the sacredness of animals and let these people die?"

"No," Hassan said, "I haven't taken a position on this. I have some emotional feelings about the use of pigs that are clearly inherited, and I hear the arguments of Nirad and Jason, but I am a doctor, and if these xenotransplants work, and I have a patient with no other options that will let him or her live, then I'm probably going to go with xenotransplants. But I am uneasy about it."

"I don't think that any of us are sure of where we stand," offered Nirad, the philosopher in the bunch. "Part of it comes down to how we understand life, Liz, and personal identity, and the place of the individual and the human species in the world. We have to care not only about preserving this individual life of ours but living it so that when we are reincarnated, we will return with a better karma, and into a better world. It's just hard to know what will make the world we return to better."

"Amen to that," concluded Jason, as they gathered up their coats and headed to their homes.

"Remember, Liz, we have an 8 A.M. consult with Dr. Levine on 15," Hassan said. Liz made a face and replied, "Right! Like Levine's ever been on time in his life!"

They all laughed as they sauntered to the parking garage.

Commentary

This case raises a variety of issues within environmental studies, beginning with how we understand the basic elements of the environment. If environmental preservation is a goal, does that mean preserving species as they are, including our own? How do domesticated animals fit into such a picture? Does genetic engineering of human animals as well as nonhuman animals violate the principle of environmental preservation? How important are the historic boundaries between species, and how should they be interpreted? As in virtually all cases of conflict within environmental ethics, disputants reach radically different conclusions depending on whether they incline toward understandings of the environment as a habitat to be preserved for the use and support of the human species as *de jure* or *de facto* steward of the biosphere or toward understandings of the human species as on par with any other species in terms of its role and rights within the biosphere.

These are not the only factors that influence stances on xenotransplants, however. Religious and spiritual attitudes toward death, religious understandings of tradition and its role in religion, and various approaches to risk assessment also affect stances on xenotransplants, as do personal experiences of and attitudes toward animals. Because trends in organ transplantation form the basis of the perceived need for replacement organs for which xenotransplants are being promoted as the solution, we should begin with an overview of the present context concerning organ transplantation.

In the more than thirty years that organ transplants have been performed on a significant scale, success rates—measured in years of survival—have increased dramatically. Meanwhile, as average life spans have lengthened, the demand for replacement organs has increased dramatically all over the world. At the end of 2002 in the United States, the demand for replacement organs exceeded the supply by an average ratio of four to one. In the less developed world, the availability of the technology, trained personnel, and the means to afford the procedure are so rare that the vast majority of persons who could benefit are never even identified and put on lists.

Throughout the developed world, attempts to increase the availability of donated human organs have been varied and numerous, but evidence suggests that it is impossible to increase the rate of cadaver donation to meet the need. Many societies have religious or cultural taboos—often based on understandings of spirit/soul as embedded in the physical body—against surrendering a part of their body to another, accepting a part of another's body into theirs, or facing judgment and resurrection with missing parts. Some societies fear the recently dead and not only fear that the spirits of family dead would haunt and curse them for allowing their organs to be given to others but also would fear accepting organs that might be accompanied by malevolent spirits of the dead. Although there are new strategies for live organ donation, such as linked exchanges between extended families with needy family members, live donation obviously is possible only for paired organs. Thus, the search for other sources of replacement organs has expanded.

Attitudes toward Death

The young doctors in this case are concerned with various strategies that are intended to meet the demand for replacement organs. The discussion begins with recognition on the part of Hassan that donor organs are not a cure for disease but merely a treatment—which requires suppression of the body's defensive immune system, which itself creates other risks for the patient. All four of the young doctors in this case have undergone extensive medical training devoted to defeating and postponing death in their patients. By discussing the case of his cousin, Suha, Hassan begins to question whether preserving life through such interventions is always for the best, noting that the quality of life of his cousin, and even that of her parents, is not satisfactory.

The others respond that such tragic cases are the minority. Liz supplies the clincher, undoubtedly true: Given a choice between certain death from heart, liver, or lung disease and life with a relatively small risk of chronic illness, the vast majority of people choose life with risk. Should this fact settle the issue?

For decades there has been critical discussion within Western medical ethics of a pervasive demonization of death, as if death were not part of the life cycle itself but an enemy to be defeated by modern medicine. Many people have charged that although medicine should have the dual task of curing patients who can be cured and caring for those who can't, our medical ethos has overemphasized curing, to the neglect of persons who cannot be cured. Medicine has been too oriented toward perfect health, perhaps, inculcating intolerance of all forms of debility and an unwillingness to recognize, prepare for, and accept death—especially the death of the young—as a part of our lives. From the perspective of such critiques, a recognition that all living beings experience both birth and death could serve to relativize the "demand" or "need" for replacement organs and help us see that what is at stake in these questions, on one hand, is an additional span of life for a given individual who has a particular quality of life and, on the other hand, some intervention in the environment that inevitably affects all other living beings as well. The choice is not best understood in the simplistic terms of "(human) life or death." One need not posit the equality of all species to understand them as irretrievably interconnected.

Animal Organs

Until recently, diseased organs have been replaced with mechanical or chemical supports, such as dialysis machines and drug treatments, or with human organs from cadavers or living (usually related) donors. Elaborate systems have evolved to support organ replacement technologies, including hospital training facilities for doctors, nurses, and various types of medical technicians; government and private insurance programs to fund transplant programs; drug research and testing programs to develop improved immuno-suppressant drugs; and elaborate systems for creating and maintaining lists of potential recipients and distributing available organs with as much equity as possible.

All of these systems inevitably affect other species in the biosphere; the recordkeeping alone utilizes paper and computers that require lumbering, mining, and the chemical industry, all of which affects forests, streams, air quality, and animal populations. As serious as some of these effects have been in specific areas of the world, however, they have been largely indirect. With a potential turn to xenotransplants as the solution to the shortage of human replacement organs, the impact on the nonhuman biosphere becomes direct.

This direct impact, in fact, already has occurred in some small areas of human medicine. In addition to the experimental, temporary use of animal organs in attempts to preserve life until human organs can be procured, surgeons have been using some animal tissue—most often valves from pig hearts—to repair heart valves in humans. These transplants have not occasioned the same extent of questioning as the prospective turn to organ transplants has engendered, largely because the risks to humans seem much lower. The valves are prepared (irradiated) so that they are not living tissue; recipients do not require immunosuppressant drugs, and there is no risk of infection from the animal.

Yet although traditional medical ethics has not raised problems with such xenotransplants, from an environmental ethics perspective the situation is quite different. Whether the issue is heart-valve tissue transplants or whole-heart transplants from animals to humans, the transfer potentially affects not only the lives of individual members of both species but also the lives and living conditions of both species. It also has the potential, perhaps even the probability, of influencing human attitudes—and later actions—toward other animal species. Before we can examine the potential impact of transplanting pig organs into humans, it may be necessary to survey the role and condition of the domestic pig in the contemporary world because, as the case suggests, most people know very little about their own food supply systems.

Pigs have been domesticated since at least the mid-Neolithic period 8,000–10,000 years ago. In many parts of the world the pig served as symbol of both fertility and abundance, often with religious significance. Sows typically have large litters of piglets (eight to twenty) who grow very quickly, forage for themselves after early weaning, and reproduce relatively quickly. Many other animals domesticated for meat-eating purposes regularly produce only one, or occasionally two, offspring at a time and bulk much more slowly.

Pig production in the developed world has been radically transformed over the past century and a half. As the percentage of the population engaged in farming has shrunk from more than 90 percent to less than 10 percent and as the world's population has more than doubled, pig production has shifted toward a factory model—as has production of poultry, cattle, sheep, salmon, and other forms of protein. Free-range food animals are rare and expensive. The typical food animal is bred on a precise schedule for specific genetic traits, inoculated, fed feed laced with growth hormones and antibiotics, reared in huge numbers of densely packed animals, and slaughtered *en masse* on a schedule determined by the rate of weight gain divided by the cost of feed and the momentary price of pork at the slaughterhouse.

Although some ecologists question whether humans had any right to domesticate animals—and thus to appropriate another species for our own life—others raise questions not about domestication per se but about this shift to factory farming. Some people find factory farming revolting, in that it removes the last vestiges of freedom from animals—even the freedom to move, to mate as they will, and to associate with the animals they choose. Others point to more systemic problems. The recent outbreak of hoof-and-mouth disease in the United Kingdom—indeed, even the outbreak of mad-cow disease (bovine spongiform encephaly, or BSE) there[1]—and the difficulty in controlling it there and throughout the world have raised additional questions about the ecological impact of factory farming. Many ecologists suggest that farming has been too reliant on economic principles, such as the economy of scale and comparative advantage, and not attentive enough to ecological principles such as maximization of diversity and the precautionary principle. Economy of scale has pushed farmers increasingly to concentrate the numbers of animals on their farms, and in many areas comparative advantage has concentrated pig (or poultry, cattle, or sheep) farms close together, often near processing plants, to cut down on transportation costs. The density of animals and concentration of farms were primary reasons that hoof-and-mouth originally was so difficult to contain.

High animal density typically creates problems with animal wastes. For example, when Hurricane Floyd flooded huge pig and turkey farms in the Carolinas in September 1999, it washed millions of gallons of animal wastes into nearby streams, wells, and coastal waters, endangering humans and animals and lowering oxygen levels, producing plant and animal kills. High animal density also creates problems of disease spread, which is why factory farmers have turned to lacing animal feed with prophylactic doses of antibiotics.[2] These antibiotic diets have now created antibiotic insensitivities in many herds. Such antibiotic insensitivity is dangerous, in that these families of antibiotics will be useless in combating new infections, which will then have no barriers to infecting whole herds. Furthermore, there is some question about the effect on humans of eating diets consisting of meat from animals living on antibiotic feed. The extent to which antibiotic insensitivity can be passed through the food chain is unknown (see chapter 12).

The economic need to maximize weight gain in farming has encouraged selective breeding; not only are whole herds impregnated by a single boar on many farms, but some large factory networks artificially inseminate all breeding stock from a very small number of prize boars. The effect has been to decrease genetic diversity at the same time that diversity in diet, living conditions, and even geography have been drastically decreased. In epidemiological terms, disaster waits in the wings.

Into this context, we now have the possibility of a new form of pig production facility. The companies involved in the development of xenotransplants insist that they are raising and will raise the animals in environments that are as close to sterile as possible. Individual animals are inspected and go through periods of quarantine before admission to the factory herd. Herds of animals are totally isolated from each other, their barns closed to outside contaminants and regularly disinfected, their food laced with antibiotics. All efforts are being made to protect the human recipients of the organs.

Risk Assessment

As in so many areas of environmental ethics in which we do not have agreed-upon principles or standards to rely on, we must begin at the other end—not applying principles or standards to specific situations but examining particular situations to see if we can tease out foundational principles and standards from our responses to these particular situations. This process is not really bad. In fact, it is how accepted principles and standards came to be accepted in the first place—by being teased out, one piece at a time, from the dominant responses to series of particular cases. The greatest disadvantage of this method of deriving principles is that it is such a slow process because the principle must be tested and refined in a variety of situations before it comes to be regarded as consistent and reliable by the majority. In the meantime, situations continue to develop. Sometimes harmful practices can be reversed later when the necessary refinements in principles and standards (as in law) have been developed, but reversals in living systems sometimes are impossible. The difficulty of reversing the damage from various types of innovations (not all of which are introduced by humans, of course) is the reason that the precautionary principle is fundamental to environmental ethics. Wisdom is incremental, so the pace of intervention in environmental systems should be slow, matched to the growth of knowledge and wisdom.

In the case of xenotransplants, the unknown risks are numerous. We have an initial set of risks we inherit with the factory farm model of meat production—risks to the animal species itself as well as to the human food supply—from the decrease in diversity and the density of production. A policy of pig factories to produce transplant organs for humans adds at least three additional risks: the risk to recipients of contracting porcine disease; the risk of importing into the human germ line porcine anomalies, including disease; and the risk of altering human attitudes toward pigs—and animals in general—negatively, in ways that affect other human actions toward animals.

Clearly, our society makes great, if unspecified, distinctions even between domestic animals in terms of what treatment is acceptable. Animals that are raised for meat are treated very differently from those raised as pets: Humans have been convicted and sentenced to years in prison for doing to household cats and dogs what is routinely done to food animals or laboratory animals. Is it cruel to pen animals so closely that they have no freedom of movement? To raise them indoors, without access to sun or sky? To cause them unnecessary pain? Our society usually avoids the question of whether animals have any rights that restrain legitimate human needs or desires in any way. We are willing to condemn humans who inflict deliberate, gratuitous pain on pets or "wild" animals, but we have little or no objection to scientific systems for killing, confining, or causing pain to animals to accommodate relatively unimportant human desires—such as in testing cosmetic compounds.

Our moral expectations of humans and our understandings of how human action, identity, and relationality are connected combine to tell us that humans who torture animals are dangerous to *humans*. Prohibitions of animal cruelty, then, are not based for the most part on an attitude that accepts animal rights, attempts to protect animals, or recognizes any analogy between human-human and human-animal relationships. Frequently people who do espouse rights for individual animals are dismissed as sentimental, often fanatic, and ultimately not practical.

On the other hand, perhaps the greatest achievement of the environmental movement to date has been its ability to persuade many people to accept a systems approach to the environment, and this shift has been changing the way many people understand the rights of animal species. Enactment of the Endangered Species Act, for example—despite controversy over some of its applications—was possible only because many Americans gradually became alerted to the way in which each species fulfills a set of functions that interlock with the functions and existence of other species, even when some of those interlocking functions remain a mystery. The human species, like all species, is dependent on the health of the biosphere as a whole, so it is dependent on all the species that make up the biosphere; in that way we do owe something to each species, if not necessarily to each member of every species. Each species has rights that inhere in it as a part of the whole that is necessary for any species to exist. We have debates on how critical it is that this particular rare species of earthworm be preserved when its preservation entails great hardships for specific groups of humans, but we do not dispute the indispensability of earthworms, termites, snails, or even the animal families humans consider to be the lowliest and insignificant, even grotesque.

It should be noted that for most of our society environmental thinking is thinking about "nature" or about the "wilderness" and does not include domestic animals or factory farms. In the division between "humans" and "nature," we have largely appropriated the latter to the human side. Although the division between humans and the rest of nature clearly is not ultimate but is humanly constructed in a variety of senses, there is some truth in this perception that pigs and other domesticated animals cleave to the human realm as much as or more than to the realm of created nature because through domestication we have transformed the pig and its role in the environment. The domesticated pig looks different from the wild boars that roamed the forests and fields of the Neolithic landscape (and still do in rare places), has been genetically altered through deliberate breeding, and performs a radically different ecological function. Should the shift to the factory farm, and perhaps to the pig organ factory, be understood simply as refinements on the original domestication of the pig? Can we—should we—sustain this division between a human realm and a realm of nature and decide that because we successfully took the domesticated pig out of nature thousands of years ago, we can now use the pig as we like without affecting "nature"?

One argument against abstracting the pig from the rest of "nature" because of its domestication is that in this case the fact that the animal in question is the pig is accidental. Were it not for immunological issues, the animal could have been chimpanzees or various apes that also are undomesticated, who were the prime candidates as organ "donors." Can one doubt that in that case the argument for using chimps would have ignored domestication—that as long as we did not seriously impact the chimp populations in the wild, growing chimps in organ factories would not be appreciably different from growing chimps to use in testing laboratories?

Perhaps the best reason for not abstracting the pig from the rest of nature, however, lies in recognizing the power and resilience of language and its role in shaping the way we think. The language we use and the categories it contains reflect a preenvironmental milieu. We understand "pig" as a part of the category "animal," and we have been taught to understand "animal" as part of a graded continuum of life. For many people, deity inhabits the top of a pyramid, followed by humans; for nonreligious people, humans are at the pinnacle, followed by animals, plants, and inanimate objects. We still use language such as the "animal nature" of humans, by which we refer to what we perceive as our baser nature. More biological language, in which we refer to ourselves as mammals, or as animals among other species of animal, has been slow to catch on. Privilege is seldom relinquished voluntarily.

Human attitudes do change, however, and they are changing. One of the things that changes our attitudes is making decisions that affect our experience. There can be little disagreement that meat eaters and vegetarians experience animals differently. If we experience pigs not only as food but also as reservoirs of human replacement organs, this perception will affect the way we understand the species; because we reason by analogy, it will affect the way we understand other species that we also classify as animals. Will it influence us to regard pigs and other animals as relatives, or will it influence us to see them as things to be used? What difference does it make? Is the difference only a moral and aesthetic difference that is unique and limited to humans, or would it affect human actions toward the rest of the biosphere—and thus the welfare of other species?

Some environmentalists have suggested that Americans and others facing environmental issues need to rethink the way we treat risk. They say that the model of risk assessment we are most familiar with comes from business, and the risks it measures and compares are the risks of losing or gaining capital. Clearly, as individuals and businesses, we frequently weigh the risks of how much we could lose against how much we could gain in a given situation and decide what level of risk to assume. Because it is impossible in a capitalist economy to gain much without some degree of risk, capitalist economics teaches us to be risk takers, at least to some degree. Sometimes the costs entailed by business decisions are the costs assigned to human life and health, as with product liability. The goal is to limit financial losses from death and injury caused by defective products to amounts that are less than the costs of attempting to remedy those defects.

The military has long used risk assessment methods, where the risks are losses of personnel and materiel and the gains are control of territory or enemy personnel and materiel. In a war, every action and inaction entails risk, and the extent of the risk often is devastating. Generals calculate how many lives must be risked or sacrificed to achieve particular objectives. In much the same way, public health officials understand themselves as being in a war to save lives against an implacable enemy that periodically mounts devastating offensives. In public health as well, calculations are made of where and how to repel the invader with the least cost—but the calculations may not be accurate, and resulting losses could be catastrophic.

Some people argue that xenotransplants raise some of the same issues as genetic engineering in the germ line (that is, genetic changes that are passed down to subsequent generations). The risks in such a move are massive not only because we do not know the magnitude of negative consequences but because once instituted, the negative consequences become morally impossible to contain. That is, if we were to discover that persons with xenotransplants, and their offspring, constituted a risk to others, they could not be eliminated or forcibly sterilized; even lifetime quarantine would be morally questionable.

The risks in the foregoing cases involve loss of lives to war and disease and loss of money. These risks are serious, and their effects may linger past the time of the persons who made the initial decision to take the risk, to invest the money, to declare the war, to fund disease treatment equally with research for a cure. But the dead get buried, epidemics die out, the living eventually rebuild their lives, new money is earned, and new investments are made.

In the case of the environment, decisions such as the proposed strategy to use pig organs in humans could introduce new diseases into not just the recipient generation but generations to come. No real risk assessment is possible because we do not know what we might be risking. There might be slight—almost zero—risk to present and future generations, or there might be tremendous risk to present and future generations.

The business model suggests that only the risk we can measure counts; in this case, if companies are well-enough insured to weather lawsuits if problems develop from pig organ transplants, then they should proceed if the prospective profits offset these insurance costs. Within the environmental model, the precautionary principle demands that intervention be limited to known risks that can be measured. In short, the environmental approach to risk assessment requires a great deal more knowledge to justify intervention and tends to justify much lower levels of risk. Are the American public and the world willing to slow down the pace of innovation to obtain more knowledge with which to do more accurate risk assessment, or is the fast pace of change, and the hope it engenders in many people, one of the benefits for which we as a people are willing to accept higher levels of risk?

Religious Perspectives

There are several different ways to classify the reactions of world religions to the issues in this case. Because xenotransplants are such a new possibility, no major religion has a developed position regarding them, but most religions do have very complex understandings and attitudes toward the human species and animal species.

Many indigenous religions have been forced by their environmental circumstances to be aware constantly of their dependence on other species and have understood themselves to have kinship relations with them. Although the discussion in this case questions how meat-eating peoples could regard animals as kin, from the perspective of many indigenous religions these two facets of life are not incompatible. Group life always requires some element of sacrifice; in some cultures—of which Inuit groups are the best known—sick elderly individuals who could no longer contribute to communal life but only consumed group resources walked out onto drifting ice floes to die. Most cultures have made heroes of those who sacrifice their lives, as in war, to protect the rest of the society. In the same way, many hunting societies thank their brother and sister animals who die at their hands for the sacrifice they have made to the cause of ongoing life. Some of these societies, such as the

Kwakiutl of the Pacific Northwest, focus their celebrations of the new year around paying homage to the animal species on which they have depended in the past year, in hopes that the Master/Mistress of those animals will continue to send the animals to be hunted.

The sacrifice of individual animals as organ donors might be understood in the same way, but from this same perspective it also might be rejected—not because of the killing of the animal but for at least two other reasons. First, the conditions under which the animals must be raised to be appropriate donors would be offensive to many indigenous religions because those conditions would greatly alter the natural environment, and hence the nature, of the animal. Second, for many participants in indigenous religious societies— the Navajo, for example—incorporating the body parts of dead animals, like dead humans, would induce fear and trembling, in that the spirit of the dead animal/human would be expected to roam the earth and haunt the living, instead of retreating peaceably to the next world.

Among the major world religions, Buddhism in some ways comes closest to sharing the perspective of indigenous religions because it understands all that exists to be interrelated. On the other hand, Buddhism traditionally has focused more on escape from the cycle of death and rebirth than on the concerns of this material world, which it understands in terms of illusion. Furthermore, Buddhism shares with many Eastern religions an appreciation of passivity, in contrast to Western emphasis on action and intervention in nature. Moreover, central to the Buddhist ethic is nonviolence to all living things; although Buddhists are not necessarily vegetarians, monks are not allowed to kill animals to eat or to accept meat that has been killed for them. The most likely Buddhist response to xenotransplants, however, would be not opposition to the means employed or the consequences to either species as much as incomprehension about why we should attempt any major and potentially disruptive interventions in nature to foil the pattern whereby old or sick persons die of organ failure. The goal of life, as Buddhists understand it, is not to prolong life but to use life well and escape the cycle of birth, death, and rebirth by discovering nirvana.

For Hindus the central issue in xenotransplants is likely to be *ahimsa*—the principle of doing no harm to any living being. Symbolized by the status of cows in Indian society, *ahimsa* has long been a central ethical imperative for individuals in Hinduism and recently and understandably has become central to Indian environmental thinking. Indian society has been very open to technological innovation—as India's role as exporter of computer scientists, engineers, and other technology personnel and its popular adaptation of diagnostic procedures such as sonograms attest. Some of these technologies can conflict with allegiance to *ahimsa*, as when millions of people use sonograms to diagnose fetal sex and abort female fetuses. Among India's people, however (soon to number 1 billion), many would see the death of the xenotranplant donor animal as morally problematic.

Although Islam developed in a natural environment that constantly reminded humans of their dependence, from its very origins Islam has been very focused on nature as given to humans by Allah for their use. Humans are understood as caliphs, or deputies of Allah, and should not abuse that role by destroying the resources Allah has entrusted to them. Because the Quranic perspective focuses on the relationship between Allah and humans, support for a Muslim environmental ethic today tends to be grounded in the care and preservation demanded by human status as Allah's deputies, rather than any intrinsic value in nonhuman creation. By itself, this ethic might lead Muslims to favor xenotransplants. Furthermore, although Islam teaches of a judgment after death and eternal rewards and punishments at that judgment, historically it has taken very seriously the material conditions of humans in this life, rather than focusing on the next. Therefore Islam could be expected to take seriously the sickness and impending death of persons who need transplant organs.

On the other hand, Muslims are forbidden to eat pork, which is understood as a dirty animal, not worthy of ingestion. Therefore, xenotransplants might be theoretically acceptable in Islam, but Muslim authorities probably would not accept pig organs. When new technologies achieve ends that are important within Islam (e.g., new reproductive technologies that relieve infertility) they tend to be accepted by religious authorities even when they have not only emerged from Western societies but are used there to fill ends that are unacceptable in Islam (e.g., new reproductive technologies to allow single women to reproduce). In such cases the technology is accepted, but often with conditions that adapt its use to Islamic values—as when *imams* have insisted that the materials used in *in vitro* fertilization must be from a man and woman bound together in matrimony. On the other hand, new technologies that intervene in Allah's creation toward ends that are not important in Islam often are understood and rejected as Western and degenerate (e.g., cloning). Such a response is more likely in this case because of the use of pigs: The identity of the animal might color judgments of the procedure itself.

As in Christianity and Islam, Judaism's primary approach to the environment is through an ethic of stewardship: The earth is the Lord's, and the Lord has entrusted its care and use to humans. Biblical texts develop at great length a conservation ethic—primarily within an agricultural framework, without much reference to nonagricultural contexts. Judaism was the first of the Semitic religions to forbid the eating of pork, and though only one segment of contemporary Jews still mandate observation of the Jewish dietary laws, at least for that segment—and probably for many more—incorporation of pig organs would be problematic. On the other hand, Judaism has been very open to technology in general and in particular to life-saving technologies in modern medicine. Action that is necessary to save life takes priority over virtually all other commands of Jewish law.

Thus, there are many different perspectives on the use of xenotransplants. It is likely that the judgments of many people, including many religious and environmental communities, ultimately may depend on balancing advantages and disadvantages—after these factors have emerged more clearly than at present. Especially important will be how successful xenotransplants are (the quality and quantity of life that they give to recipients), how accessible they are to the bulk of the global population, how much human genetic material is transferred to the animal and vice versa, how successfully the modified organism can be isolated from the domesticated version, and what degree of suffering the process is understood to entail for the animals involved.

Questions for Discussion

1. Why are many scientists looking to other species, especially pigs, for transplant organs? What advantages do these species offer?
2. What are the various risks of xenotransplants, and which of them seems to be the most significant? To whom or to what is this risk posed?
3. Are you convinced by Liz's arguments? Why or why not? How is the nature of her arguments different from the arguments of Nirad? What is the role of emotion in each of their arguments? To what extent does emotion have an appropriate role in moral reasoning?
4. How important do the environmental concerns implicit in this case loom against the human medical concerns? Is that appropriate? What might an environmentalist add to this debate among doctors?

Notes

1. The spread of BSE has been traced to the practice of using rendered animal products to lace animal feed, so that if an animal with BSE is rendered and used in animal feed, the animals that receive the feed could develop the disease, and those receiving that feed that are rendered (often, those that fail to thrive and therefore are more likely to have some form of disease) continue to spread the disease. The use of animal products in feed was developed to speed growth by raising the protein intake and thus shortening the time before the animal could be slaughtered (and lowering costs).

2. In Denmark, concern over antibiotic levels in food animals recently led the government to fund experiments comparing the costs of disease in factory farm herds raised with and without prophylactic antibiotics; these experiments found that if farmers adopted thorough disinfectant washings of barns between herds and wore coveralls that prevented them from carrying germs between barns, deaths and weight gains remained the same between antibiotically treated herds and those without, with some advantages to those without.

For Further Reading

Almond, Brenda. "Commodifying Animals: Ethical Issues in Genetic Engineering of Animals." *Health, Risk and Society* 2, no. 1 (2000): 95–105.

Balzer, Philipp, Klaus Rippe, and Peter Schaber. "Two Concepts of Dignity for Humans and Non-Human Organisms in the Context of Genetic Engineering." *Journal of Agricultural and Environmental Ethics* 13, no. 1 (2000): 7–27.

Center for Bioethics and Human Dignity. On Human Ethics and Stem Cell Research: An Appeal for Legally and Ethically Responsible Science and Public Policy. 1999. Do No Harm website: www.stemcellresearch.org.

Fisher, Lawrence M. "Down on the Farm, A Donor: Breeding Pigs that Can Provide Organs for Humans." *New York Times*, 5 January 1996.

Heeger, Robert. "Genetic Engineering and the Dignity of Creatures." *Journal of Agricultural and Environmental Ethics* 13, no. 1 (2000): 43–51.

Kaplan, A. L. "Is Xenografting Morally Wrong?" *Transplantation Proceedings* 24, no. 2 (April 1992): 722–27.

Munro, Lyle. "Future Animal: Environmental and Animal Welfare Perspectives on the Genetic Engineering of Animals." *Cambridge Quarterly of Healthcare Ethics* 10, no. 3 (2001): 314–24.

Parker, William, Shu S. Lin, and Jeffrey L Platt. "Antigen Expression in Xenotransplantation: How Low Must It Go?" *Transplantation: Baltimore* 71, no. 2 (January 27, 2001): 313–19.

Singer, Peter. "Transplantation and Speciesism." *Transplantation Proceedings* 24, no. 2 (April 1992): 728–32.

Stolberg, Sheryl Gay. "Company Using Cloning to Yield Stem Cells." *New York Times*, 13 July 2001.

Takefman, Daniel M., Gregory T. Spear, Mohammad Saifuddin, and Carolyn A. Wilson. "Human CD59 Incorporation into Porcine Endogenous Retrovirus Particles: Implications for the Use of Transgenic Pigs for Xenotransplantation." *Journal of Virology* 76, no. 4 (February 2002): 1999–2002.

Appendix

Using Environmental Case Studies in the Classroom

Case study method has a long history in Western ethics, beginning with the development of medieval casuistry within Christian moral theology and spreading in the twentieth century to many different areas of ethics, religious and secular—especially professional ethics.[1] Within environmental studies today, case study method is one of the most common, effective approaches to environmental ethics, for several reasons. Many case studies acquaint readers with particular situations in which the environment has been or is being threatened or damaged, thereby promoting environmental awareness. In addition, the fact that case studies explore a particular situation in some depth, examining a variety of different interlocking sets of relationships within the nonhuman environment and between humans and the rest of the environment, means that case study use contributes to the development of deeper knowledge of the complexity of ecosystems and the difficulty of treating any one element of an ecosystem—or, for that matter, of the entire biosphere—without impacting the rest of the system. Thus, the case study method in environmental ethics helps to dispel the individualistic, unintegrated approach that is common among American university students in favor of an approach to problem solving that is more social, more systemic, and more open to interdependence.

Perhaps the most important reason for the prevalence of the case study method in environmental studies concerns the youth of that field. In most fields of ethics there is an established body of principles that is applied to particular situations in case studies. The existence of this body of principles does not make their application to the case cut and dried; more than one principle may apply to the case, and those multiple principles may push resolution of the case in conflicting directions. Many sets of principles are not hierarchically ranked, so one must decide in specific situations which ones take priority. Sometimes the appropriateness of a principle to a particular case can be unclear, as when a code of behavior that is clear and appropriate in general is proposed for a minor; for a mentally ill person; or for a person with language, cultural, or other communication obstacles. Even well-developed areas of professional ethics have cases that are engrossing because they are difficult to decide.

Environmental ethics, however, is an infant field. Although we can point to the writings of Aldo Leopold in the late 1940s,[2] until Rachel Carson published *Silent Spring* in 1962[3] there was little public awareness or reflection within which an ethic could develop. The extreme youth of environmental ethics in comparison to other areas of ethics—such as sexual ethics, the ethics of war, or medical ethics, which were treated in ancient religions and philosophies—means that the foundational principles and concepts are still in the process of development and argumentation. The youth of the field of environmental ethics offers students the possibility of participating in the process of formulating, testing, and refining the foundational principles that will characterize environmental ethics in the next decades—perhaps even centuries and millennia.

Principles: Not Revealed, but Discerned through Testing

People often assume that ethical principles do not have to be discerned but always have been known because they were somehow revealed from on high. If we examine the vast majority of ethical principles that guide behavior in the various areas of human life, however, we find that very few, if any, represent infused knowledge. Most represent wisdom that has been learned the hard way, through long processes of trial and error. Although some of the most basic and universal ethical statements (the Golden Rule; love your neighbor) are found in religious and philosophical teachings all over the world, the form those ethical imperatives take in specific areas of life are seldom spelled out in divine revelation. The imperatives remain very general. That very generality gives them universal applicability.

As we have seen, in environmental studies there is an ongoing need to develop relevant principles and norms because so many of the existing anthropocentric principles and norms that are applied to the environment have been shown to be grievously and destructively inadequate. Although those values, norms, and principles for dealing with the environment and the mythical and literary sources from which they come in the industrial West often appear particularly inadequate, those from other cultures or times, though often more cognizant of the interdependence of all forms of life, can seem irrelevant to and irreconcilable with the prevailing structures of human life in our late-modern world. Human societies inevitably rely on experience, one specific case at a time, for developing and refining principles and norms. Case studies in environmental studies not only present situations that test the principles and norms (such as those in chapter 1) that have been proposed to date in environmental ethics, helping to further refine them; they also force readers to grapple with new situations that may inspire the proposal of new principles and norms that will then be tested and refined in later cases. Thus, case studies constitute not only the experiments through which hypotheses are tested and refined on the way to becoming theories but also the steps in the process by which a particular theory continues to develop on the way to perhaps becoming the paradigmatic lens through which the environment is interpreted.

Many teachers of ethics are clear that case studies teach analytical and critical-thinking skills. Many also find, however, that students can become so bogged down in the specifics of the cases that without supplementary materials on theory they emerge from their studies without a sufficient grasp of the body of theory in the field. Such a criticism is particularly frequent in Christian and other religious ethics where the body of theory (e.g., Christian ethics/moral theology) is so extensive. New ethical areas such as environmental ethics, which are long on information about the environment and short on inherited, developed theories about values and priorities within the environment, therefore are ideal for case studies. Not only is there no large body of theory that could be obscured by the data; in fact, systematic questioning of the data is the very process through which new prototheory is discovered, tested, and refined. Thus, although the case study method always offers students the opportunity to participate in decisions about which principles apply to specific situations, and in what priority, the case study method in environmental ethics today offers students the opportunity to participate in the very formulation of the foundational principles of the field. It is difficult to imagine a more participative model of education.

Good Case Studies

A good case study is complex because life situations are complex. If the conflicts in the cases were easily resolved, they would not be interesting, much less absorbing. There would be nothing to talk about—everyone would agree about what should be done. There also would be nothing to be learned because none of our assumptions or interpretations would be challenged. Good case studies are challenging and engaging precisely because they are complex.

Environmental issues and conflicts develop amidst other conflicts, tensions, and differences, all of which affect the actors in an environmental case. Sometimes the motives and intentions of individuals in the cases who support attractive options nevertheless seem unclear or unsavory. Students often will take particular stances within a case study not only because one's worldview is anthropocentric and another's is ecocentric but also because of personal factors such as regional, gender, class, racial/ethnic, occupational, or other characteristics and experiences that influence students' reactions to the agents and situations in the case. Decisions in environmental ethics have rippling consequences in many areas of social life, in economic aspects of production and distribution, and in health care and intimate lifestyle issues such as the style and efficiency of flush toilets in our homes. Anticipated outcomes are important influences on our decisions; very few of us are pure deontologists with regard to our incomes, health, or lifestyles. One of the more important roles of an instructor who is using case studies is to remind students to be aware and self-critical of the effects of their own social locations and the attitudes they learned in those locations. An occasional question along the lines of, "Who speaks for _____ in this case?" can be very effective in reminding students of the limits of their own perspectives and experiences and calling them to grapple with alien perspectives and experiences.

Yet our propensity to be influenced by our life experiences and ascribed characteristics should not simply be dismissed as "bias." The designation of "bias" should be reserved for disproportionate privileging of our own experience that deafens us to the expressed experience of other groups whose needs are equal to or greater than ours. All members of society must represent their own experiences if sharing our own situations and perspectives is to allow us as a society to make decisions for the common good. Our representations of our own experience must always be tempered, however, by openness to the representations of others.

Using the Case Method

Precisely because there are so many different things going on at the same time in a good case, cases can be used in a variety of ways. Much will depend on the questions the instructor presents to the class regarding the case. The general tendency of undergraduate students in cases is to focus whenever possible on the personal relationships in the case. This is especially true when the relationships in the case are those that are most important in the lives of most students: sexual relationships, familial relationships, personal friendships. Undergraduates respond disproportionately to personal relationships both because this individualist focus is culturally normative in the United States and because most students feel more experienced in and knowledgeable about personal relationships than they do about politics, economics, technology, or ecological systems. They feel comfortable in discussing what individuals should do personally in dealing with a lover, a parent, or a boss. Many students feel comfortable discussing individual options vis-à-vis conserving the environment, such as decisions about automobile gas mileage, water conservation in the home, and whether to eat meat or not. They are more likely to identify with Kyle, the ag student, than with his farmer father who wants to plant GMO corn, and more likely to identify with the American-trained coral reef restorer, Ismail, than with his Balinese staff or clients, for cultural reasons.

One way to attempt to overcome such identifications is to role-play in the classroom. The "River Run or River Ruined?" case, for example, lays out three stances—removing the dam altogether, enlarging the dam, and refitting the dam to be more efficient but the same size—each of which has its own set of advantages and supporters. Although some students will take positions immediately, discussion of the alternatives will allow many students to move from an uncommitted stance to identification with one of the alternatives. Roleplaying often can be added to a case by extending the time frame. The class presumes, for example, that the staff of *Medios Nuevos* has one more meeting to decide what stance their Peruvian delegate should take at the POPs conference or that Ismail's staff meets once more with the different stakeholders in the Binging reef, and the different roles can be played by class members. It then becomes the responsibility of specific individuals to speak for the different positions.

Most instructors feel the necessity of leading students away from an exclusive focus on personal issues and forcing them to deal with more social, structural, and policy issues. What should the public policy decision about the environment be in this situation? the instructor asks. Most students find these questions difficult. Many are uncomfortable even beginning a discussion. They say things such as, "Well, I have my own opinion, and everybody else has their opinion, but there's no way to tell who is right, so there's no sense in talking about it. We'll disagree, and that is okay." They are suspicious of propaganda and public relations methods of building support. Such skepticism can be a strength in class discussion because it can furnish the basis for critical approaches. When such suspicion leads to complete cynicism about how public policy gets made, and about possible alternatives, however, it becomes problematic. Instructors can chip away at this cynicism by pointing out within the cases not only how much American and other attitudes throughout the world have changed toward aspects of the environment over the past half-century but what steps contributed to that change—the studies and reports, the scholarly meetings of scientists, the government conferences, the newspaper and magazine articles, and the formation of citizen action groups that kept up pressure for all the above. There have been major improvements in air and water quality in the United States since the 1970s as a result of regulation. On a global basis, although there has been no movement on CO_2 or greenhouse gases in general, the 1987 Montreal Protocol on banning the chlorofluorocarbons that were destroying the ozone layer has stopped that deterioration, and some progress has been made on ocean dumping. Many developing nations have begun conservation programs for wildlife and animal habitats, and some have begun to turn their attention to urban industrial problems such as air and water pollution. A global problem that was virtually unrecognized fifty years ago is now widely understood as a serious threat to the future of life on the planet.

Although student preference for personal rather than public policy approaches to cases can be problematic, student interest in individuals and personal relationships does have some uses in the classroom, as well as some real relevance to ethics. In many case studies it is appropriate to deal not only with policy issues but with character issues. This approach often is called virtue ethics. We all want to live in a society that is just and healthy, peaceful and sustainable. We also want to live in a community made up of persons with good character, persons we can trust and depend on, persons we can love and expect to love us in return. So when we make decisions, in these cases or in real life, we need to do the "right thing" and to do what helps make all the people involved, including ourselves, good people. "Doing the right thing" and doing "what makes good people" often are overlapping and not so different. There are cases, however, in which it is necessary to ask to what extent taking the proposed step—for example, approving xenotransplants—affects the character of humans and their attitudes toward the rest of the biosphere. Character is important because it can never be divorced from agency. What we do affects who we become, just as who we have become affects what we choose to do, in a never-ending spiral.

Attention to character issues can be accomplished easily within role-playing. Another way to teach the cases is to have students read and discuss the case before they read the commentary. They would then discuss the case again after they have read the commentary, being careful to note what aspects of the case they had missed or what new aspects or approaches they had discovered that the commentary failed to treat.

Some instructors have guided their classes through several cases and then divided the class into writing groups, with instructions to create a case study on the basis of some real-life local environmental issue. Each member of the group attempts to represent a major group in the local community within the local environmental conflict and to get their perspective into the text of the case. Such an assignment has the advantage of demonstrating to students the relevance that environmental ethics has to their own lives, as well as encouraging students to consider new forms and levels of civic responsibility.

The Problem of Language in the Classroom

Students often are frustrated by the lack of adequate language in classroom discussions of environmental ethics. They become aware, suddenly, that the words they are using have implications and attitudes attached to them that they do not wish to invoke, implications and attitudes that give them pause and make them search—in vain—for more adequate language. In deciding between the interests of humans and (an)other species, for example, students quickly realize that they are accustomed to using rights language and concepts in conflict-of-interest situations between humans but that although they have well-developed theories of *human* rights with which to work, they have no consensus on theories of the rights or value of other species or whole ecosystems. The anthropocentrism of ethics to date has permeated all of its principles and theories, as well as the very language it uses, but this inadequacy often is invisible until we are faced with the demands of a particular situation in a case study. The inadequacy of inherited ethical approaches for working with the environment invariably forces students to deal with the anthropocentric bias by constructing new language, concepts, and principles that are answerable to broader constituencies and reflect more social, more interspecies, perspectives.

Our conceptual framework for all of reality in the West has been very theologically based: Humans have understood themselves as unique among the creatures of the world because we are made in the image and likeness of God. That likeness to God has been variously defined in terms of mind, the ability

236

to reason, the aptitude for agency and for self-conscious subjectivity. Both temporality and materiality, which humans have been understood to share not with God but with other creatures, were understood as lesser, eclipsed not only by the eternity and transcendence of God but also in humans by the higher purposes of the human soul/mind. For classical theology, the good and perfect (God) was characterized by permanence, stasis, hierarchical order, and discreteness. What was temporal, material, constantly changing, and interdependent was flawed and lesser, created to serve the higher. The more temporal, material, changeable, and interdependent an entity was, the lower it ranked in the hierarchy of reality. Thus, in the worldview inherited from the Western religious traditions, the human species was of higher value than, and in charge of, the rest of creation. Carolyn Merchant, in *The Death of Nature*, explains how this theological view underlay the foundations of modern science in thinkers such as Francis Bacon:

> Due to the Fall from the Garden of Eden (caused by the temptation of a woman), the human race lost its "dominion over creation." Before the Fall, there was no need for power or dominion, because Adam and Even had been made sovereign over all other creatures. In this state of dominion, mankind was "like unto God." While some, accepting God's punishment, had obeyed the medieval strictures against searching too deeply into God's secrets, Bacon turned the constraints into sanctions. Only by "digging further and further into the mine of natural knowledge" could mankind recover that lost dominion. In this way, "the narrow limits of man's dominion over the universe" could be stretched "to their promised bounds."
>
> Although a female's inquisitiveness may have caused man's fall from his God-given dominion, the relentless interrogation of another female, nature, could be used to regain it. As he [Bacon] argued in *The Masculine Birth of Time*, "I am come in very truth leading to you nature with all her children to bind her to your service and make her your slave."[4]

Thus, modern science was understood as salvific, in that it restored that which had been lost to sin—human dominion over nature—and in so doing also restored the original likeness between humans and God: dominion.

A review of the early scientists and philosophers of science illustrates the fact that nature—all of creation—was understood, especially by Protestants, as disordered and deformed by human sin. Thus, it was not surprising that

Protestantism was more engaged in the early development of modern science—understood as controlling and harnessing chaotic nature—than Catholicism, which understood the effects of the Fall more conservatively and salvation as a matter of divine grace building on the foundation of nature (human and other). As the scientific revolution developed, of course, it shaped the worldview of Protestants and Catholics as well as Jews and other socioreligious groups in the West.

Images of nature as disordered, chaotic, and therefore threatening permeated Western thought. The only good land was land that had been cleared, planted, and homesteaded—civilized. Wilderness came to designate places of dark, danger, and violence. The most basic characteristics of the biosphere came to hold the least value. The dynamism of the biosphere was interpreted in terms of profligate fertility, disordered chaos, and unstable temporality. Its interdependence was interpreted in terms of weakness, of contingency, and its complex diversity was interpreted as proof not only of disorder but of deliberate and irrational willfulness. Today this modern, theologically based scientific paradigm, this lens for interpreting the universe—particularly the biosphere—is dissolving under the impact of greater attention to, and more data about, the environment of earth. This paradigm is not eradicated, however; it retains a great deal of power, much of it embedded in the meanings of everyday words and the boundaries they evoke for the people who use them. For example, when we use the word "human," or "human being," or even "human species," for most of us there is a major boundary line between humans and all other species of animal—even humans and other mammals. Although most of us accept the theory of evolution as more or less historical, we do not have an evolutionary perspective that understands humans as part of a common animal spectrum, in contrast to plants or other elements of the ecosystem. In the same way, despite our acceptance of evolutionary theory we have tended to read evolution backward into the past rather than forward into the future. Thus, many people regard the human environmental task as one of preserving the present by preventing any change or development within the natural world—as if this strategy did not contravene the evolutionary process.

In some ways we are in the midst of reclaiming our language back from the modernist paradigm and refashioning our interpretive paradigm. Many people in our society still think of wilderness as space not yet utilized, a commodity to be used, a resource to be transformed to fill some human function, such as suburban housing, highways, parks, agricultural fields or malls, and utility plants. Increasing numbers of people in our society, however, see wilderness as an image of richness, diversity, interdependence, equilibrium—and as a planning norm for land whose alternatives require justification. More and more people are beginning to think in terms of ecosystems and to conclude that using human convenience as the deciding factor in all policy decisions about the earth has pragmatic and moral problems. We may be uncomfortable with programs to reinstate a wolf population in our region of the country, but more and more of us can understand that ecosystem equilibrium is impossible when the top predators have been eliminated.

What this means for us today in environmental ethics is that the same words may have very different connotations to different persons in our society. For example, to some people the phrase "the human animal" may still evoke theological discussions of "man's lower, bestial nature," with hints of savage violence and uncontrolled sexual drive, whereas for others the same phrase may evoke an understanding of humans that recognizes all other living creatures as entities with whom we are related and interdependent and for whom we share responsibility. A cleared, planted field may represent beauty, order, fertility, and human productivity to some people and the loss of wetland and the hundreds of species that inhabited it to others. In environmental cases, this variety of images, associations, and emotions evoked by the very language we use complicates discussion and agreement.

All of this makes the environmental ethics classroom a very complicated scene to navigate, much less to manage. Generally it is helpful to point out to students at regular intervals the difficulties with which they are wrestling and the reasons such wrestling is difficult. Most students have more patience with themselves and others when they understand the nature of the paradigm shift within which they are working, the lack of adequate language, and the range of positions that individuals can and will occupy in the shift from an anthropocentric ethics to a more open systems approach to the environment.

Often it works well to encourage compromises on the use of language, so that the class does not waste time rehashing the same disagreements over language usage in each new case. For example, a recent class agreed after discussion that references to "human" would not entail assumptions of more value than was assumed to inhere in animals or other living things, though arguments for the greater value of individual humans or the human species were acceptable and would be judged on their own merits, in general and in specific case situations. That is, students opted to try to use language in as value-neutral a way as possible (recognizing that full value neutrality is impossible), while they recognized that it was essential to tackle the value question directly, in explicit arguments.

One area that was not settled cooperatively in this class was the admissibility of the term "creation" as an alternative term for biosphere or universe. Nonbeliever students thought the use of "creation" privileged faith and traditional values and priorities; believer students insisted that the concept of deliberate and satisfying creation is the ultimate foundation of all value in the material world. In other classes in the past, this issue too has been successfully compromised.

Notes

1. Richard B. Miller, *Casuistry and Modern Ethics: A Poetics of Practical Reasoning* (Chicago: University of Chicago Press, 1996).
2. Aldo Leopold, "The Land Ethic," in *A Sand County Almanac* (New York: Ballantine, 1970 [1949]).
3. Rachel Carson, *Silent Spring* (New York: Fawcett, 1962).
4. Carolyn Merchant, *The Death of Nature: Women, Ecology, and the Scientific Revolution* (San Francisco: Harper and Row, 1980).

Index